THE MEASURE OF MAN

THE MEASURE OF MAN

Incursions in Philosophical and Political Anthropology

by
David J. Levy

Claridge Press
St Albans

First published in Great Britain 1993

by The Claridge Press
27 Windridge Close
St Albans
Herts
AL3 4JP

Copyright © David J. Levy

Printed by University of Missouri Press
Columbia, USA

ISBN 1-870626-43-5

1.   Philosophy
2.   Politics

CONTENTS

PREFACE

The studies composing *The Measure of Man* were written over a ten year period between 1981 and 1991. Individually, each is an attempt to explore and clarify one or another aspect of the enigmatic character of human existence through an approach — the approach of a philosophical anthropology of *homo politicus* — that takes seriously both the permanent defining features of man's nature and condition and the extraordinary variety of responses which this situation permits. Together, the chapters of the book represent complementary aspects of a single effort to continue the work of theoretical clarification of the human sciences and of the reality that is their object begun in *Realism* (Manchester, 1981) and continued in *Political Order* (Baton Rouge and London, 1987).

If the title of the work recalls the famous saying of Protagoras that, "Man is the measure of all things," that recollection must be taken in an ironic and even dialectical sense. For, if there is one single message to be gleaned from the book, it is that man must learn anew to measure himself and his achievements not only against his own aspirations and ideals but against the broader encompassing reality of a world that he did not create and which is, at best, indifferent to his most cherished goals. Man is not the measure of all, but rather the finite being in whose existence all the tensions of the cosmos, spiritual as well as material, rise to consciousness in the historical effort to endure and flourish. This is the point at which the most urgent of contemporary ecological concerns reawaken and restore that ancient consciousness of human fragility that prompted the rituals of world renewal on which the religious life of the first civilizations was centred. On such a reawakening our very survival may now depend.

Alongside art and religion, politics and philosophy embody the record and the promise of an adventure that must continue so long as men may be. Out of the encounter with the things of the world and man's accompanying awareness of the mysterious process out of which both he and his world have emerged — the no less humanly constitutive awareness of divine transcendence — history arises as the destiny of a being uniquely fated to live with the consciousness of his own limits. These are limits which man may seek to transgress but with whose consequences he must always continue to cope.

The Measure of Man falls roughly into three sections. The first four chapters examine aspects of the ways in which, through the twentieth century, a number of significant but hitherto neglected thinkers have sought to respond, intellectually and politically, to the troubles of the time. The particular choice of themes and thinkers is dictated by the conviction not only that these are figures who, at least potentially, can make a significant contribution to our understanding of the real possibilities now open to the human race, but that, in the wake of the fall of Soviet communism and the new period of self-doubt into which what we knew as the free world has entered, the styles of thought they exemplify are likely to find a new and wider audience than before. Chapters Five to Seven attempt to apply some of the insights derived from such ways of thinking to problems of the present; while the final four chapters examine a particular problematic aspect of man's condition through a necessarily selective survey of the sensed tension between the political imperatives of worldly survival and the absolute demands of divine revelation as we encounter them in various religious traditions, ancient and modern.

This book appears at a time when, despite, or perhaps because of, the recent disappearance of the military threat of an obviously less pleasant totalitarian alternative, the political foundations of liberal democratic order, and of the creeds that gave its claim to universal legitimacy a certain credibility, appear, in some ways, more fragile than at any time since before the Second World War. The present eclipse of any viable institutional alternatives to what, with all due recognition of the inadequacy of the term, we may term liberal democracy has had the effect, only at first sight surprising, of raising once more all the questions of the continuing political viability and intellectual validity of what have become the guiding assumptions of the modern world. Without a clearly defined and obviously threatening enemy, our now established systems of political institutions and beliefs find themselves faced again with the unanswered questions that have accompanied them ever since their origins in the decline of the old order of religious orthodoxy and particularist loyalties to prince and place

In seeking to renew interest both in some of the most searching twentieth century critics of those assumptions and in drawing attention to the sometimes elusive continuities that link the present predicament of man with his primordial and still, in many ways, definitive state of being, *The Measure of Man* seeks to contribute not to the further destruction of the decencies of which modern liberal polities can be rightly proud, but rather to their preservation in a world where the myths on which such polities have traditionally depended — the Enlightenment myths of unconstrained individual autonomy and limitless economic and technological advance — become less believable as every day goes by.

David J. Levy (London, December 1992)

Acknowledgements

Many elements of this book have previously been published in various forms elsewhere and I wish to thank the following for permitting me to bring them together in the present work: the organisers of the 1989 Arnold Gehlen Conference in Speyer for "Gehlen's Anthropology and the Foundations of Hermeneutic Understanding", the publisher and editors of *Man and World* for "The Life of Order and the Order of Life", the publisher and editor of *The British Journal for Phenomenology* for "The Limits of History", Paragon House, New York, for "Liberalism, Politics and Anti-Politics", the editor of *The Salisbury Review* for "Carl Schmitt as a Conservative Thinker", Cambridge University Press and the editors of *The Political Responsibility of Intellectuals* (C.U.P. 1990) for "Politics, Technology and the Responsibility of Intellectuals", the editor and publishers of *Continuity* for "Israel and Judah", the editor and publishers of *The World and I* for "The Religion of Light", and the publishers of *Modern Age* for "Paul Ricoeur: Christianity and the Space of Politics".

In addition, I would like to thank Roger Scruton and Beverly Jarrett, at once good friends and publishers, for their trust and generous encouragement in bringing this book to press. Andrea Downing and my brother Peter Edward Levy have both greatly helped me in the preparation of the manuscript, and the moral support of Denis and Mary O'Keeffe has also sustained me in an effort whose results will, I hope, prove worthy of their trust.

Finally I thank the Earhart Foundation for helping me financially with a grant that has made it possible for me to consult with many of the sources, human and textual, that have enriched my thinking and with it this work of thought and order.

THE MEASURE OF MAN

1

THE MEASURE OF MAN

Gehlen's Anthropology and the Foundations of Hermeneutical Understanding

1. Theory, Truth and Method

My purpose in this chapter is to explore the relationship between philosophical anthropology, particularly the conception of anthropology advanced by Arnold Gehlen in *Der Mensch, seine Natur und seine Stellung in der Welt, Man: His Nature and Place in the World*,[1] and what we may broadly term philosophical hermeneutics. Under the latter heading I include both the conception of hermeneutics as designating the general and distinctive methodology of the *Geisteswissenschaften*, the human sciences, proposed by Emilio Betti and E. D. Hirsch,[2] and the rather different view of the matter, developed under the influence of Martin Heidegger and pre-eminently represented by the work of Hans-Georg Gadamer.[3] According to the latter view, hermeneutic understanding is to be seen, not merely as a distinctive methodological requirement of the human sciences, but, more radically, as characterizing the fundamental, defining feature of man's being-in-the-world. In the opinion of Gadamer and other post-Heideggerian theorists, the term *hermeneutics* is thus, primarily, an ontological rather than a methodological category: it designates not or not only a condition for the understanding of the human other, a requirement of human-scientific theory, but an originally pre-theoretical accomplishment necessary to the very survival of the human being in the world. So conceived, hermeneutics is not the specific difference of the human sciences, as it is for Betti and Hirsch, but of man's being as such.

Adopting a useful terminological distinction from Josef Bleicher, I shall refer to the first, methodological, current of philosophical hermeneutics as 'hermeneutical theory' and the second, ontological, one as 'hermeneutic philosophy'.[4] In Husserlian terms, the distinction is one between a conception of hermeneutics as pertaining to the theoretical attitude insofar as this is directed toward the understanding of other subjects, and a view that regards hermeneutic understanding as a constitutive feature, perhaps *the* constitutive feature, of the 'natural attitude' of man in the life-world, the *Lebenswelt*.

Just as Molière's *bourgeois gentilhomme* is speaking "prose" even when he has not yet been taught the fact, so, as the second, Heideggerian, view affirms, man in the 'natural attitude' is always practising hermeneutics without realizing it. It is, however, a primary feature of the 'natural attitude' that man, born always at a temporally and culturally distinct moment in the human story and facing the seemingly self-evident reality — the order of accepted fact and truth, of his particular life-world — does not 'naturally' perceive the hermeneutic dimension of his existence. Believing himself to inhabit a given reality, an objective and inevitable 'order of things', he is unaware of the extent to which the work of human imagination has already entered into the structure of what he experiences as what he normally refers to as the 'outside world'. In the normal context of the life-world, man does not readily recognize that the particular reality he inhabits is neither a given determination of brute nature nor an unmediated gift of the gods, but the result, the civilizational sediment, of prior interpretations which, over time, have become objectified in the taken for granted world-view of his culture — a culture to which he, no less 'hermeneutically', must respond.

As phenomenological philosophers, in particular, have argued, in order to become aware of this intrinsic but normally hidden, 'hermeneutical' dimension of existence, one must be prepared, as it were, to step outside the natural, common-sensical attitude, which takes the objective reality of the world for granted, and adopt the distinct, self-consciously reflective attitude of theory. This is not because the actual existence of the surrounding world is seriously in doubt, but because, as Husserl taught, one will only understand the nature of the reality it does possess if he learns to distinguish, within the fabric of the real, the different threads, natural and cultural, anthropologically constant and historically variable, that are enmeshed together in the world as we experienced it to be. It is precisely such distinctions that are blurred in the undifferentiated world of common sense. Unnecessary to the everyday business of practical life, they become vital when our attention turns from survival to self-reflection. And such a turn is, for better or worse, an intrinsic part of the human vocation — a matter not of choice but of our fate as self-aware if never exclusively rational beings.[5]

In Husserl, the theoretical attitude is strictly identified with an idealized view of the objectifying, socially and historically de-contextualized, perspective of what he refers to as pure or rigorous science, *strenge Wissenschaft*. This places him in a somewhat ambiguous relationship to his positivist contemporaries. By this I mean that, although Husserl rejects the positivist claim that there is any one single model of scientific method —typically, for the positivist, the method of Newtonian physics, which can with minor variations be applied to every area or, to use a Husserlian term, 'region' of reality —he does maintain that every field of inquiry reveals, on examination, its own 'regional ontology'; that is, its own particular ontological structure whose proper analysis will, in turn, require the development and application of the regionally appropriate scientific method. This is the meaning of Husserl's claim that his phenomenological method, for the first time, transforms philosophy into a genuine science, and, more startling still, that it is his rejection of the positivist claim for the unity of scientific method that makes him the truest positivist of *all*.

For, according to Husserl, philosophy does not become scientific by adopting a method, the method of experimental physics, originally developed in a quite separate region of inquiry, but by developing for its own chosen region, the region of immediate perception, a no less rigorous method but one specifically tailored to its own distinct, ideal rather than material, object.[6] The proper scientific object of philosophy is the realm of objects as they appear to consciousness, phenomena, and its proper method is, consequently, a pure science of appearances, of intentional mental objects, that proceeds without regard to any question of whether or not such objects exist outside the mind of the subject who perceives them. For Husserl this and this alone is pure phenomenology: and its very irrelevance to practical or existential questions, entailed in the requirement that it maintain a strict neutrality with regard to the metaphysical question of whether or not the particular object, horse or unicorn, heaven or earth, *actually* exists, ensures the unique status of phenomenology as a truly scientific philosophy.

In Gadamer's work, by contrast, the notion of a theoretical attitude denotes, not the discovery of a privileged method that will grant access to truth, but a more generally reflective, philosophical stance toward reality as a whole. Unlike the Husserlian conception of a scientific method specific to philosophy — an ideal pursuit directed toward purely ideal objects — Gadamer's notion of theory stands in continuity with rather than contradiction to the world of practice. Based in the all too material business of existence, it can hardly avoid questions of the ontological reality of whatever it considers. Indeed, if anything, like the pre-reflective experience from which it historically emerges, it tends rather to assume, unless otherwise convinced, that what is experienced is real and has, as such, a being that is independent of its being perceived.

So seen, theory entails, not a radical break with the common-sense understanding of the life-world, but rather the reflectively conscious pursuit of the same task of understanding — the constitutively human attempt to understand self and world —that is already present, pre-reflectively, in what Husserl calls the 'natural attitude'. This is, incidentally, also the position taken by Eric Voegelin, when he emphasizes the extent to which classical philosophy is, in essence, the systematic, *noetic* or self-reflective articulation of common sense, and by Paul Ricoeur in his claim that philosophy thinks nothing that is not pre-reflectively articulated in popular myth and symbol.[7]

What is, perhaps, particular to Gadamer's formulation of the issue of the relationship between the world of theory and the world of practice, or, to put it in another way, between the activity of interpretation and the anthropological framework in which interpretation occurs, is the extent to which, in opposition to Husserl's attachment to an ahistorical conception of the theoretical, scientific and/or philosophical, pursuit of truth, Gadamer stresses, alongside this quest, the historical factors that are inescapably involved in the process. Gadamer insists that we have to recognize, as a primary *datum* of theoretical self-awareness, the rootedness of every theoretical inquiry, including one's own, in the distinct historical conditions of the life-world in which it arises.

This insistence reflects the difference between two philosophies. The first, exemplified by Husserl, sees an absolute distinction between the timelessly true world of theoretical inquiry, defined by its equally timeless adherence to the regionally appropriate scientific method, and the historically contingent world of practice. The second is that represented for present purposes by Gadamer, which sees truth, not as the result of the application of the correct method to a defined subject matter, but as something, sensed but indefinable, for which man struggles as part of his vocation as a primordially self-interpreting or hermeneutic being — one who must understand in order to survive and survive in order to understand.

2. Contexts of Reference

The legacy of Husserl, though differently appropriated and evaluated by each school, is, alongside the thought of Wilhelm Dilthey, a recognized part of the inheritance of both contemporary hermeneutical theory and hermeneutic philosophy. The two are, even when seemingly most opposed to one another, *frères ennemis*: creatures sharing an intellectual genealogy who enter into dispute, and can so do, because, behind the issues dividing them, there are overlapping, if not always identical, concerns, as well as a mutually intelligible vocabulary of debate. The champions of each school engage with the issues and utilize the terms of debate, almost as a matter of course, by virtue of their common and commonly acknowledged heritage. These shared issues and terms are, as often as not, matters originally brought to the centre of the philosophical agenda by Husserl himself. They are family traits which those who stand in a certain line of philosophical descent take for granted as constitutive of the activity of philosophy as such. In this way, as Gadamer sees it, the Husserlian ideal of a presuppositionless philosophy is ultimately betrayed by its own dependence upon the unwarranted presupposition, inherited from Descartes, that such a de-contextualized philosophical ground can ever be attained. For, to each philosophical tradition there belongs, as it were, a 'natural attitude' of its own.[8]

One obvious consequence of this is that the shared terms and issues that constitute philosophy for one tradition are by no means necessarily nor even likely to be obvious or transparent to those outside the family circle, to whom they may appear as utterly devoid of merit and meaning —not philosophy but its negation. It is thus that the devotees of analytical philosophy, for whom not Husserl and Heidegger but Frege and Wittgenstein define the proprieties of modern philosophical debate, have, at least until recently, regarded the whole area of discourse within which my paper moves.[9] So long as a state of utter theoretical *apartheid* prevails this situation is philosophically regrettable but without intellectual consequence. Each cultivates his philosophical acre, imagining it to be the universe, and all survive in a peace that rests if not on ignorance then on mutual disbelief.

However, when, for one reason or another, the barriers begin to break down, when academically significant individuals, like Richard Rorty, once analyst now hermeneut, begin to move between traditions, odd things begin to happen.[10] Mutual understanding across barriers of intellectual tradition, desirable in itself, may sometimes lead, on both sides, to a misunderstanding of the very ideas which are supposed to provide the new common ground. This is not always a bad thing. There is, as the practice of hermeneutics reminds us, such a thing as creative misunderstanding — a misunderstanding out of which an as yet undiscovered truth emerges. But there is as well another side of the coin that must also be taken into account. That is the fact that one possible consequence of misunderstanding is the loss, from the tradition that is misunderstood in the course of cultural translation, of one or more of the essential truths that are embedded, sometimes uniquely, within it.

I mention this matter in this context because the present consideration of the relationship of philosophical anthropology to hermeneutics is spurred, at least in part, by the strong impression that, in the recent reception of hermeneutic philosophy in the English-speaking world, but especially in the United States, a considerable, theoretically and practically unfortunate misunderstanding may actually have occurred.

Because German hermeneutic philosophy, not merely hermeneutical theory, has been taken on board without any equivalent appropriation of the philosophical anthropology which, for Gadamer at least, is its necessary concomitant, the idea has taken hold that an historically oriented hermeneutic philosophy can dispense with, and is even incompatible with, any notion of human nature or of anthropological constants that define or delimit the being of man.[11] Let us have, the message goes, a human science without a notion of human nature and, along with that, a human society that is unprecedentedly humane because, in the name of the ideal of pluralism — which means, in practice, the refusal to endorse or defend any distinctive ideal at all — it no longer exalts one possibility of human being over any other, nor has any philosophical grounds for ever doing so.[12]

Between German and English language philosophy what I have termed cultural translation has not, of course, been a one-way process. In the post-war world, but especially in the last two decades, cross-fertilization has been the order of the day. This being the case, and Gehlen being one of post-war Germany's leading importers of the ideas of the American Pragmatists, one is led to ask, in his case as well, whether a destructive rather than creative misunderstanding may not have occurred? If Rorty takes hermeneutic philosophy, wrongly as I believe, to imply a position of cognitive relativism inscribed only by the bounds of good taste — which I take to be the meaning of his notion that philosophy can never be more than "edifying discourse" — can Gehlen be said to have been either more faithful or more pragmatically successful in his successive appropriations of American pragmatism to suit the conditions of both pre-war and post-war Germany?

For the moment I leave the question open, pausing only to remark that any answer we give is bound to affect our judgement of Gehlen's status both as a theorist of philosophical anthropology and as a politically engaged social critic. For what seems to be implied in Gehlen's espousal of the pragmatic tradition is this: that, as a resolutely anti-metaphysical philosophy, which raises practical success to the status of theoretical truth, pragmatism is uniquely suited to provide the minimal philosophical legitimation required both by an objective, theoretical but non-speculative, science of man and by a social order that that no longer seeks to justify itself by appeal to the disaggregated absolute of disputed ideals, but in terms of its systemic efficiency alone.

Here, however, it should be noted that Gehlen's reading of the political "consequences of pragmatism", to echo the title of Rorty's recent book, [13] is strikingly different from Rorty's own. This is awkward, for it renders questionable an assumption which I take to be one of the principle reasons for

Gehlen's attraction to pragmatism. That is the assumption that the pragmatic criterion of practical effectiveness provides at least one indisputable point of reference for settling disagreements in a world which, if it is to avoid a repetition of the ideological wars of our century, must learn to do without the sort of consensual consciousness that characterized previous forms of stable social order. Ask once, "Effectiveness for what?" and the appeal of pragmatism diminishes greatly.

That said, I return briefly to Husserl. I concede that much of the Husserlian, phenomenological legacy of philosophical hermeneutics of both varieties, though relevant to general discussion of the nature of the human sciences, is of secondary importance to the specific matter of this chapter . Acknowledging this, I shall not discuss it as a topic *per se*. Nevertheless, reference to Husserl does more than help us to distinguish between varieties of philosophical hermeneutics. Invocation of his name, and so of phenomenology in a restricted, Husserlian sense, also calls to mind two issues pertinent to our attempt to establish the significance of Gehlen's anthropology for philosophical hermeneutics. The first is the disputed matter of the relationship between theoretical reflection, its historical context and its practical implications — a point already touched on when contrasting Gadamer's view with that of Husserl. The second is the related but not identical question, posed originally and most dramatically by Nietzsche, of how far the aims of theoretical reflection, of pure, practically disinterested science, are continuous or even compatible with the imperatives of life. Neither issue will be examined here in its purely phenomenological context, but both will recur in the course of reflections in which comparison of Gehlen with phenomenologists *de plus stricte observance* can play a useful part.

In addressing the relationship between anthropology and hermeneutics, phenomenology provides us with an essential third point of reference. In the present context, this is not primarily a function of the influence that phenomenological ideas exerted on the major theorists of both philosophical anthropology and hermeneutics — an influence that would, in itself, guarantee phenomenology a prominent, perhaps a preeminent, place were our main concern with the genealogy and history of ideas. More important here, is the fact that in recalling certain issues addressed by phenomenology we are led to see why there can, in the last analysis, be no question of having to choose between the perspective of philosophical anthropology and that of hermeneutic philosophy. For what we will seek and be able to show is that neither stands alone; that each requires the other, and equally so, if we are adequately to conceptualize both the task of the human sciences and the limitations to which they are subject.

This sets me in opposition to theorists who, ignoring both Max Scheler and the rich vein of post-Schelerian philosophical anthropology, simply assume that hermeneutic philosophy has made methodologically redundant and ontologically obsolete all reference within human scientific theory to the idea of a constant human nature. But it also distances my position from that of philosophers, like Ludwig Landgrebe and Calvin Schrag, who do indeed discuss the claims of anthropology, but conclude that Heidegger's *Dasein* analysis effectively undermines the foundational claims of any theory of human being which, like Gehlen's, rests its case on what it takes to be scientific knowledge of the ontologically constitutive, structural conditions of man's nature and place in the world.[14]

3. The Challenge to Anthropology

Such arguments derive ultimately from the analyis of human existence, of *Dasein*, originally presented in *Being and Time*. There Heidegger seeks, among other things, to establish the ontological primacy of *Dasein*'s self-interpretive dimension — the ever questioning and questionable character of man's being-in-the-world — over the sort of structural conditions of existence in terms of which more conventionally anthropological philosophers had sought to delineate the being of man.[15] It is however not in *Being and Time* itself but in a slightly later work, *Kant and the Problem of Metaphysics*, that Heidegger explicitly deploys the results of his analysis in an argument designed to show that the Schelerian project of developing, alongside a renewed metaphysics, a scientifically informed, foundational discipline of anthropology is, by comparison with Heidegger's own "fundamental ontology", a derivative, and even a philosophically misbegotten undertaking.[16]

What Scheler conceives as an inquiry rooted in the universal metaphysically determined peculiarity of man's place in the cosmos — his conception of philosophical anthropology as the necessary self-clarifying discipline of a being in whom the originally separate principles of drive and spirit, *Drang und Geist,* are uneasily joined[17] — is presented by Heidegger as a specific *historical* problem of Western metaphysics as it emerges from the ordeal of Kantian critique. According to this view, metaphysics and anthropology do not represent, as Scheler supposes, parallel projects in the self-clarification of human being as such. They are not theoretical tasks imposed upon man by ontologically given features of his being, or universally valid inquiries bearing on matters that may be questionable in theory, but which must, practically speaking, be accepted as inescapable facts of life. Instead, Heidegger maintains, they are developments that occur only as specific functions of the historically distinct tradition of Western, 'metaphysical' thought — the tradition of Platonic and post-Platonic philosophy. And this tradition has its origins, not in any uniquely privileged encounter with self-evident truths of being, but in, what remain to this day, powerful but still questionable *interpretations* of what it is to be first developed by the Hellenic philosophers.

According to Heidegger what we in the West have long known as metaphysics, the universal science of being as such, as well as the more recent project of a general philosophical anthropology, originate in the historically and culturally decisive yet still provisional answers to what he calls the question of Being which we inherit from the thinkers of ancient Greece. Only the passage of time and the authority of a philosophical tradition that is now itself to be called into question give the founding, formative questions of Schelerian anthropology their apparent self-evidence. To question the tradition in this way is, Heidegger stresses, not necessarily to reject it, but rather to emphasize its hermeneutic origin as founded in the interpretation and not an imagined facticity of Being.

In his illuminating survey of contemporary philosophy, Landgrebe invokes a foreshortened version of Heidegger's argument against Scheler in order to criticize the anthropology of Gehlen's *Der Mensch*. Landgrebe accuses Gehlen of attributing ontologically necessary, foundational, status to what is, in reality, no more than an inevitably selective complex of features of human life. What is more, Landgrebe argues, the features of man's being on which Gehlen places particular stress reflect, not the unchanging reality of the human condition as such, but only a particular, historically conditioned interpretation of that condition.

Gehlen, he maintains, presents " *The self-understanding of man as a function of the facticity of life regarded as an ultimate*;" and so sees consciousness as only "an auxiliary means of the organic process." In Landgrebe's view, this position needs to be reversed. Gehlen's " *interpretation of human existence* " — as a kind of life which by its very constitution excludes the capacity of answering the question concerning its meaning — *must be understood as the function of a very specific manner of self-understanding*. For a certain kind and amount of self-understanding pertains inseparably to human existence, and this is more than a powerless reflex of a static constitutional condition of this existence. In his self-understanding man designs a blueprint . . . of what he can be and should be, and in doing so he reaches out beyond everything that he has been. It is precisely when the problems implicit in the anthropological approach are consistently followed to their conclusions, as is done in exemplary fashion in Gehlen's treatise *Der Mensch*, that it becomes clearly evident why *these are not and cannot be narrowly self-confined* but point beyond themselves to a different plane upon which the approach to the phenomenon of man tries to derive its justification from the structure of human self-understanding." [18]

Here, from the position of an essentially Heideggerian hermeneutic philosophy, Landgrebe wields a sword that is meant to cut away the claim of philosophical anthropology to provide a secure, scientific foundation for the human sciences. Gehlen claims that his account of man's nature and place in the world describes an experimentally, historically and archaeologically attested framework of anthropological constants, rooted in and explicable by reference to the unchanging survival needs of the morphologically unique, human form of life. In Landgrebe's words, Gehlen believes that he has, thereby, provided "a scientifically established starting point for the question which man asks concerning his own self." But this, according to the same author, is not the achievement it claims to be but "rather a sign and symptom of the wayless forlornness which Nietzsche described as one of the symptoms of European nihilism."

Anthropology, Landgrebe claims, cannot "rise to a mode of self-reflection which would be capable of penetrating with its glance to the sources of its historically conditioned origin." Philosophical anthropology, in the sense we understand it here, neither is nor can be a foundational science of man, as Scheler hoped and Gehlen claimed. Its interest, for Landgrebe, is not as a secure modern *science* but rather as a *symptom* of modern insecurity. Its ambition to achieve the status of foundational science only serves "to illustrate the situation of modern man: its characteristic self-satisfied readiness to accept life in its striving for self-preservation and self-exaltation as an ultimate unquestioned and unquestionable fact." What is more, Landgrebe adds ominously: "When translated from theory into practice, this assumption is believed to justify any amount of brutality in the struggle for naked self-preservation, whether it be of the individual, of a people, or of a state." [19]

Landgrebe's case, and with it the Heideggerian and post-Heideggerian claim to have established the unequivocal primacy of hermeneutics over a structurally oriented anthropology is something I shall seek to counter below. It is, I have suggested, a claim whose validity is generally assumed without further examination in recent Anglo-American work in the philosophy of the human sciences; and it is one that must be answered if we are to make good our case for the mutual and equal entailment of hermeneutic and anthropological approaches to the question of man. However the proper place for such an answer lies not at this point in our argument but later, when we turn to a critical review, an alternative presentation, of the relation between anthropology and the type of philosophical approach exemplified above by Landgrebe. Before doing that, however, we must first look at the part played by anthropology, or rather the essential place of what I call anthropological reference, in the logic of inquiry of what Bleicher terms 'hermeneutical theory', as distinct from its relation to a 'hermeneutic philosophy' of Heideggerian provenance.

4. Hermeneutical Theory

Here let us recall that Bleicher's distinction between 'hermeneutical theory' and 'hermeneutic philosophy' is intended to signal the difference between the view that 'hermeneutics' designates, "the methodology and epistemology of interpretative understanding practised as a science," [20] and the view advanced in *Being and Time* that the term serves primarily to denote, not a mode of theoretical inquiry specific to the human sciences, but a primordial feature of man's being-in-the-world, of *Dasein*. The priority accorded here to establishing anthropology's relationship to hermeneutical theory is not however decided on the usual, historical grounds that the methodological conception of hermeneutics, as represented pre-eminently by Dilthey, precedes Heidegger's ontological view in time. Indeed, though of undoubted use, the distinction between a 'methodological' and an 'ontological' hermeneutics can become thoroughly misleading when conceived, as so often it is, merely in terms of nineteenth- and early twentieth-century intellectual history. It is particularly confusing in relation to Dilthey himself, whose conception of the range of hermeneutics is not primarily methodological at *all*, but based in a distinct philosophy of human, cultural reality which is, in anything but Heidegger's own peculiar sense of the term, an indubitably 'ontological' theory.[21]

I do not say that there is, historically speaking, no such a thing as a purely methodological conception of hermeneutics, only that we do not find it in Dilthey. If we want an example of hermeneutics conceived as method alone we have to delve back, beyond Dilthey and the nineteenth century, to the older, Post-Reformation tradition of biblical hermeneutics, in which the hermeneut's task is defined as being to provide a philologically informed supplement to what would otherwise be an incomplete exegesis of the word of God. In place of the Catholic appeal to the collective wisdom of a divinely instituted Church, embodied in an authoritative interpretive tradition, Protestantism must enlist the knowledge and techniques of the individual scholar, the professional philologist, in order to settle any matter of doubt which may arise concerning the proper meaning of scripture. This is the whole task of biblical hermeneutics as originally conceived. The forensic methods of philology are employed purely as means in the service of a theological and evangelical end —the exposition of the divine Word —that cannot itself be the subject of any equivalent inquiry.

This is indeed a methodological conception through and through. Hermeneutic deliberation is of means, not of ends. For, in an exegetic variation on the classic Lutheran theme of justification by faith alone, the end is removed from the scope of examination. The privileged status of scripture, as the record of divine revelation, is vouchsafed purely by faith, and is thus in principle held to be beyond the competence of a human scholarship whose only purpose is to make plain the sometimes mysterious word of God. Such a biblical and theological hermeneutics is purely methodological not in the tautological sense that it makes use of the specialist methods of philology, but, more deeply, because its scope of inquiry falls short of reflection on either the truth or the ontological status of its object. It leaves untouched the philosophical question of what sort of reality its object may possess or be.

Now this clearly is not the case in the work of Dilthey. Nor is it true of the hermeneutical theories of his immediate predecessors, Schleiermacher and Droysen, in whom, respectively, the philosophical standing of the claims of Christian faith and the ontologically distinctive status of historical reality as a realm within yet also apart from nature, are central objects of interpretive reflection. These are philosophical, even ontological, questions, and the fact that the major figures of nineteenth-century hermeneutical theory all present hermeneutics as a *method* of inquiry should not blind us to the fact that the questions to which the interpretive method is now to be applied are the central, ontological questions of philosophy itself.

In a hermeneutics conceived, as Dilthey conceives it, as the general and distinct *method* of the human sciences, the question of method is already inextricably implicated with the question of the ontological status of its intended object — the being of human, social and historical reality. This engagement with ontological questions is the mark of a new, philosophical as opposed to purely philological or methodological, hermeneutics. And the fact that Dilthey himself continues to describe hermeneutics as a *method* should not prevent us from seeing that underlying and provoking his methodological concern, is a distinct view of the ontology of the life-world. In truth, what sets Dilthey and his immediate predecessors apart from the older tradition of biblical hermeneutics, and from traditional legal hermeneutics as well, is not the extension of a pre-existing method to new areas, as Dilthey's own 'methodological' presentation of hermeneutics may at times suggest. It is the fact that the new hermeneutical theory of the nineteenth century is, from the beginning, a mode of *philosophizing* as the older theological hermeneutics was not.

5. Towards Philosophical Anthropology: The case of Dilthey

In other words, hermeneutical theory in the Diltheyan tradition, distinguished though it is by its overt concern with presenting interpretation as a method, is already a fully philosophical hermeneutics. It differs from post-Heideggerian hermeneutic philosophy not because it is any less concerned with ontological issues, within which we must include the question of the nature of man, but because it refuses to prioritise, in anything but an epistemological sense, the interpretive dimension of man's being over what it takes to be given, inescapable features of human life. Thus, when Landgrebe indicts Gehlen for presenting "the self-understanding of man as a function of the facticity of life regarded as an ultimate," it is ostensibly a thoroughly Diltheyan 'crime' of which the anthropologist is being accused. For, in Dilthey's philosophy, the case for the universality of hermeneutics as the method of the human sciences is founded in the prior ontological conviction that every cultural, historical reality must be understood as an historically particular expression and objectification of the universal, specifically and distinctively human, form of 'Life'.

Here, though, we must enter a word of caution; for while Life, *Leben*, is the fundamental category of Dilthey's ontology of human existence, his *Lebensphilosophie*, it is a term which, as Marjorie Grene notes, he tends all too readily to identify with the historical field of human activity.[22] The bio-physical reference, present in the word itself and stressed in the work of subsequent philosophical anthropologists, is underplayed and even ignored in Dilthey's own use of the concept of Life. Indeed, much of the future task of philosophical anthropology, notably the development of what Gehlen terms his 'anthropobiological' approach and the non-Heideggerian ontology and anthropology of Nicolai Hartmann, may best be understood as an extended attempt by Dilthey's successors to identify the distinctiveness of man's being in a more conceptually adequate way than that represented by Diltheyan *Lebensphilosophie* in its original form.[23] For the moment though let us remain with Dilthey in order to bring out more clearly what I have termed the essential anthropological reference of his hermeneutical theory.

Justifying the claim of hermeneutics to represent the proper mode of human scientific inquiry as distinct from the methods appropriate to the natural sciences, Dilthey writes that: "Life is to be understood in its peculiar essence through categories which are foreign to the knowledge of nature. What is decisive here is that these categories are not applied to life in an *a priori* fashion as from without, but that they lie implicit in the essence of life itself." [24] *Selbstbesinnung*, self-reflection or, in our terms, self-interpretation, is, for Dilthey, a fundamental aspect of man's mode of being-in-the-world. It is an essential part of the way in which human Life achieves expression in the objectified form of an historically concrete culture. Interpretation, the method of *Verstehen*, is thus the privileged method of human scientific inquiry primarily because the object of such inquiry is always already itself the objectified product of an historically specific form of self-understanding.

It is thus that Dilthey seeks to vindicate the methodological claim of interpretive understanding, hermeneutics, by reference to the distinction of human being as a life-form in which the element of interpretation is already implicit as an indisputable, but not exclusive formative element. For there is, Dilthey argues, more to the structure of life than self-understanding alone. Hermeneutics, as the form of inquiry through which alone the human life-form is to be understood, seems, therefore, to require further reference, beyond the self-interpretive dimension of Life, to the reality of an ontologically structured human nature that is prior to all historically particular varieties of self-understanding. "What man is, only history can tell him," he writes; but then again, what he learns from history is that "the nature of man . . . is always the same." [25] The constancy of human nature which we discover only through interpretation of the variety of historically given forms of self-understanding belies the idea that the identity of man is ever a matter of interpretation alone. [26]

In Dilthey's philosophy, beneath and before the question of hermeneutics as method, we find ourselves in the presence of a powerful vision, not yet fully articulated, of the ontologically given reality of man's being, the variable yet finite constancy of his nature and condition, conceived as both object and condition of inquiry. This is what I meant when I referred above to the essential ontological and anthropological references of Diltheyan hermeneutical theory; and it is interesting here to note that Dilthey himself describes the ultimate task of hermeneutics in terms of what he calls 'anthropological reflection', *anthropologische Besinnung*—meaning by this an overall reflection both on life and on the primary self-reflection *Selbstbesinnung*, which is an inexpungeable element not only in the life of the species but in the biography of every individual. Self-reflection, he suggests, rises to the level of anthropological reflection when the individual becomes conscious of his place in historical life and of the sense or meaning of life as a peculiarly human project. [27] While this idea may be given an Heideggerian interpretation it is no less compatible with the alternative conception of life held by Dilthey himself.

Life, in this view, is indeed an 'ultimate', the perennial and perennially questionable object of interpretation but not its creature. For Dilthey, as for Gehlen, the interpretation of man's being by reference to imperatives of life is not to be seen, as Landgrebe sees it, as simply "the function of a very specific manner of self-understanding." Rather, interpretation, the domain of hermeneutics as a whole, must be seen as the expression of a particular form of life which pertains to man as such. If this is to be described as a "specific manner of self-understanding," it is one that is, in its claim to embody certain enduring truths about man as an identifiable life-form, specific to the species as a whole and not, as Landgrebe implies, merely the product of a particular historically limited world-view.

To put matters in more general terms, what we are trying to suggest is that, though the mode of human inquiry is always interpretive, what is discovered through interpretation is, in hermeneutical theory, always acknowledged to be something more than the product of the process by which it comes to be known. Here we may invoke Husserl's fundamental distinction between *noema* and *noesis*, between the object of knowledge and the means or act of knowing. For it is a distinction that serves to underline the crucial point that interpretive knowledge of man, though bearing inevitably upon prior interpretations of the meaning of the life-world, bears no less surely, both on its own account and by way of the particular historically given world-interpretations which stand in its interpretive path, upon those constitutive features of the human condition which pre-exist articulation and which, from the beginning, provoke interpretation as a perennial and necessary project of man's being. Where there is life-world, there also is life.

In epistemological terms we may admit that knowledge of the world comes to us through interpretation; but, speaking ontologically, what we know there to be, though known only in part and always from a particular perspective, is more than a mere function of self-understanding or even of understanding as such. The epistemological universality of hermeneutics in our knowledge of man, and even, to concede a point to the Heideggerians, in man's primary awareness of his being, is, *pace* Heidegger, no proof of its ontological priority as the defining feature of man's being-in-the-world.[28]

The point at issue can be illustrated by reference to a passage from the journal of the historian of religion Mircea Eliade where he writes: "Even if we wanted to, we couldn't give up hermeneutics because we are the result of a millennial hermeneutical effort. Ultimately, we are the result of interpretations of life, death, consciousness, creativity, etc. elaborated since the pre-Socratics, and even before since the discovery of agriculture and metallurgy for example."[29] One may take issue with Eliade's use of the term *ultimately* in this context, but the significance of his words is plain enough. What he is pointing to is the fact that the identity of human beings and of the cultures they form is not something utterly determined by nature but rather a creative accomplishment—one that is, however, achieved over history through a process of continuing interpretation and reinterpretation of certain inescapable features of existence. Seen thus, man is indeed an hermeneutic being but life and death, consciousness and creativity provoke interpretation at all times and places precisely because, alongside the no less inevitable facts of human physiology, they are not themselves creatures of the interpretive process. Rather, they must be understood, just as much as the hermeneutical effort they provoke, to be elementary and inescapable features of man's being-in-the-world. As such they form in sum a finite anthropological framework—a more or less complete catalogue of anthropological constants—whose recognition and acceptance is the measure of interpretive truth.

Reference to such an anthropological framework is present not only in Dilthey's work, as evidenced by his reference to the constancy of human nature, but thoughout the tradition of hermeneutical theory in which he is the central figure. Before Dilthey, we find it in Droysen for whom, "The method of historical inquiry is determined by the morphological character of its material," and, a century later, in Betti's characterization of hermeneutics as the investigative 'inversion' of the creative processes through which the common humanity of man achieves expression in the objectified form of cultural artifacts.[30] In all three authors, the ultimate, ontologically determined sameness of human nature—what we may term the postulate of anthropological constancy—founds the possibility of understanding the real variety in which the material of human history consists. That this postulate of constancy is no dogmatic assertion but a necessary consequence of inquiry itself has recently been shown with unequalled eloquence and clarity by Hans Jonas in his *Wandel und Bestand* "Change and Permanence," an essay which, significantly if somewhat ironically, first appeared as Jonas's contribution to the *Festschrift* published in celebration of Heidegger's seventieth birthday.[31]

Following Jonas, we may say that in hermeneutical theory the epistemological claims of hermeneutics as a method of human scientific inquiry must invariably be justified, if only in the last analysis, by reference to the ontologically enduring nature and condition of man as a peculiar sort of being whose trans-historically given life-form is essentially active, creative and expressive and yet, at the same time, limited by the worldly state in which he finds himself to be. In its fundamental features this life-form, though always expressing itself historically, is the precondition and not the product of history —not the creature of interpretive inquiry but both its presupposition and the cognitive result, the intentional ontological object, to which the pursuit of hermeneutic understanding must inevitably lead.

6. Anthropology Attained: Scheler and Plessner

What then is the connection between the anthropological reference we find in Diltheyan hermeneutical theory and the type of philosophical anthropology exemplified for our purposes by Gehlen's *Der Mensch*? Without going into the historical affiliations, evident for example in the work of Erich Rothacker, we may say that whereas in Dilthey the ultimate reference to human nature represents an appeal to an element whose constancy is taken for granted, in twentieth-century philosophical anthropology the 'nature' of human nature has itself become the central problem.

In keeping with the heritage of German idealist and romantic thought, Dilthey *assumes* that man, while always expressing his being in historically particular forms through which alone he can be known, is an essentially unchanging being. Because, in Dilthey, the enduring identity of man is, generally speaking, taken for granted, the focus of the philosopher's interest falls overwhelmingly on the historical particularity of human achievements rather than on the transhistorical conditions which make every such achievement possible. It is for this reason that in Dilthey's work the concept of Life, as a designation of the peculiarly human form of being, is so exclusively identified with the sphere of action and culture — the realm of the historically mutable. Secure in his anthropological convictions, Dilthey assumes a constancy in human nature, which he rightly takes to be confirmed by historical inquiry, but takes no interest in further delineating the physiological, cosmological and ultimately ontological conditions in which that constancy consists and which delimit the range of historical possibility.

Thus, despite Dilthey's characterization of human scientific inquiry as a mode of what he calls 'anthropological reflection', the anthropological reference implied throughout his work never issues in anything approaching a fully articulated philosophical anthropology. Life, in its Diltheyan sense, is an irreducible term, an explanatory category that designates, in an inclusive and conceptually undifferentiated way, the totality of man's nature and place in the world, *seine Natur und seine Stellung in der Welt*. In this philosophy 'life' is, in Landgrebe's sense, indeed an 'ultimate' —an unquestionable point of final reference in terms of which the particularities of historical existence may be explained, and not, as it was to be for Gehlen, a category requiring further anthropological reflection and differentiation. Considering the relationship between the two, we might even say that only where the logic of hermeneutical inquiry finds its completion, in the Diltheyan notion of human 'Life', does the specific task and challenge of anthropology begin.

When Dilthey writes that, "Life is to be understood in its peculiar essence through categories which are foreign to the knowledge of nature," he is presupposing not only that there is a constant core, life's 'peculiar essence', that allows understanding to occur, but that the distinctiveness of the human life form is identifiable by historical inquiry alone. In contrast, when Gehlen begins his work some fifty years later, the situation has altered. The enduring identity of man, taken for granted in romantic hermeneutics, has become problematic. Not only can history no longer be relied on to show that "the nature of man is always the same," but advances in knowledge of the human life-form, attained as a result of natural scientific inquiry, have rendered questionable Dilthey's attempt to isolate the human sciences from the sciences of nature.

Here we may cite in evidence the words of Max Scheler, who writes, in 1926, in justification of his own anthropological project: "In no age have views concerning the *essence and origin of man* been less sure, less determinate and more varied, than in our own... In approximately ten centuries of history, this is the first in which man finds himself completely and utterly 'problematical', in which he no longer knows what he is and simultaneously *knows that* he does not have the answer." Faced with this situation the primary task of the philosopher is to construct a philosophical anthropology: "a basic science which investigates the essence and *essential constitution* of man, his relationship to the realms of nature organic, plant, and animal life as well as to the source of all things, man's metaphysical origin as well as his physical, psychic, and spiritual origins in the world, the forces and powers which move man and which he moves, the fundamental trends and laws of his biological, psychic, cultural, and social evolution, along with their essential capabilities . . .. Only such an anthropology can furnish an ultimate philosophical basis, as well as definite, certain aims of research, to all sciences concerned with the object, 'man', to the natural, medical, archaeological, ethnological, historical, and social sciences, to normal and developmental psychology and character analysis." [32]

The essay from which this passage is taken is entitled "Man and History" but, as Scheler's remarks make clear, the relationship between the two terms of the title is no longer conceived as it was in Dilthey's *Lebensphilosophie.* Whereas Dilthey focusses on historical *inquiry* as providing us with a privileged route to knowledge of human nature, Scheler, influenced both by the phenomenological emphasis on immediate experience and by the civilizational crisis through which he is living, directs his attention on an historical *situation* in which political events and the disaggregation of knowledge resulting from the growth of the special sciences have conspired together to render questionable all our traditional assumptions about the nature of man. In the historical past Dilthey finds the objectified marks of human constancy: in the historical present Scheler discovers only the clash of competing anthropological visions — mutually contradictory images of man — each of which founds a distinctive view of politics and history and none of which seems able to prevail over its rivals. Thus the project of a philosophical anthropology takes its characteristic twentieth-century form as an attempt to integrate diverse fields of knowledge with a view to answering the twin Kantian questions, "What is man?" and "What ought he to do?"

It is this ambitious research project to which, in 1928, the last year of his life, Scheler gives expression in *Die Stellung des Menschen im Kosmos (The Place of Man in the Cosmos)* — a work which, despite its distinctively Schelerian reference to metaphysics, is generally regarded as the "manifesto" of the new, scientifically and, in particular, bio-physically informed philosophical anthropology of which Gehlen is a pre-eminent representative.[33]

Scheler's metaphysical orientation, articulated in his image of man as the being in whose life originally world-transcendent Spirit becomes, for the first time, present in the world, decisively sets his anthropology apart from the mainstream of *Lebensphilosophie*. Man, Scheler maintains, can only be understood against the background of "the total world of living things," but ultimately his real distinctiveness must be comprehended in terms of the presence within his essentially dual nature of an element, Spirit, which is originally foreign to the world of Life and whose imperatives stand ever in potential opposition to the requirements of organic existence. Thus conceived man is indeed a distinctive life-form but one whose metaphysical distinction as incarnate spirit separates him from imperatives of life with which, nonetheless, he must continue to cope.

In contrast, in the anthropology of Helmuth Plessner, whose early writings are contemporaneous with Scheler's final works, metaphysical speculation is set aside in the interests of extending the purview of Diltheyan *Lebensphilosophie* to encompass, within the concept of life, our knowledge of man as a particular sort of organism. Man is not spirit incarnate but a purely bio-physical entity characterized, as Plessner puts it, by the distinctive 'position' which he occupies *within* the broad realm of nature. Man's spirit is not to be seen as something originally apart from life but as an original manifestation or expression of a life-form exclusively identifiable in terms of its peculiar 'positionality' in the natural world.

In *Die Stufen des Organischen und der Mensch 1928 (The Stages of Organic Being and Man)*, Plessner seeks to identify the specific difference of human being against the background of a hierarchical conception of increasingly differentiated life forms. Seen thus, the peculiar position which man occupies within nature, the key to his relative freedom from organic impulses and the source of the adventure of historical existence, is explained in terms of the reflective, self-aware character of human consciousness. The animal lives purely out of the centre of its sensual experiences, aware of the world only as a source of life-enhancing or -threatening stimuli. Man, by contrast, occupies an 'ex-centric' position in the world; bound to bodily existence, and so a centre of sensations, yet able, reflectively, to comprehend, quasi-objectively, the place he occupies within the order of things and so to seek to order his fate.

As Axel Honneth and Hans Joas put it, Plessner takes over the methodological conception of Diltheyan hermeneutics, the reference of interpretation to the explanatory category of 'Life', while "giving it a decisively important naturalistic turn: a hermeneutics of human expressions of life can do theoretical justice to its object only if it also systematically takes into consideration the human being's organismal constitution."[34] Or, as Plessner puts it: "the idea of laying the foundation for sensory experience of the kind appropriate to the socio-cultural sciences necessitates reflection upon problems that reach into the sensual-material sphere of 'life', the sphere of the objectual-instrumental body; it necessitates, therefore, a philosophy of nature, understood in its broadest and most original sense."[35]

In this way Plessner integrates the Diltheyan concept of 'Life' into our broader knowledge of organic life as the form of being characteristic not of man alone but of all living things. The distinctiveness of man is explicated not by reference to life as such, but in terms of the uniquely human-specific 'position' that pertains primordially to man's form of living in the world. In consequence, Plessner argues, "An idea of the mode of existence of the human being as a natural occurrence and as a product of the history of his mode of existence can only be obtained by contrasting it with the other forms of animate nature that are known to us."[36]

Here, as in Scheler, the philosophical-anthropological project is envisaged, in part at least, as a philosopher's response to an historically conditioned situation of acute human self-doubt and confusion. But Plessner goes beyond Scheler in regarding self-doubt not merely as a symptom of crisis but as an enduring feature of man's mode of being. He presents anthropology as "a theory of man with a philosophical purpose, based on his *essential* dubitability"; meaning by this that no metaphysical theory of the essence of man can ever finally still the unquiet interrogation of his being which arises from the intrinsically reflective, self-questioning character of man's ex-centric position in the world.[37]

7. Elemental Anthropology: The Case of Gehlen

Plessner's strategy of anthropological distinction within a philosophy of nature is also the starting point for Gehlen's inquiries; though here the naturalization of *Lebensphilosophie* is carried a stage further; to the point at which Gehlen, no longer satisfied with the characterization of anthropology as a fundamental *philosophical* discipline, albeit one informed by the findings of the special sciences, designates it not as philosophy at all but as an empirical

science in its own right. This move is signalled in Gehlen's displacement of
the notion of anthropology as *Lebensphilosophie* by the new terminology of
what he calls an *Anthropobiologie.*

Plessner mobilizes the findings of the natural sciences in the service of
anthropology in order to inform what remains and, in terms of his image of
man, must remain an essentially open exercise in human self-interpretation.
Thus his anthropology remains philosophical in the strict sense that it entails
reflection on the proper ends and purposes of human existence considered in
the light of what we know of man's nature and condition. Gehlen by contrast
finds in the data of the special sciences not merely the limiting conditions
within which human action takes place — findings which both form the
objective measure of theoretical truth, the *noema* of human-scientific *noesis*,
and reveal the conditions of practical judgement. He also considers scientific
knowledge to be capable of providing a legitimate criterion of the validity of
every such judgement. Practical success, measured in terms of scientifically
calculable survival chances, becomes not a measure but the very definition of
anthropological truth.

As Gehlen's work develops from the early essays written under the dual
influence of phenomenology and Fichtean idealism, philosophical reflection
on the ends of human life is increasingly replaced by a growing acceptance of
the radically anti-speculative premise that, insofar as these ends can be known
at all, they are knowable only as determinations inherent in a life-form to
which the special sciences, social as well as natural, can alone give access.
This process, already well advanced in the anthropology of *Der Mensch,* is
carried much further in the post-war writings; marked as they are by Gehlen's
sense that the catastrophe of the Third Reich was due, in no small measure,
to the pollution of an essentially healthy desire for national political survival
by extra-scientific considerations derived from the speculative realms of
volkisch metaphysics and myth.

In the pre-war years the already pragmatic Gehlen had effectively endorsed
the racial ideology of National Socialism not because he accepted its claim to
scientific truth, but because, pragmatically speaking, he considered it capable
of mobilizing the German nation for effective action in the world. This comes
out very clearly in his reaction to Eric Voegelin's book *Rasse und Staat* 1933
where Gehlen accepts Voegelin's argument that the race idea is not, as it
pretends to be, a body of established scientific knowledge but rather an
activating myth — in Voegelin's terms, a political idea or symbol and not a
scientific theory. However, while recognizing this, Gehlen goes on to
conclude that just such a myth is what may presently be required.[38] It is the
practical failure of National Socialism, as much or more than its crimes, that
leads the later Gehlen, on the same, essentially pragmatic, grounds, to disown

and condemn not merely the ideology to which he had once given his, again essentially practical, assent, but everything that smacks to him of political mythologizing.

From the German catastrophe Gehlen draws the conclusion that, whatever may be the mobilizing power of political ideology and myth over the human mind, and hence its effectiveness as a contribution to the possible success of practical endeavour, the dangers inherent in its use are, in the potentially all-destructive conditions of the modern technological world, too great to make the risk worth taking.

What we witness in the development of Gehlen's thought is what we might term the attempted *exodus* of anthropology from the realm of philosophy — the attempt to found the interpretive logic of the *Geisteswissenschaften* in an empirical science of man constituted out of testable data alone and thus free from the toils of philosophical dispute. Here we are reminded irresistibly of the equivalent ambition of Auguste Comte, a century before, to erect a positive science of society, sociology, in place of the conflicting interpretations of what constitutes a viable and desirable social order represented by competing traditional political philosophies. The resemblance is all the more marked when we consider the motivation that underlies both projects. For both Gehlen and Comte the appeal to empirical science, the emphatic disavowal of what was, in each case, a precocious and highly developed taste for philosophical inquiry, reflects the discovery, or at least the personally compelling conviction, that, while philosophy leads only ever deeper into the mire of irresolvable dispute, scientific investigation discloses a realm of fact that, while not absolute, is, at any point in the development of scientific knowledge, capable of commanding recognition and assent from every rational being. Scientific knowledge, while always provisional and capable of revision in the light of further evidence, represents, at every moment, a relatively certain reference point for political decision making.

In the absence of any universally acceptable metaphysics, and where apparently irresolvable philosophical dispute concerning the truth of man's being takes a practical turn, as it does in post-revolutionary France and, infinitely more bloodily, in the ideological wars of the twentieth century, four possibilities seem to suggest themselves.

The first, represented by such latter-day Marxists as Jürgen Habermas, is to cling desperately to whatever may be salvaged from the Hegelian notions of the absolute and substantive reason, even if this means falling back behind Hegel to a form of Kantian transcendentalism. The second is to seek, in the manner of Eric Voegelin, to show that underlying the clash of incompatible doctrines, the situation of what he calls, in a typically suggestive Hellenizing neologism, 'dogmatomachy', is an undeniable if also undeniably questionable experience of existential tension which only issues in mutually contradictory ideologies when, under the pressure of this tension, men seek to concretize this experience in the inevitably inadequate form of propositional metaphysical or ideological systems. The third, which we find in Carl Schmitt's "Decisionism" and the voluntaristic sociology of Hans Freyer as well as in the young Gehlen's conception of *Erlebnis*—the rationally unjustifiable but subjectively compelling experience which imposes a certain decisive direction upon subsequent action—involves an acceptance of irresolvable conflict and so of the necessity to take one's stand on the basis of the choice one finds oneself compelled to make. And the fourth, as already indicated, is the Comtean option, adopted by the older Gehlen in the name of pragmatism, which involves the disavowal of the philosophical quest for anything more than provisional truth and the prudential reference of every action to the exclusive measure of testable, empirically established scientific data.

To these four positions, each of which endeavours to provide a foundational reference point both for the human sciences and for human conduct, we might add the presently fashionable "post-modernist" option, which, not without occasional reference to Gehlen's concept of the contemporary world as in some sense 'post-historical', disavows the whole "foundationalist" enterprise. [39] When Richard Rorty disowns the quest for philosophical and/or empirical scientific foundations within the sphere of practical judgement, he remarks that "all we require is anthropology." But here the reference is not to anything resembling a philosophical or empirical science of man's nature and condition in the sense we have been using the term hitherto, but simply to the body of ethnographic data whose strictly non-evaluative accumulation and classification constitutes the whole task of social or cultural anthropology in its Anglo-Saxon sense.

Where philosophical anthropology still conceives its task as to deduce anthropologically universal truths from the variety of historical and ethnographic evidence — a truth which may, at the Schmittian limit, entail merely the recognition of mutually contradictory and so potentially warring conceptions of the human good—post-modernist thought requires us simply to marvel at the variety of man. Pluralism is the order of the day, but above all a playful pluralism. However seriously they may regard themselves we must regard the given forms of human life, including our own, only as so many forms of play. One exists alongside the other as tennis exists alongside football. The rules of the games are incompatible but, lacking any foundation for discriminatory judgement, we can have no intellectual grounds for choosing between them. Nor dare we do so. For where a choice must be made, the games may turn serious and resolve themselves in the single ancient, but now potentially universally fatal game of war. [40]

   This post-modernist position, which, as already indicated, seeks residual philosophical corroboration in the post-Heideggerian notion of *Dasein*, man as a purely self-interpreting being, is, in its fundamental motivation as well as its political implications, closer to Gehlen than may at first appear. The exodus of philosophy from itself, its disavowal of its truth-seeking vocation and re-emergence as what Rorty quaintly calls "edifying discourse," continues the process of the exodus of anthropology from philosophy already noted in connection with the development of Gehlen's ideas. In both cases the apparent inability of philosophical inquiry to determine definitively what truth may be — without irresolvable debate and hence polemic that may lead literally to *Polemos* war — provokes a disengagement from the quest for philosophical foundations for the human sciences. In both there is a turn toward what is seen as a purely empirical starting point. The difference being that while Gehlen still envisages this as an empirical science of anthropological constants entailed in the biophysical constitution of human being — constants that underly, make possible, and ultimately set the limits to political and cultural variety — post-modernists see variety itself as the only constant feature.

   This, in turn, can only seem intellectually credible if man's nature and place in the world is assumed to be fixed by nothing more ontologically fundamental than the immediate source of this variety, self-interpretation and expression. Thus the post-modernist exodus of philosophy from its previously constitutive vocation of truth-oriented inquiry must be accompanied by a removal of anthropology from the sphere of science and, as Gehlen had already shrewdly noted in a comment on the significance of Heidegger, its reincarnation in an expressive form that might still call itself "knowledge" but which former generations had known as "art." [41]

8. The Limits of Elemental Anthropology

In this context Gehlen cites Gottfried Benn's dictum: "The philosophers must now make poetry; for the moment discursive thought has reached an impasse." Being unwilling to follow the aesthetic path, and regarding as no longer scientifically tenable the alternative, properly philosophical strategy of Hartmann's critical ontology, Gehlen abandons philosophy to the aesthetes and turns to what he regards as the hard business of empirical science. Again, the parallel to Comte is striking; though now the path of science is no longer seen as leading to a rational reordering of the world but, in a quasi-Weberian spirit of resignation, to a more or less uncritical acceptance of what are taken to be the inevitable socially formative dynamics of a technologically conditioned industrial system. No longer may the system itself be criticized; a wise Führer would have contented himself with being a good managing director. Instead Gehlen's undiminished critical energies are directed against anyone who, like the theorists of the New Left, still seeks to call the existentially necessary social order into question in the name of obsolete philosophical or political ideals.[42]

The Fichtean philosophy of willed existential commitment, so marked an element in Gehlen's early writings, is abandoned in the wake of its historical wreckage in Germany's defeat. In its place we find an exclusive commitment to scientific fact and a social-psychological, rather than historical-political, diagnosis of the reasons for the lingering discontents of modernity. The world may no longer be reordered in the image of the existentially compelling idea —the activating fantasy or myth. Rather whatever ideas may remain must be submitted to the implacable logic of irreversible events. What once seemed a healthy practical manifestation of the intrinsic freedom of the human will is now diagnosed as a pathological failure to recognize the reality of what must be.[43]

And pathos it truly is; for, as Gehlen's late writings make plain, the transition to a post-historical world, materially comfortable but without any overall meaning or commanding ideals, beyond the imperative of conformity to technological necessity, cannot be accomplished without great cost to some of the most deep-seated features of man's nature. Above all the creative imagination, which, from the beginning, had guided man's practical ordering of the world, his re-creation of nature as culture, must be excluded, in anything but the most narrowly instrumental form, from the realm of political action and confined to the "native reservations" of art and religion. Here imagination may still hold sway. Within these reserved areas discontents may be expressed and purely imaginary comforts developed and indulged. But woe betide the man who seeks to carry his imaginative ideals back into the public sphere or the society that allows him to do so.

Thus, a generation after Gehlen, and so removed from the pressures of the pre-war imperative of fateful decision, the uneasy legacy of Gehlen's philosophy of action and institution resolves itself in the systems theory of Niklas Luhmann, for whom not the freedom of deciding will but the inescapable, mutually entailing inputs and outputs of cybernetics provide the model of a viable social order.[44] Philosophy can be safely left to aestheticizing Heideggerians and Deconstructionists, for in a self-regulating cybernetic system even the most apparently disturbing output can be expected to generate an equivalent restabilizing reaction. In such a social science not interpretation but model-making is the name of the game. Thus, in the wake of its exodus from philosophy, the newly scientific anthropology of the social actor makes its exodus from itself. *Homo Sociologicus* becomes, in every instance, a microchip in the already decided programme of the social system of modern industry and technology. The system may be analysed but even the attempt to subvert or 'deconstruct' it can do no more confirm it on its course. This is something which many post-modernists and deconstructionists seem inclined to accept. Some even welcome it, in the name of that attitude of playful irresponsibility or vocationally conformist 'critical' nonconformity whose display is the sole remaining, recognised public responsibility of the authentically post-modern, 'critical' intellectual.

For such a bohemian intelligentsia the late Gehlen reserves a more or less tolerant contempt —the degree of his tolerance varying, almost from year to year, on the extent to which the vestiges of once great philosophical questions actually disturb the smooth running of the social order. Lecturing in 1961, he recalls his "indignation as a student upon reading Spengler's remark to the effect that he hoped his writings would contribute to converting philosophy students into technicians. Such advice," he writes, "seems entirely reasonable to me today." Nietzsche, his and his generation's youthful hero, had wanted "to derive clear-cut prescriptions for action from a comprehensive interpretation of the world." But such a "great key attitude," *grosse Schlüsselattitüde*, depended upon "that blindness toward the fundamental laws of technology and industry which runs through Nietzsche's entire work." All such attitudes and the "systematic world views" that went with them are now, for both theoretical and practical reasons, obsolete.

Reflecting on the history of his times, Gehlen continues: "It soon became evident that the realization of ideas that is, the adjustment of reality in the direction of the purity of the idea inevitably leads to bloodshed. Reality is not compatible with the ideal, which consequently takes revenge upon it.... After two world wars, which were fought at enormous sacrifice under the banner of ideas, the only ideas and world views that now seem to have a future are those that have already become a functional part of the established social order and of the operating rules of large industrial societies. They have emerged as the true constituents of industrial societies and, as a reality which was paid for dearly, are now beyond discussion." To this practical consideration, formed in the shadow of the threat of universal extinction, Gehlen adds the theoretical point that scientific specialization has now reached such a point that no purportedly scientifically founded, comprehensive world view could represent anything other than dilettantism. Not only the extra-scientific, Nietzschean dream of the triumph of the will must be disowned: "It is also clear that global views of the world can no longer be formulated within the sciences, just as fundamental reforms can no longer be instituted somewhere within the total system of social practice. Fundamental reforms in government or education are similarly impossible. Given the abundance of data available in those areas, such reforms would have to be thought out at such a high level of abstraction and with such a lack of transparency that only dilettantes could imagine that their views could remain relevant." [45]

This is not a matter I can pursue here except to note my conviction that for all its insights into what are, truly, indispensable aspects of contemporary social order, this systems theory leaves out of account the enduring dependence of every social system upon the identity and self-image of the beings who make it up. Though, from a systemic standpoint, these are indeed elements in a self-regulating order for which cybernetics provides as good a model as any, the programming of any of them can never exclude that element which Plessner calls the essential 'dubitability' of man. The potential for re-programming by the self or another remains an element in the substance of the human stuff of which social systems are composed.

My reference here to Plessner rather than to Gehlen is not accidental; for if we are to pin down a particular point in our story at which the development of anthropology begins to lose touch with the fullness of human reality, and so to diminish in terms of its foundational value to the human sciences, it is the point at which Gehlen, disowning the inclusive, phenomenological notion of experience as a key to reality, confines the scope of the anthropologically given to what is established by the data of the special sciences or may be derived necessarily therefrom. With this move what is lost is, precisely, the constitutively human character of a life-ordering reflection which is not merely reflective of the particular, historically given circumstances of the present.

In the disavowal of fundamental, philosophically critical reflection on the historical process, conceived as the inescapable *logos* of *techne*, Gehlen sees the only hope of avoiding further and perhaps final catastrophe. And so far as this entails rejection of the reborn "critical theory" of the new Marxism of the 1960s, he is, in my view, wholly correct. But, as reference to the equally anti-utopian Plessner and, for that matter, to Eric Voegelin makes plain, the practice of fundamental reflection is not necessarily incompatible with uncompromising recognition of the real organizational imperatives of a civilized modern political order and rejection of all ideological fantasies. Indeed, as Hans Jonas argues in his *Imperative of Responsibility, Das Prinzip Verantwortung* 1979, only such a reflection, amounting to a new metaphysics of morals carried out in the spirit of a scientifically informed *Lebensphilosophie*, may be capable of protecting us against destructive developments inherent in the very techno-industrial imperatives which the late Gehlen seeks to absolutize. [46]

Anthropology remains the necessary reference point of any hermeneutical theory directed toward the clarification of the actuality and prospects of the human condition. But, *pace* Gehlen, such an anthropology must remain properly philosophical, radically interrogative of the present, if it is to fulfil its practical, guiding function. It is not merely that man will, as a matter of fact, remain radically self-questioning regardless of any attempt to delimit the scope of reflection in the name of the practical imperative of the species' survival, but that only such radical reflection is capable of ensuring that the road recommended in the name of obedience to systemic necessity does not lead, as surely as the pursuit of fantasy, to the very extinction it is meant to avoid. A philosophically clarified recognition of ontological necessity —the conditions for the species' survival — is a necessary element of such a reflection; but such necessity is not to be identified exclusively or even primarily with the established, ecologically destabilizing dynamic of present technological-industrial civilization, to which, increasingly obviously, it may even stand oppposed.

9. Vindicating Anthropology: Project and Prospect

Finally let us return, perforce briefly, to the relationship between anthropology and Heideggerian hermeneutic philosophy. Here, following the arguments of Plessner, Jonas and Marjorie Grene, my point is that no truly self-aware interpretation of man's being-in-the-world can leave out of account the given cosmological and biophysical conditions of that being.[47] In *Sein und Zeit*, Heidegger forgoes the anthropological project of seeking to *establish* the distinction of man against the background of a philosophy of nature. Instead, for the sake of giving a purely phenomenological account of existence, one that takes nothing for granted except the inescapable reality of reflection in the life of a being conscious of his own mortality, he allows the worldly conditions of human being to re-emerge, where at all, as creatures of interpretation —which is, of course, how they actually *appear* to reflective consciousness.

When Heidegger writes that "only as phenomenology is ontology possible," he is, for all his departures from the Husserlian ideal represented by his recognition of the radical situatedness of consciousness, remaining true to the Husserlian rather than the Schelerian concept of phenomenology as a knowledge that must refrain from discriminatory judgement as to the ontological reality of its objects. Not the Schelerian 'intuition of essences' but the Husserlian self-clarification of a now existentially situated consciousness remains the guiding principle of Heidegger's early reflections. In the pure phenomenology of *Dasein* as the point in Being, the 'existential' questioning being, in which awareness of Being uniquely appears, the ontologically given becomes itself a matter of pure appearance. Thus the Husserlian distinction between *noema* and *noesis*, what is known and the act of knowing or rather 'encountering', is effectively undercut. Everything is knowable only as a structure of *Dasein*, who is both knower and known; a point of especial significance in connection with Heidegger's self-consistent relativizing of the concept of 'world', *Welt*.

Contrary to what is commonly supposed, I am therefore inclined to think that, at least in its influence on the further anti-naturalistic and anti-ontological direction of contemporary post-modernist thought, the most important thing about *Sein und Zeit* is not its departure from the Husserlian ideal of self-evident certainty but its fidelity to it. For it is in the name of the exclusive evidence of the phenomenologically apparent truth of the being of *Dasein*, its self-interpretive, hermeneutic character, that the ever provisional character of the knowledge of world-structure granted us by empirical science and critical ontology alike can be ruled out of account as somehow inauthentic and secondary. The question that remains, as posed pointedly by Plessner and Grene, is whether this does not remain a further variation on the old Cartesian theme of prioritizing, for the sake of immediate and irrefutable certainty, conscious experience over the conditions which we otherwise know to be presupposed by the existence of any conscious being at all?

As Grene puts it, "Human being, as Being-in-a-World . . . is possible only as the achievement of a certain kind of living being, with certain organic endowments and a certain kind of biological as well as social environment. *Animalia* are a necessary presupposition of *existentialia*." To reject this claim, which represents, in truth, a condition of being, as Heidegger and his followers do, constitutes "an *ontological* ommission, not a reasoned dismissal of ontic claims from an ontological analysis." [48] Or, in Plessner's words: "Only he can exist who lives, regardless of the level on which he lives. To close oneself off to life in its fullness, and to found living upon just one of the human being's possibilities, namely existing, means to let the pursuit of the human being's enquiry about himself count as the sole legitimate directive for an anthropology carried out with practical intent . . . . What conditions must be fulfilled so that the dimension of existence is founded on that of living?" [49] It will not do to take account of the body of man, as Plessner accuses Heidegger of doing, only insofar as it is destined to die. Heidegger's evocative notion of 'Being-unto-death' describes the reality of our existence but what is fated to die, and to know itself so to be, must be a form of life and so subject to whatever we may know to be the conditions that make life possible. To deny this shows not philosophical acumen but an ontological obscurantism which no appeal to the principles of phenomenological evidence can justify.

Notes

1. Arnold Gehlen, *Man. His Nature and Place in the World* trans. Clare McMillan and Karl Pillemer, Introduction by Karl-Siegbert Rehberg (New York: Columbia University Press, 1988. [*Der Mensch, seine Natur und seine Stellung in der Welt* Berlin 1940].

2. Emilio Betti, *Allgemeine Auslungslehre als Methodik der Geisteswissenschaften* (Tübingen: J.C.B. Mohr, 1962);. Betti, 'Hermeneutics as the General Method of the *Geisteswissenschaften*', in Joseph Bleicher (ed.) *Contemporary Hermeneutics. Hermeneutics as Method, Philosophy and Critique* London: Routledge and Kegan Paul, 1980 pp.51-94; E. D. Hirsch, *Validity in Interpretation* (New Haven, Conn: Yale University Press, 1967).

3. Hans-Georg Gadamer, *Truth and Method* trans. William Glen-Doepel, (London: Sheed and Ward, 1975 [*Warheit und Methode* Tübingen 1972].

4. Bleicher, *op.cit.* "Introduction".

5. The question of how far the late works of Husserl, notably *The Crisis of European Sciences*, conform to the model of a presuppositionless philosophy cannot be addressed here.

6. Edmund Husserl, "Philosophy as Rigorous Science," in *Phenomenology and the Crisis of Philosophy*, ed. Edmund Husserl trans. with an "Introduction" by Quintin Lauer (New York: Harper and Row, 1965).

7. See especially Eric Voegelin, *Anamnesis*, trans. Gerhart Niemeyer University of Notre Dame Press, 1977 and Paul Ricoeur *The Symbolism of Evil*, trans. Emerson Buchanan (Boston: Beacon Press, 1967).

8. Gadamer, *Philosophical Hermeneutics*, trans. David E. Linge (New Haven, Conn.: Yale University Press, 1976).

9. Note here the remark of Michael Dummett. "When I was a student in Oxford in the late 1940s... Heidegger was perceived only as a figure of fun, too absurd to be taken seriously as a threat to the kind of philosophy practised in Oxford". In 'Can Analytical Philosophy be Systematic, and Ought It to Be?', collected in *Philosophy. End or Transformation*, ed. Kenneth Bayes, Joseph Bohman and Thomas McCarthy (Cambridge, Mass. MIT Press, 1987) p. 189. It is interesting to recall that the dominant figure in Oxford philosophy at the time was Gilbert Ryle — Dummett refers to "Ryle's Oxford." Ryle had, when young, been an early English exponent of Husserl's philosophy, and had, in 1929, published a critical but respectful review of Heidegger's *Sein und Zeit*. This review may be found in *Heidegger and Modern Philosophy*, ed. Michael Murray (New Haven, Conn.: Yale University Press, 1978) pp.53-64. The opening words of Ryle's review are worth citing. "This is a very difficult and important work, which marks a big advance in the application of the 'Phenomenological Method' — though I may say at once that I suspect that this advance is an advance towards disaster." Unlike Ryle himself, philosophy students in "Ryle's Oxford" seldom had the opportunity to judge for themselves.

10. Richard Rorty, *Philosophy and the Mirror of Nature* (Princeton, N.J.: Princeton University Press, 1980).

11. Apart from Rorty, see, for example, Susan Hekman, *Hermeneutics and the Sociology of Knowledge* (Oxford: Polity Press, 1986). For an illustration of Gadamer's positive attitude to philosophical anthropology, note his remark, in *Die Aktualität des Schönen*, that, in his discussion of play, he is "following the insights of philosophical anthropology developed by Scheler, Plessner, and Gehlen under Nietzsche's inspiration." Gadamer, *The Relevance of the Beautiful and Other Essays,* trans. Nicholas Walker, (Cambridge: Cambridge University Press, 1986), p.46.

12. I am well aware that the ideal of pluralism may, despite its refusal to endorse any distinctive ideal of its own, develop its own form of intolerance; directed, of course, at those who cannot accept the free-for-all of the pluralist vision. The new Enlightenment, like the old, has its own versions of the need to *Écrasez l'infâme.*

13. Rorty, *Consequences of Pragmatism* (1983).

14. Ludwig Landgrebe, *Major Problems in Contemporary European Philosophy* trans. Kurt F. Reinhardt, (New York: Frederick Ungar, 1966); [*Philosophie der Gegenwart*] Calvin O. Schrag, *Radical Reflection and the Origin of the Human Sciences,* (West Lafayette, Ind.: Purdue University Press, 1980).

15. Martin Heidegger, *Being and Time* trans. John Macquarrie and Edward Robinson, (Oxford: Blackwell, 1962).

16. Heidegger, *Kant and the Problem of Metaphysics* trans. James S. Churchill, (Bloomington, Ind.: Indiana University Press, 1962).

17. Max Scheler. *Man's Place in Nature* trans. Hans Merhoff, (Boston: Beacon Press, 1961).

18. Landgrebe, *op.cit.* pp.26-27.

19. *Ibid.*

20. Bleicher, *op.cit.*

21. See below, section 6.

22. Marjorie Grene. "The Paradoxes of Historicity" in *Hermeneutics and Modern Philosophy* ed. Brice R. Wachterhauser, (City: State University of New York Press) pp.168-189.

23. David J. Levy, "The Limits of History. Ontology, Anthropology and Historical Understanding". *Journal of the British Society for Phenomenology* 20; 2 (May 1989) pp.46-62. See also Levy, *Political Order: Philosophical Anthropology, Modernity and the Challenge of Ideology* (Baton Rouge and London: Louisiana State University Press, 1987).

24. Wilhelm Dilthey, *Gesammelte Schriften,* VII: p.232.

25. Dilthey, *Gesammelte Schriften,* VIII: p.224 and V p.xci cited by Herbert Schnädelbach. *Philosophy in Germany 1831-1933,* (Cambridge: Cambridge University Press, 1984) p.231.

26. Hans Jonas, "Change and Permanence: On the Possibility of Understanding History" in Jonas, *Philosophical Essays,* (Chicago: Chicago University Press, 1974) pp.237-260.

27. Dilthey, *Gesammelte Schriften* VII: pp. 200ff. See the discussion of this in

Rudolf A. Makkreel, *Dilthey: Philosopher of the Human Studies*, (Princeton, N.J.: Princeton University Press, 1975).

28. I have discussed this in "The Limits of History" *loc. cit.* note 23.

29. Mircea Eliade, *No Souvenirs* (New York: Harper and Row 1973) pp. 289-90.

30. J. G. Droysen, cited by Schnädelbach, *op. cit.* p.53. Emilio Betti "Hermeneutics as the General Method of the *Geisteswissenschaften*" in Bleicher *op. cit.* pp.51-94.

31. See note 26.

32. Max Scheler, "Man and History" in Scheler, *Philosophical Perspectives* trans. Oscar A. Haac, (Boston: Beacon Press) p.65.

33. See note 17.

34. Axel Honneth and Hans Joas, *Social Action and Human Nature* trans. Raymond Meyer, (Cambridge: Cambridge University Press, 1988) p.73.

35. Helmuth Plessner, *Die Stufen des Organischen und der Mensch* (Berlin: de Gruyter, 1975) p.24, cited by Honneth and Joas *loc. cit.*

36. Plessner, *op. cit.* p.xix.

37. Plessner, *Laughing and Crying. A Study of the Limits of Human Behaviour*, trans. James S. Churchill, (Evanston: Northwestern University Press, 1970).

38. Arnold Gehlen, "Rasse und Staat," *Die Erziehung*, IX, (1933): p.201ff.

39. Gianni Vattimo, *The End of Modernity* trans. Jon R. Snyder, (Cambridge: Polity 1988).

40. Gehlen, "An Anthropological Model", *The Human Context*, I (1968/9) p.13.

41. Gehlen, "The Crystallization of Cultural Forms" trans. Clare A. MacMillan in *Modern German Sociology* ed. Volker Meja et al.(New York: Columbia University Press, 1987) pp.218-231.

42. Gehlen, *Moral und Hypermoral* (Frankfurt, 1973).

43. See note 41.

44. See, inter alia, Niklas Luhmann, "Modern Systems Theory and the Theory of Society" in *Modern German Sociology*; see note 38, pp.173-186.

45. Gehlen, "The Crystallization of Cultural Forms," *loc. cit.* note 41, pp.219-224.

46. Hans Jonas, *The Imperative of Responsibility. In Search of an Ethics for the Technological Age* (Chicago: Chicago University Press, 1984).

47.

48. Grene *op. cit.* p.184-5.

49. Plessner. *Die Frage nach der Conditio Humana* (Frankfurt: Suhrkamp, 1976) pp.188-9.

2

THE LIFE OF ORDER AND THE ORDER OF LIFE

Eric Voegelin on Modernity and the Problem of Philosophical Anthropology

1. Setting the Scene

"The motivations of my work are simple: they arise from the political situation." [1] With these words, recorded in the summer of 1973, Eric Voegelin returned from the high meditative ground of his current concerns to remind us, lest we had forgotten, of a point that is crucial both to his conception of his own work and, if the overall thesis of that work is to be accepted, to the understanding of the philosophical enterprise as a whole. Philosophy, Voegelin avers, is neither a technical academic discipline, designed to bring a little linguistic order into the special sciences, nor a purely intellectual quest for clarity or truth carried out in some imagined ontological or historical vacuum. Rather, it is a human spiritual activity, an act, at once of existential response and resistance, in which an individual soul, embodied in the person of the philosopher, becomes conscious both of the particularity of his historical situation and of the generality, or anthropological universality, of the features that define the *conditio humana*. In this awakening to reality, the philosopher discovers or rediscovers the essence of man as lying not or not only in his worldly position but in the relationship of the human soul to God, the world-transcendent ground of being.

If, in Voegelin's view, the essence of philosophy is to be found in the discovery of the relationship of the human soul to a God who transcends the immanent things of the world, its characteristic historical occasion — the moment of the happening of philosophy as an event and thus, potentially, an ordering force in the world — is the experience of worldly disorder. In anxious or uneasy response to the disorder of his time, the philosopher discovers the gap, more or less but always to some degree present, between what I shall term the life of order and the order of life. By this I mean the sometimes apparently abysmal chasm that seems to separate the actual conduct of human affairs, the historical course of what Aristotle calls *anthropina*, from what, through meditative exploration, is discovered to be their anthropologically and, as it emerges, divinely proper order.

Thus, taking what is for Voegelin the paradigmatic case of Plato, the *corpus* of Platonic writings is taken not as the expression as a personal doctrine — a theory of truth and order expressing the opinion of the man Plato — but as the linguistic articulation, through the then novel symbols of what we subsequently know as 'philosophy', of a meditative experience of divine order which stands, actually and perhaps forever, in tension with the established disorder of the life-world. It is not the business of the philosopher to abolish this tension, which Plato symbolizes in terms of man's life in the *Metaxy* — his existence in the in-between of a divine beginning and a no-less divine, because world-transcendent, beyond. Rather, the philosopher's task is to delineate as clearly as he may the outlines of this definitively human situation and, in doing so, to call man to awareness of the truth of his condition as one in which the life of order, though known in the soul, is never perfectly realized in the order of life.

The important practical point in this cautionary programme is that, while it may be utopian to seek to embody the life of order in the order of life, a life lived in awareness of the world-transcendent character of divine order, and therefore conscious of its historical unattainability in the form of a perfect worldly polity, is one in which, personally and politically, the measure of divine truth is able to operate as the standard by which the actual conduct of human affairs is to be judged. To this salutory programme, which freely admits the world-transcendent character of its measure of truth and order, stand opposed both the dangerous utopianism of those who seek to recast the meditative ascent toward truth as an historical struggle for the perfect society, and the self-styled 'realism' of those who, having recognized the political unattainability of the philosophical vision of transcendent order, dismiss it as a potentially life-threatening irrelevance, and so choose, instead, to identify the quest for order exclusively with the struggle for mastery in whatever may happen to be the prevailing order or disorder of biological and historical life.

Lest all this seem over-abstract, let it be recalled that the political situation in which Voegelin's work arose, that of central Europe between the wars, was one awash with ideological currents dominated by one or other of these two mistaken views. Sometimes, as in the work of the Italian marxist, Antonio Gramsci, as well as among Germans who dreamed of a projected non-conflictual order of racially homogeneous *Volksgemeinschaft*, elements of both might be combined in a personal ideological synthesis. However, generally speaking, while the political project of the Marxist left was governed by the conviction that worldly perfection had now become attainable through Communist revolution, the world-view of the Fascist and National Socialist revolutionary right was dominated by an image of existence in which the violent struggle for continuing personal, ethnic and national survival was elevated to a point at which it appeared to be the ultimate truth, as both origin and destiny, of man's being in the world.

Despite moments of temptation,[2] Voegelin's thinking was overwhelmingly formed in opposition to the ideological climate of his time. By this I mean not only that Voegelin was, as a matter of intellectual and political judgement, opposed to the revolutionary ideologies of left and right, but also that his philosophy takes on its characteristic form as a result of his confrontation with the phenomenon of ideology as such. In view of the ubiquity of ideological discourse at the time, Voegelin's quest for a form of political thinking that was not itself ideological could lead to confusion as to his intent among his readers. Voegelin recognized the danger, but saw it as one which, in the circumstances, he could not avoid.

By way of example of such misunderstanding I cite the remarks on Voegelin in Aurel Kolnai's *The War against the West* 1938 . Here, based on a careful reading of Voegelin's two books of 1933, *Rasse und Staat* and *Die Rassenidee in der Geistesgeschichte*, as well as some personal acquaintance, Voegelin is described as "a fascist *savant* of rare acumen and coolness," and a "shrewd thinker of a counter-revolutionary society whose greatness is only partially due to his stupendous erudition." Voegelin's books appear in Kolnai's remarkably inclusive bibliography among those described as "representative of Nazism or at least its general trend and atmosphere." And his analyses of the historical and ontological sources of the race idea and appreciation of the symbol of "race" as a formative political idea — one founded anthropologically in elementary human experiences, and historically in the secularization of the Christian idea of the Church as the *Corpus Christi mysticum* that binds all believers in the one body of the Church — are treated not as attempts to analyse objectively a real political phenomenon but as admittedly nuanced justifications of the new racial politics.

In his work Kolnai takes full account of Voegelin's indictment of the materialist reductionism entailed in the Nazi appeal to anatomic 'indices'; and notes, with characteristic irony, Voegelin's critical description of National Socialism itself as a "mass ideology analogous to Liberalism and Socialism" embodying the fallacious, quasi-egalitarian doctrine of an "equality between all bearers of a certain complex of bodily properties." But Kolnai sees these observations, not as elements in a diagnostic effort directed at the identification of what is, in sum, a pathological distortion in human self-understanding — remember Voegelin's words in *Die Rassenidee*: "The knowledge of man has come to grief" —but as efforts to purify and so fortify racial thinking from within.[3]

Kolnai's was a careful reading, and, moreover, one undertaken by a man influenced by sources, Christian anthropology and the philosophy of Max Scheler, that overlapped with Voegelin's own. If such a reader could so misconceive the tenor and intent of Voegelin's early work it could only be because, as Voegelin himself noted, in a climate suffused by ideology — one in which, as Jürgen Gebhardt puts it, "intellectual dishonesty is not accidental but is the very structure of reality of a social world he had to live in" — it becomes all but impossible to distinguish scholarly analysis, carried out in the spirit of truth, from the ideological effort to legitimize the phenomena one seeks to explain. In such a climate, the spiritual realist, as Voegelin then described him, will, where he is not depicted as the partisan of one party or another, "remain socially ineffective to the point of not even being misunderstood." [4]

It is therefore understandable that Kolnai, trying, as he was, to explain a potent and threatening ideological phenomenon to an English audience hardly aware of its scope and power, misrepresented, if not the content of Voegelin's early work, then, at least, its reflective distance from the mendacious context in which it appeared. And yet this can hardly be the end of the matter. Reference to Kolnai's reading of Voegelin's discussion of the ideology of race not only brings out the difficulties of making sense of a work of non-ideological theory in an ideological age, it also raises the matter of Voegelin's real affinities, intellectual and political. And here there are a number of difficulties that must be cleared from our way.

In part, these difficulties are a function of our historical distance from the situation of Voegelin's early writings. In this, our problem is the reverse of Kolnai's own. For while Kolnai, fully engaged as a combatant in the ideological struggle against National Socialism and related currents of thought, finds himself, in an ironic echo of Carl Schmitt, classifying the relevant literature under the mutually exclusive headings of "friend" and "foe", we are likely to turn to Voegelin's early writings only in the distancing light of his post-war work. And then, what is more, almost inevitably under the influence of Voegelin's frequent but perhaps over-stated protestations of his distance, even before the war, from the mainstream of German philosophy.

Leszek Kolakowski begins his masterly survey of the development of

Marxism with the reminder that: "Karl Marx was a German philosopher." [5] Perhaps, I suggest, we need a similar reminder in the case of Voegelin. With this difference: that while the labelling of Marx serves to remind us of the extent to which the structure of his work, and so the implications he draws from his material, remain determined by the inherited assumptions of the Hegelian system, which was for Marx identical with German philosophy at its highest point of development, the reminder that Voegelin too was a German philosopher helps us merely to identify elements in his environment that were significant and formative for his subsequent achievement.

In so contrasting Voegelin with Marx, even while emphasizing their shared rootedness in the German philosophical as well as political cultures of their respective times — cultures which each, in his way, disowns — I am seeking here to bring to light not only the difference between two men and two mind-sets, but also a distinction that separates the characteristic ambitions of two philosophical epochs. Contrasting the two men, we might say that whereas, in Marx, German philosophy, identified with the self-sufficient Hegelian system, forecloses, even where unrecognized, the imaginative horizon of Marx's own, avowedly post-philosophical thought, in Voegelin the more uncertain background of the post-Nietzschean German philosophy of the early twentieth century prepares the way for the author's recovery of the open horizon of philosophy itself.

Working in the shadow of the Hegelian pretence to have solved the riddle of the universe through the attainment of absolute knowledge, Marx proposes his own alternative, more limited but at the same time supposedly more realistic, answer through the expedient of transposing Hegel's theme of self-resolving historical dialectics into the key of his own historical materialism. Not the self-expression of an imagined World Spirit, but the self-transforming activity of men, labour, is presented as the key to the meaning of history and so to the riddle, if no longer of the universe, at least of human life. Thus Marx seeks, as he conceives it, to bring Hegel's discovery of ultimate meaning back to earth as a problem of practical action. Not theory but practice will resolve the enigma of a distinctly human life-form marked hitherto by an apparently impassable tension between, on the one hand, human aspirations and will and, on the other, the resistance of the surrounding universe.

Just as Hegel sees the prior history of the human spirit as preparation for his own resolution of the enigma of being in the unity of subject and object, so Marx conceives all history up to his own day as preparing the day when man will become master in his own house. Philosophy, as the exploration of enigmatic being, will become obsolete. The life of order, sought hitherto in the imagined harmony of a no less imaginary heaven, will become incarnate in an order of life where no human need is unmet and no question, except the now obsolete questions of philosophy, will remain unanswered.

Seen thus, Marx's thought belongs to a species of thinking — the species of self-sufficient systems embodying definitive, because historically guaranteed, answers to the fundamental questions of human existence —that seemed to most philosophers of Voegelin's generation to be itself historically obsolete. As Karl Löwith was later to analyse it, Marxism, which pretended to provide the key to the realization of Hegelian dreams of ultimate metaphysical harmony, was itself only a moment in the dissolution of the Hegelian system and its associated claims to rational certainty.[6] It was not, as Engels had claimed, in Marxism and "the German working class movement" that German idealist philosophy found its historical resolution but, Löwith argued, in the breakdown of all claims to ultimate truth and meaning associated with the name of Friedrich Nietzsche.[7]

In other words, the really significant movement of thought runs not from Hegel to Marx but, in the title of Löwith's great work, *From Hegel to Nietzsche*. What this means is that far from the legacy of systematic philosophy finding its true home in what is ultimately an equally harmonious system of social theory and organization, its destiny is to be exhausted and dispersed in the conflict of world-views, *Weltanschauungen*, of which Marxism is merely one not particularly attractive example.

According to Nietzsche, the potential success of each of these world-views depends not on its truth as measured by the standard of historical necessity, still less in terms of some mythical, trans-historical absolute of reason, but on the strength of the will with which it is asserted. This was something which the few politically successful Marxists recognized in practice, even if, with the exception of the maverick figure of George Sorel, they were unwilling to admit it in theory. Thus the Hegelian necessity of the ultimate realization of reason in the world revealed itself to the disenchanted Nietzschean or post-Nietzschean eye as the absurdly pretentious legitimizing formula of one particular will to power. Correspondingly, the Marxist claim to present a unique substantively rational solution to the problem of human social order appeared, as Max Weber noted, for what in fact it was: one option among others and one that, for all sorts of personally compelling reasons, ranging from the aesthetic to the historical-experiential, one might find it better to reject.

If Marx wrote in Hegel's shadow, Voegelin and his generation, despite all differences, worked alike in the shadow of Nietzsche. This is not to say that they were all Nietzscheans. Voegelin, for one, was certainly not. It was rather the case that Nietzsche's great creative-destructive enterprise, by undermining the credibility of every philosophy that claimed that the world's reality could be encompassed and explained within the bounds of an intellectually transparent, self-sufficient philosophical system, created a new agenda of thought and, with it, a new sense of the limits to which philosophical reason must forever be subject. This is a crucial element in the contextual background of Voegelin's work; and it is one which we must now examine a little further.

2. Voegelin and Philosophical Anthropology

Here we encounter, in relation to Voegelin, what is perhaps the central problem in the theory and practice of interpretation. This is the problem of understanding a work, and especially a philosophical work, out of the interplay of its achieved content with its original context. If, with an eye to the recovery of the author's original intent, we concentrate on a work's content alone we are likely, despite our best intentions, to understand it, not in terms of what its author actually meant, but only according to our own historically conditioned understanding of what its terms have now come to mean to us. If, on the other hand, we concentrate too exclusively on the work's historic context, we are likely to miss precisely what in it is most significant. That is, the work's particular and unique meaning —that which sets it apart from other productions of the same epoch and which, in its very distinctiveness, makes it worthy of special attention. In other words, responsible interpretation must tread a careful path between the utopian ideal of understanding the text according to the intentions of the author as revealed, whether explicitly or, as Leo Strauss would have it, "esoterically", in the body of the text, and the interpretive anarchy that follows from the denial of any knowable connection between meaning and authorial intent.

I call the Straussian ideal 'utopian' because, whatever may be an interpretor's intent and however deep his historical scholarship, every act of interpretation necessarily involves what Hans-Georg Gadamer has called a 'fusion of horizons' between the historically conditioned horizon of meaning opened up by the text and that of the interpreter.[8] We may fairly assume that any text embodies in a more or less determinable way the intentions of its author. However, not only is the meaning of a text irreducible to what its author may have originally intended to convey, but every such meaning, insofar as it can be comprehended at all, must be one to which the interpreter is already existentially open and to which he is, therefore, intellectually receptive. This means not only that a work may convey more or other than was originally intended by its creator, but also that certain elements of the original meaning of the work may be lost.

To put it in a more Voegelinian way, understanding is always an *anamnetic* undertaking; an exercise in rememberence or recollection, where what must be recalled is not only whatever may be known of an author's intent but, more important, the nature of the experience that motivates the work and renders it intelligible. Recognition of textual meaning may therefore be seen to entail re-cognition — a knowing once more — of the experiential substance that is responsively articulated in the linguistic symbols of the text. Seen thus, understanding is only possible on the basis of a certain actual or potential commonality of human experience; and true understanding of any human expression can be said to occur not in the sensual-objective encounter with its textual or other embodiment, its surface *qua* work alone, but in the reactivation, within the interpreter's psyche, of the experience that underlies it and which, as it were, provokes it into being.

It is doubt concerning the very possibility of such re-cognition, which depends in turn upon our acceptance that there is indeed a high degree of ontologically formative constancy in the defining features of man and world alike, that fuels the epistemological scepticism of much contemporary literary theory. But for Voegelin at least, the commonality of human life in what he, following Plato, calls the *Metaxy* — the historically enduring structure of man's life between beginning and beyond which he finds attested in the symbolic record of history—provides the ultimate ground for the possibility of the fusion of horizons that occurs in understanding. In this conception, however, it is not anatomical indices, nor any other material or physical measure, that tell us what is essentially common to the human race and what, hardly less essentially, divides it, ethnically and historically, but rather the survival of intelligible indices of relative openness to an enduring truth of being — to the reality of the human condition — as we encounter them in the symbolic expressions that come down to us in the form of hardly less enduring cultural works.

Plato was a Greek philosopher, as Voegelin was a German one. The ethnocultural adjectives, Greek and German, are hardly irrelevant to our understanding of either man. They serve, indeed, to point us to the concrete contexts that determine both the language and the initial trajectory of their respective works. But it is the second, shared term, *philosopher*, that, in Voegelin's view, directs us to the heart of the matter. This is to be found in the characteristic, originally and constitutively 'philosophical', openness of each — and so, by implication, of every authentic 'philosopher' — to a more embracing, supraethnic and even supra-historical context of being as the defining framework within which the dynamics of human order and disorder must ultimately be understood. This may be further characterized as an openness to the humanly formative significance of what Voegelin calls the world-transcending process of the Whole — a process in which even the *Metaxy itself* is experienced to be only an enduring though anthropologically definitive moment. It is this openness of soul to the reality of transcendence which permits the spiritual "race" of philosophers, the exemplary tribe of the *daimonios aner*, to communicate, though never exhaustively, the truth of man's being across the barriers of language, time and place.

What though is this truth? And why do we call its bearers exemplary? It is that the term *man* not only designates a biologically distinct species, constituted as he is by a shared evolutionary inheritance, and only subsequently differentiated along distinct ethnic and cultural-historical paths: but, more deeply still, that, in our self-identifying recognition of man as a unique, ontologically distinctive life-form we find ourselves talking about an essentially 'world-open' being. By this we mean that we find in man a being not only open to the various possibilities of earthly being but, ultimately also, to an experience, or, perhaps, to multiple experiences, of transcendence which even the plenitude of the world cannot fulfil. Man, in other words, is a being in whom the life of order consists, not in submission to what is experienced as a given order of biological or historical life, but in the struggle to attune the conduct of life to divine truth.

Thus Voegelin writes: "The discovery of transcendence, of intel-lectual and spiritual order, while occurring in the souls of individual human beings, is not a matter of 'subjective opinion'; once the discovery is made, it is endowed with the quality of an authoritative appeal to every man to actualize it in his own soul; the differentiation of man, the discovery of his nature, is a source of social authority. The assertion of such authority, as well as the appeal to the ignorant to actualize the potentialities of their humanity, is a permanent factor in the dynamics of order." [9] And again: "The truth of the philosopher is not a recipe for transforming mankind at large, but creates a new type of man among others. The very study of the nature of man reveals it as something which man does not have flatly but as a potentiality which requires actualization in the process of life." [10]

Voegelin's confident, some might say reckless, identification of man's "discovery of his nature" with "the truth of the philosopher" — a truth, in turn, identified with 'the discovery of transcendence' — is what leads him to claim, in relation to Aristotle's idea of man, that: "The metaphysical construction of human nature as an immanent form. . . an immanent essence like the form of an organic being. . . is technically inadequate because it is supposed to cover structures of the soul that are formed by transcendence. . . The self-understanding of man is conditioned and limited by the development of his existence toward transcendence." And so, "At the border of transcendence the language of philosophical anthropology must become the language of religious symbolization." [11]

It is worth dwelling a moment on this passage. The critical thrust of Voegelin's remarks is ostensibly directed at what he sees as the ultimate shortcoming of Aristotle's philosophical anthropology. The crucial failing in this anthropology lies, according to Voegelin, in Aristotle's definition of human nature as "an immanent essence like the form of an organic being" or, to use other terms, as a species-specific life-form, distinct from others but still of the same ontological type. Aristotle teaches that man's constitutive form of being is that of a quite peculiar, political, spiritual and even philosophical animal, a *zoon politicon* etc. but of an animal, *zoon*, nonetheless. As Voegelin reads him, Aristotle follows Plato in penetrating the religious character of noetic life, of the *bios theoreticos*, as the encounter with divine transcendence. He even conceives the result of this encounter as ultimately to be actualized only in the immortalization of the human soul. Yet this possibility is, at the same time, contradicted by the metaphysics of immanent form which "requires the immanent actualization of human potentiality." So seen, Aristotle's conception of man's being remains and must remain, in Heidegger's suggestive terms, a mode of 'being-there-in-the-world', *Dasein*, and so, despite the meditative ascent toward immortalization, a 'being-toward-death', *Sein-zum-Tod*.

Voegelin continues thus: "From this conflict (between immortalization and the metaphysics of immanent form) results the construction of an immanent actualization of the supranatural potentiality of the soul. We shall meet with a similar theoretical situation at the end of the Middle Ages when, with the disintegration of Christianity and the new wave of immanentism, political thinkers began to evoke the idea of an intramundane realization of perfect human existence. The immanentization of transcendental fulfilment resulted at that time in the development of political "ideals", and ultimately in the political chiliasm of transforming society into a terrestial paradise by means of organization and violence. . . . A similar movement of political idealism and chiliasm would have lain in the logic of Aristotelian metaphysics." If neither Aristotle nor Plato followed the path of "catastrophic derailment which characterizes modern politics," it was due, Voegelin says, to the "spiritual sensitiveness and the magnificent realism" that they shared. [12]

Here I am tempted to ask whether one element of this "magnificent realism" was not precisely the common, Platonic and Aristotelian, inheritance from the ancestral religious consciousness of their forefathers. For, despite recognizing man's desire for immortalization as a troubling part of his nature, Greek religion had always identified the specific difference of man from god with the ontological distinction between mortal and immortal beings. In the light of this heritage, even man's existence toward divine transcendence, which Voegelin sees as the philosophers' novel, more adequate because more differentiated, reformulation of man's primordial experience of the existential presence of the gods, remains, insofar as the philosopher is, despite everything, aware of being never more than a man, limited *inter alia* by the awareness of his mortality, of his *Sein-zum-Tod*.[13] In the pre-philosophical Hellenic conception of man's nature and place in the cosmos as that of a mortal and so finite being — a typically Hellenic, religious sense of the constitutive finitude of man's being that may be qualified but is never denied either by Plato or Aristotle —there is, *pace* Voegelin, quite enough force to have prevented the derailment of Aristotelian metaphysics toward a political chiliasm directed as the attainment of heaven on earth. Why then does Voegelin think otherwise?

In seeing a chiliastic direction as entailed in the anthropology of Aristotle, Voegelin is, I suggest, reading back into the theory supposedly necessary lines of development that are not in fact there. And this he does for two reasons. The first is the extent to which, at this stage of his development, the period of *The New Science of Politics* and of the first three volumes of *Order and History*, Voegelin's understanding of Aristotle's metaphysics and anthropology of immanent form is overly conditioned by his experience of apparently equivalent, naturalistic anthropologies in his own day — theories whose political implications he had good reason to distrust. And the second is his unwillingness to accept that the real source of potential derailment toward chiliasm is not the tension between the discovery of transcendence and continuing awareness of finitude that we find in the classic philosophers, but the wholly un-Hellenic conviction, which surfaces first in Hebrew apocalyptic and finds a peculiar confirmation in the Christian belief in the incarnation of God as man, that mortality itself may be overcome in the dissolution, by divine grace, of the barriers that, as the Greeks believed, forever separated man from God.

Here is a case where the relationship between the content of Voegelin's work and its motivating context assumes crucial importance. For we will only understand the significance of his criticisms of Aristotle, and hence the distinctiveness of what, in the 1950s, he still terms his own 'philosophical anthropology' if we set them against the background of the pre-war, Central European situation of ideological conflict and post-Nietzschean philosophical endeavour sketched in the first section of this paper. Indeed the very term *philosophical anthropology* which plays so prominent a role in Voegelin's writings of the time, and which we have, hitherto, treated as historically and hermeneutically unproblematic, only reveals its true significance when viewed against this background. For *philosophical anthropology*, a term which appears in Kant and which Voegelin applies only retrospectively to Aristotle, is a key term of German language philosophy in the inter-war period. As Voegelin appropriates it for his own work, it refers, not so much to a single school of thought, but to a number of related, distinct but often mutually opposed, approaches to the problem of human order and disorder. These approaches take, as their common starting point, the attempt to understand empirically the nature of man as an identifiably distinct sort of being occupying a no less distinct place in the totality of things.[14]

So conceived, *philosophical anthropology*, in both its naturalistic and non-naturalistic variants, denotes the attempt, carried out in the wake of Nietzsche's destruction of the claims of all comprehensive philosophical systems that purport to unlock the secret of universal truth and order, to achieve a more limited but nonetheless objectively true account of the historically and ontologically given nature of man's being.

3. The Example of Max Scheler

In Voegelin's *Autobiographical Reflections* we read: "As the first chapter of my volume on *Rasse und Staat* shows, I adopted at the time the philosophical anthropology of Max Scheler, as expressed in his recent publication *Die Stellung des Menschen im Kosmos*." Somewhat unrevealingly, he adds: "It proved sufficient for the purpose of analysing the race problem; its defects were of no importance to the issue at hand, though I discovered them later when I started on my original work on Classic philosophy."

Scheler was not among the earliest influences on Voegelin's thinking, and his name does not even figure in the account of what Voegelin termed the formation of "my own horizon" which he prepared, under the title of "Remembrance of Things Past," for the English version of *Anamnesis*.[15] Yet, in the opinion of Gregor Sebba, it was the encounter with the philosophical anthropology of *Die Stellung*, and especially the final sections in which Scheler conceptualizes the relationship between man and what he calls the 'Ground of Being' in terms of the 'becoming' of God in the world through the being of man, which provided the starting point for what was to become Voegelin's distinct philosophical outlook.[16]

Sebba's view of the significance of Scheler for Voegelin's intellectual development deserves particular attention. For, of all Voegelin's critics and commentators, Sebba was closest to him in the crucial formative period of the 1930s. However, even apart from Sebba's testimony, it is not hard to find echoes, not only of Scheler's themes but of his arguments too, in Voegelin's later writings. Thus Alfred Schutz, in a letter written in November 1952, notes the Schelerian resonances in the chapter on "Representation and Existence" in *The New Science of Politics*; and the same Schelerian theme of the interplay of what Scheler calls 'real' and 'ideal' factors plays a vital if unannounced role in the argument of Voegelin's important essay "The Growth of the Race Idea" 1940 which was one of the first articles he published after his arrival in the United States.[17]

My purpose in stressing the Schelerian connection in this context is not to provide an exercise in hermeneutic detection directed only at the uncovery of early influences on Voegelin's work. Voegelin was a great philosopher, and his achievement stands on its own, quite regardless of the currents of thought that originally fed his philosophical imagination. No more would I wish to quarrel with Voegelin's own judgement, that what he initially found in Scheler, a theoretical standpoint from which to refute the naturalizing claims of racially oriented anthropological theory, he later found better done in the classic philosophy of Plato and Aristotle. Rather what I suggest is, first, that Schelerian anthropology provided the exemplary model for what was to become Voegelin's own distinctive conception of the relationship between the life of order and the order of life; second, that this anthropological model significantly influenced Voegelin's subsequent understanding of the classic philosophers themselves; and, third, that Scheler's example, and particularly his conception of the mind-opening task of philosophy in the peculiar conditions of modernity, continued to influence the broad development of Voegelin's thought long after he had come to reject Schelerian theory as such.

Thus, it seems to me that the Schelerian influence not only persists in Voegelin's continuing use of the term *philosophical anthropology* through the 1950s; it also penetrates, in a formative sense, even the meditative essays in which the work of his final period consists. These are works from which the characteristic language of anthropology has all but disappeared but which, as I hope to show, remain none the less significantly bound by an originally Schelerian anthropological premise.

There are, of course, other aspects of Voegelin's work in which a focus on influences other than Scheler's would prove more revealing. Here I think particularly of the example of Max Weber in determining both Voegelin's scrupulous attention to the lessons of historical scholarship, an attitude foreign to Scheler and all too rare among philosophers in general, and his rejection in the name of an Aristotelian, no less than a Weberian, ethics of responsibility, of all totalizing political solutions based on ideological certainties or 'inner' personal conviction. Nevertheless, in relation to our present topic, it is the figure of Scheler who is most important. For in Scheler we find, albeit in a different, perhaps less adequate, formulation, the prototypical themes that guide, throughout, the direction of Voegelin's philosophical quest.

Three of these shared themes deserve special mention. The first is the identification of man's essential distinctiveness with his openness, not only to the things of the world — what in the common language of German philosophical anthropology is identified with man's 'world-openness' *Weltoffentlichkeit* as such—but to the world, transcendent yet paradoxically no less experiential presence of God. The second is the tendency, Schelerian as much as Voegelinian, to understand the crisis of modernity in terms of man's loss of awareness of this divine presence. And the third is the claim that the future of order, as the condition for a fully or 'truly' human life, depends on man's recovering the experience of divine presence as the fount of order in his worldly conduct.

These three themes, the theme of immanence and transcendence, the theme of modern consciousness as a mode of existential and cognitive deficiency, and the theme of the ultimate dependence of the order of life on a proper appreciation of the divine source of the life of order, run as related motifs in the rich counterpoint of Voegelin's thought. And each is already to be found, in outline at least, in the texts of Max Scheler.

Here is not the place to attempt an overall account of Scheler's influence upon Voegelin, still less of the much underestimated importance of Scheler as a philosopher in his own right.[18] Rather, I shall confine my remarks to those aspects of the Schelerian *corpus* which clearly prefigure Voegelin's own conception of the problem of order, especially as man encounters it under the conditions of modernity. As Voegelin's autobiographical reference to *Die Stellung des Menschen im Kosmos The Place of Man in the Cosmos* indicates, it is to that work that we must primarily refer; even while noting that there were other works of Scheler, such as his *Problems of a Sociology of Knowledge* 1924 , in which the theory of 'real' and 'ideal' factors is developed, that also contributed substantially to the formation of Voegelin's outlook.

Even within *Die Stellung* we must be selective. We must leave aside any account of Scheler's careful delineation of the distinctiveness of human being as a unique life-form situated within a hierarchy of organic forms extending upwards from plant, through animal, to man, in order to focus on the point in the text where Scheler, subsuming all that has gone before, avows the inadequacy of all attempts to conceptualize the being of man within a world-immanent philosophy of the organism.[19] Since it was just such a comparative philosophy of life-forms, in which man's mode of existence was understood exclusively by reference to its scientifically knowable distinctiveness from that of other worldly beings, that characterized the main lines of development of German philosophical anthropology in the years following Scheler's death, we are, in referring Voegelin's starting point to the moment of ontological rupture in Scheler's text, also pointing to the crucial divide that separates Voegelin's thought from that of his one-time *confrères*.

This, I want to stress, is not essentially, and perhaps, as Kolnai for one thought, not originally a political divide; even though this is how the historical and ideological context of Voegelin's early writings and subsequent career must now make it appear. The contextual motivation of his works on racial theory may indeed, as Voegelin says, be political but the distinctiveness of their content is certainly not. It is emphatically a philosophical distinction, and a Schelerian-philosophical one at that. In other words, the point where Voegelin breaks ranks with the majority of his fellow post-Schelerian anthropologists is a matter of ontological conviction concerning what is to be regarded as a philosophically adequate conception of man's nature and not a function of his political distance from the prevailing ideologies of the time.

What I am getting at here is that though Voegelin is right to point to an ideological affinity between National Socialism and the sort of naturalistic anthropology he rejects, there can be no question of identifying the division between naturalistic and anti-naturalistic or, better, 'trans-naturalistic' anthropologies with any one pattern of political alignment. It is probably true that, if consistently adhered to, an anti-naturalistic anthropology that identifies the specific difference of man, considered as a single biological species, with his orientation and openness to divine presence, would prove ultimately incompatible with the sort of ideological affinities that Kolnai, in 1938, seemed inclined to attribute to Voegelin.[20] On this matter, examination of the intellectual and moral difficulties faced by the more conscientious theologians of *volkisch* or Germanic Christianity would prove revealing.[21] On the other hand, it would be quite wrong to imagine, as both Kolnai and Voegelin often seem inclined to do, that the attempt to think through the problem of philosophical anthropology from essentially naturalistic, a-theological, though not necessarily anti-theological, premises, predisposes a thinker to some form or other of brutalizing ideological politics.

Here we may mention the case of Helmuth Plessner, a philosophical anthropologist of the first order, whose early anthropological writings are contemporaneous with Scheler's. Even more than *Die Stellung*, Plessner's *Die Stufen des Organischen und der Mensch The Levels of Organic Life and Man*, which appeared in 1928, the same year as Scheler's work, provides, in its structure and style of approach, an unequalled model for the type of approach to the problem of human distinctiveness through the comparative delineation of life-forms that was, at the time, coming to typify German language anthropology in general. The example of Plessner is telling, not only because he was fiercely opposed to National Socialism — his half-Jewish origins would be enough to explain that — but also because in 1924, four years before *Die Stufen*, he had already published a work, *Grenzen der Gemeinschaft (Limits of Community)*, in which he developed, within the bounds of the premise that man must be understood as a world-immanent being, the creature and partial creator of the life-world of nature and history, a theory of humanly proper political existence that is at least as incompatible with mass ideological politics as Voegelin's own. Unlike Voegelin, Plessner remained convinced, throughout his long career, that philosophical anthropology, in the strict sense of a discipline concerned, in a quasi-Aristotelian way, with theorizing man's being as a distinct life-form 'positioned' within the world, was the only adequate way to make sense of our existence.[22]

Despite a common starting point, Voegelin's position is quite different from this; and the key to the difference has already been given us in a sentence cited above: "At the border of transcendence the language of philosophical anthropology must become the language of religious symbolization."[23] My claim here is twofold: first, that this position, which grants a uniquely privileged anthropological significance to the experience of divine transcendence relative to every other, is already anticipated in the final section of Scheler's *Die Stellung*, which carries the heading "Philosophical Anthropology and Religion"; and, second, that Voegelin's turn to religious symbolization, no less than Scheler's move in the direction of a more ambitious if less concrete religious metaphysics of the becoming of divine spirit in the world, presupposes, as its starting point, the totality of the anthropological analysis that precedes it.

In other words, man's encounter with the world-transcendent reality of God, though unaccountable in purely anthropological terms, is, *qua* experience, which is to say phenomenologically, nothing more nor less than an anthropologically given fact of life. Or, putting it yet another way, that man's awareness of divine presence is, both as a matter of historical record and of philosophical experience, an indubitable item of the historically given reality of man's being in the world. To refuse to recognize the sense of divine presence as such a constitutive element in human being, and so of the movement of history — one given non-speculatively but primitively in human experience and one which may, when encountered in its full force, become the overwhelmingly important factor in determining the course of a man's life, *vide* St. Paul — amounts to what Voegelin, adopting a term from the Austrian novelist Heimito von Doderer, calls the 'refusal to apperceive' *Apperzeptionsverweigerung.*

It was this 'refusal to apperceive' that Voegelin came to see as the root phenomenon of what he was to call the 'eclipse of reality' that typically characterizes the consciousness of modern man. The eclipse of reality occurs insofar as the given structure of experienced reality, which includes the reality of the experience of divine transcendence, is distorted, and so subsequently denied, by the refusal of ontological recognition to one of its constituent elements. That is, to the experience of the presence of the Divine entailed in the awareness of transcendence.

As the opening paragraph of *Order and History* makes plain, this divine presence is not something that awaits discovery by the philosophers or, for that matter, by the prophets. Rather, it is, Voegelin insists, known to man by virtue of his participation in what he calls "a primordial community of being" —one which is *primordially* experienced as comprising "God and man, world and society." According to Voegelin, the contribution of the philosophers and the prophets is not, therefore, the discovery of God as such but, through the equivalent yet very different symbolizations, Greek and Hebrew respectively, of philosophy and revelation, the adequate articulation of the world-transcendent quality of His being.[24]

"The community (of being)," Voegelin writes, "with its quaternian structure (God and man, world and society) is, and is not, a datum of human experience. It is a datum of experience in so far as it is known to man by virtue of his participation in the mystery of its being. It is not a datum of experience in so far as it is not given in the manner of an object of the external world but is knowable only from the perspective of participation in it."[25] Voegelin terms the historical events of philosophy and revelation 'leaps in being' because they differentiate the transcendent quality which is the ontologically distinct mark of God's presence in the community of being—a presence to consciousness that is emphatically not the presence of another immanent object of the world. Equivalently, the characteristic thinking of modernity, which refuses to recognize the reality of anything that is not knowable or even conceivable as such an object — a refusal on principle to admit the reality of any being which is not a thing or, as such, part of the scientifically ascertainable order of things — represents a fall from the once attained, though ever mysterious truth of divine being disclosed in the parallel but quite separate symbolizations of Greek philosophy and Israelite revelation. Participation in being, according to Voegelin, entails the apperception of God, or, at least, of some world-transcendent element of spirit, as part of, and, perhaps, partner in, the drama of existence. The denial of this can, he thinks, only be the fruit of the refusal of apperception and so of a more or less deliberate falsification of experience itself.

Whatever Voegelin took to be Scheler's philosophical shortcomings, and despite the latter's late disavowal of theism in the conventional sense, at least he did not refuse to apperceive in this way. Indeed, Schelerian anthropology culminates in the unequivocal assertion that it is man's relationship to the divine ground of being, and nothing else, that is the single most important distinguishing element in the human form of being. And this, he warns, is a relationship that we must not even try to objectify in the mode of the immanentizing sciences of nature. It is, Scheler says, a relationship known only in man's awareness of the participatory presence of the divine in his consciousness. And every such consciousness, the consciousness of an individual 'person', is, at the same time, also and only to be understood as a particular moment in man's general, participatory presence in the process of the cosmos. We may and must speak of the presence of divine being as an event in our worldly being because we experience it as such; but if we once attempt to "make an 'object' out of this being" — something tempting in view of our desire for evidential, scientific or objective, reassurance, as well as because of the intrinsically objectifying character of language as the medium in which experience must be embodied if it is to be communicated at all — we will, Scheler thinks, lose sight of its distinct quality as the ultimate ordering presence in the cosmos, which is to say in world and soul alike.

Alone among the masters of modern philosophical anthropology, Scheler refuses what, to use Dante's phrase, Voegelin regards as the 'great refusal' of modernity. This, of course, is not the refusal of the world for the sake of salvation to which Dante refers, but the refusal to apperceive the founding and formative presence of the divine in our experience of being. And if the Schelerian metaphysical language of the interpenetration of spirit and drive, *Geist und Drang*, is somewhat crude, this requires, not abandoning an evidentially unwarranted transcendental reference, as most of Scheler's legatees supposed, but the attainment or recovery of a more adequate vocabulary. For Voegelin, this meant a return to the linguistic symbols in which the mystery of transcendence was first differentiated, those of classic philosophy and biblical revelation. In recovering these languages as intelligible articulations or indices of experience, we can, he claims, be reawakened to the experience of transcendence whence their intelligibility derives.[26]

4. Anthropology and Beyond

In the preceding pages we have raised more hares than we can presently hope to run to ground. Nevertheless we are, I think, now in a position to make some general points about Voegelin's philosophy of order that are not without interest. These are points of substantive importance which may be overlooked by readers who take simply at face value Voegelin's sincere but overstated declarations of his independence from the mainstream of the German philosophical tradition. It may, as he avows, be true that following his early exposure to American life and thought he was rendered immune to the seductive charms of Heidegger's *Sein und Zeit*, which enraptured so many of his German contemporaries and which is now perhaps the single most important reference point for American philosophers as well. It is certainly the case that the period of Voegelin's first visit to the United States coincides with his abandonment of the epistemologically oriented, neo-Kantian perspective which marks his earliest writings. But none of this should distract us from the observation that while Voegelin's philosophical terminology is, over the years, increasingly divorced from that of the German tradition, phenomenological as well as neo-Kantian, his identification of the central problem of philosophy with the substantive problem of the order of man's being in the world is a legacy, not from an Anglo-American tradition that has, in its modern, post-Hobbesian phase, tended to take the substance of that order for granted, but from the more troubled, less secure experiential storehouse of German-speaking Central Europe.

Along with the classics, it is Hegel and, more implicitly, Nietzsche and Heidegger, not Dewey and John Commons, who provide the enduring reference points for Voegelin's thinking. And if these German figures are sometimes treated in polemical style as 'Gnostic' masters of deception, these references are balanced by the occasional but highly significant acknowledge-ment that in their works, however flawed, there is to be found a depth of philosophical penetration of issues unparalleled in other post-classical tradi-tions.[27] Nor should Voegelin's post-Schelerian turn to Plato and the classics be considered as signalling a rupture with his German past. As Gadamer has recalled, the understanding of Platonic philosophy as a whole in terms of its political background, which characterizes Voegelin's approach, was also typical of the direction of German Plato scholarship in the interwar years.[28] Even in the matter of terminology it is notable that the philosophically central notion of the 'It-reality', which Voegelin in his last writings uses to denote the non-objective flow of the process of the Whole — as in 'It happened that. . .' or 'It seems to me. . .' — is not only of Nietzschean origin but is more or less precisely paralleled in Heidegger's view of the philosophical significance of the equivalent German grammatical form " *Es gibt. . .*"[29]

None of this casts doubt on the uniqueness of Voegelin's achievement or the distinctiveness of his thought. If he was and remained a German philoso-pher he was hardly typical of the breed. But even here one could argue that the distinction evident in the experientially concrete character of Voegelin's analyses — his 'meditations' as he came to call them — and of the terms in which they are articulated, is the fruit of a depth and range of philological and historical inquiry which is typical, not to be sure of German speculative philosophy, but of the best scholarly traditions of the German academy. It was, we should recall, the academic ethos of systematic, professional and, above all, non-dilettante scholarship, as institutionalized in the German universities of the nineteenth century, that provided the first and best model of what we have come to regard as academically respectable work. To this tradition of scholarship, as much or even more than to his native philosophical tradition, Voegelin is an authentic heir. In his work the lively acuity and experiential sensitivity of the philosopher is conjoined with the scrupulous attention to the full range of relevant data that marks out the great historical scholar. Thus he unites, in the living out of a single biographically formative vocation, two aspects of the life of the mind that were and still are too often to be found only in isolation from one another.

To put it in relation to two significant intellectual "markers" in Voegelin's early manhood, his work combines the broad historical sweep of an Oswald Spengler with the scrupulous philosophical rigour of an Edmund Husserl. The result is an historically concrete philosophy of order, a primarily historically rather than biophysically oriented anthropology, that avoids Spengler's over-schematized historicism as much as the equally schematic ahistoricism of Husserl. Not for Voegelin the cavalier treatment of philosophical inquiry we find in *The Decline of the West* nor the distortions of history that mar the otherwise acute analyses of our civilizational crisis to be found in Husserl's *Crisis of the European Sciences.* By taking seriously the programmatic implications of his own claim, announced in the preface to *Order and History*, that "the order of history emerges from the history of order," he overcomes, in the interests of anthropological truth — the truth about what Scheler calls 'man's nature and place in the cosmos' — the disciplinary gulf between history and philosophy; or, in terms of this essay's title, between the empirical-historical study of the given order of life and the no less empirical-philosophical study of what men experience to constitute the life of order.

I have argued that much that is distinctive in Voegelin's outlook is best understood against the background of Scheler's philosophical anthropology; and, as my references to Nietzsche and the metaphysically sceptical and anti-systematizing quality of German philosophy in the post-Nietzschean age are meant to indicate, I believe that the character of this philosophy, and, more generally, of the wider contemporary turn to philosophical anthropology as a new, cognitively modest but empirically warranted ground of inquiry, is crucially influenced by Nietzsche's destruction of the claims of more speculative philosophical systems — systems which make sense of the order of the whole only by ignoring the particularity of the historically and naturally determined items in which our experience of this putative whole actually consists. Voegelin's philosophy, though it moves beyond the conceptual universe of Schelerian thought and eventually abandons altogether the distinctive terminology of philosophical anthropology, is a recognizable product of this shared post-Nietzschean determination never to ignore the rootedness of thought, however abstract, in the hard business of historical and hence biophysical life.

Although in biographical terms a means of overcoming the tutelage of Scheler, Voegelin's penetration of the Platonic philosophical experience as paradigmatic for philosophy as a whole is thus doubly indebted to the Schelerian example. For, from Scheler, Voegelin brings to his understanding of Plato not only the common post-Nietzschean conviction that the thought of a man must be understood out of the context of his life, and so anthropologically out of the general determining conditions of human existence as such, but, more particularly, that this context is not limited to the human encounter with worldly things but, at the limit, extends beyond immanence to the encounter with the world-transcendent Ground of Being.

However, in a post-Nietzschean age we cannot grant this encounter, however anthropologically privileged and ontologically unprecedented it may seem to be, any degree of metaphysical certitude beyond the primitive certitude that attaches to our being in the world as such. By this I mean simply that even the experience of what is other than the world —I think here of Rudolf Otto's phenomenological analysis of the Holy in terms of man's experience of the "wholly other" [30] —is, however paradoxically, knowable only as an item of experience in the world. The reality of the human experience of divine transcendence, as attested against all immanentist anthropologies by Scheler and by Voegelin, is simply, and as surely as any other, a matter indicated in the record of human historical existence — in the existence of cognate others, the men we know as the prophets and the philosophers, if not always of oneself. In other words, it is a fact of life, no more but also no less deniable than others, that men at certain times and places find themselves responding not only to stimuli induced by the presence of external objects in the world but also to what Scheler, in terms heavily mortgaged to the very traditions he wishes otherwise to overcome, calls "the ideal demands of *deitas*." On the relative importance a theorist attaches to this fact of human life as compared to others will depend the particular perspective of his anthropology. And what is really odd here is not that Scheler and Voegelin find it necessary to introduce the topic of divine transcendence as an integral element of their philosophical reflections, but that most other modern thinkers do not.

In Scheler as in Voegelin, the presence of God, though known as the presence of world-transcendent being, is, however, only known within the world in the medium of human consciousness on which, experientially, it exerts, always potentially and often compellingly *vide* once more St. Paul, a formative influence. It is again simply a matter of historical record that the man who has encountered this presence, who has had what we call a revelatory experience, does not normally continue to act in the world precisely as he did before; even if, as is also known historically to be the case, the world is not otherwise changed by what has occurred.

Correspondingly, in Voegelin as in Scheler, the identification of the experience of world transcendent divinity presupposes as its experiential ground and so as condition of its possibility, the full range of world immanent experiences. By this I mean the range of our experiences of definable objects which endure as they are despite every leap in being. This must be the case because, according to Voegelin as to Scheler, it is only insofar as God is known to be something utterly other than another such an object that He is properly known at all. It is, therefore, only because man knows the things of the world as such things, and in a way that tells him that they are truly world-immanent items, objects of science, that he is able, in the revelatory encounter, to know that what is encountered is no such thing at all. The distinctiveness of the experience of divine transcendence thus presupposes experience of that from which it is knowably apart.

This is why, although, as Voegelin says, "At the border of transcendence the language of philosophical anthropology must become the language of religious symbolization," this must not be taken to mean that the anthropological perspective is somehow itself transcended by the symbols of religion. After all, even what is, in some traditions, called 'revealed' as opposed to 'natural' theology is an undeniably human undertaking —one practised from and within the specific perspective of man, even if, in the eyes of the faithful, there is nothing humanly constituted in its object.

Even the original theophanic or revelatory event, however ontologically unique it may be, is also an anthropological event, and only as such can it be known. It is an event, which though apparently coming from without, happens within the partial reality of a world, the anthropologically definitive life-world of the *Metaxy*, that is itself known to be nothing more than a lasting event in the transcendent but anthropologically unfathomable process of the whole. *Ontologically*, we are aware of our finitude and know that the *Metaxy* is bounded by the boundless reality which Anaximander, at the birth of philosophy, termed the *apeiron*, the 'unbounded', out of which all has come and into which it must in time return—an awareness which, following Voegelin, we symbolize in terms of the beginning and the beyond.[31] *Existentially*, we may sense ourselves to be drawn beyond the anthropologically given reality of our being. But *cognitively*, there is no getting beyond anthropology; for even what seems most surely to point beyond, our sense of our potential for immortality for instance, is encountered only subject to the natural and cultural historical conditions of life.[32]

It is this experience of transcendence encountered out of immanence which, according to Voegelin, structures the specific tensional structure of human being. He agrees with the mainstream of modern philosophical anthropology that man is and must remain a being of the world — a full participant in the order of life and subject, throughout the adventure of history, to its empirically knowable trials and conditions. Yet at the same time he stresses, against the naturalizing implications of this position, that man, no less knowably, experiences the source of order within this life, as well as beyond, to be itself no part of the given order of biophysical existence. We already find this point of tension in Scheler, where it is expressed in what are almost purely Kantian terms, and subsequently resolved, if only speculatively, by reference to the metaphysics of the convergence of Spirit and Drive, ideal and real being, in the being of man — a form of being which Scheler, in his last writings, conceives as nothing less than the destined form of God's becoming in the world.

In Voegelin there is no equivalent speculation and so no comparable resolution. What there is is the resolutely historical, anti-speculative and anti-metaphysical, observation that, insofar as God may be said to make His presence known in the world it is uniquely on the plane of consciousness. So encountered, He may, as we know from the record, form the conduct of those who experience the divine presence, whether directly or through the transparent symbols of a living faith, but He does not otherwise alter the conditions to which even divinely oriented human action remains subject. Consequently, the life of order remains in tension with the order of life and must do so long as things may last. That is the enduring problem of man and the final word of an anthropology that takes his being, in the plenitude of its openness, as its object of inquiry.

Notes

1. Eric Voegelin, *Autobiographical Reflections* ed. Ellis Sandoz (Baton Rouge: Louisiana State University Press, 1989) p.83.

2. See on this Voegelin's remarks in *Autobiographical Reflections* on his brief Marxist period in the immediate aftermath of the First World War and his reaction of disgust at the behaviour of the Western democracies following the *Anschluss*.

3. Aurel Kolnai, *The War against the West* (London, 1938). The quotation from Voegelin appears in *Die Rassenidee in der Geistesgeschicte von Ray bis Carus* (Berlin, 1933) p.1.

4. Voegelin, "Last Orientation" *ms.* cited by Jürgen Gebhardt in "Toward the Process of Universal Mankind" in Ellis Sandoz, ed. *Eric Voegelin's Thought: A Critical Appraisal* (Durham, N.C.:Duke University Press, 1982 p.68.

5. Leszek Kolakowski, *Main Currents of Marxism: Volume I* (Oxford: Oxford University Press) p.1.

6. Karl Löwith, *From Hegel to Nietzsche* (Holt, Rinehart and Winston 1964).

7. Friedrich Engels, *Ludwig Feuerbach and the End of Classical German Philosophy* 1888, in *Karl Marx and Engels Selected Works* (International Publishers, 1968) pp.596-632.

8. Hans-Georg Gadamer, *Truth and Method* (Sheed and Ward, 1979). For a useful exchange between Gadamer and Strauss see the correspondence published in *The International Journal of Philosophy*.

9. Voegelin, *Order and History: Volume Two* (Baton Rouge: Louisiana State University Press, 1957) p.186.

10. *Ibid.* 3: p.358.

11. *Ibid.* pp.363-4.

12. *Ibid.* p.365.

13. For useful criticism of Heidegger's characterization of man's being as *Sein-zum-Tod* from the point of view of philosophical anthropology see Helmuth Plessner, "Der Aussagewert einer Philosophischen Anthropologie" in Plessner, *Die Frage nach der Conditio humana* (Frankfurt, 1976).

14. On the significance of philosophical anthropology as a distinctive current in modern German philosophy see Herbert Schnädelbach, *Philosophy in Germany 1831-1933* (Cambridge: Cambridge University Press, 1984) and Odo Marquard, "Zur Geschichte des philosophischen Begriffs 'Anthropologie' seit dem Ende des achtzenten Jahrhunderts" in Marquard, *Schwierigkeiten mit der Geschichtsphilosophie* (Frankfurt, 1973) pp.122ff.

15. Voegelin, *Anamnesis* translated by Gerhart Niemeyer, (South Bend, Ind.: University of Notre Dame Press, 1978).

16. Personal communication to the author from Professor Sebba.

17. *Review of Politics*, (1940). pp.283-317.

18. I have discussed this is in my book *Political Order: Philosophical Anthropology, Modernity and the Challenge of Ideology* (Baton Rouge and London: Louisiana State University Press, 1987) See also David J. Levy "Max Scheler, Truth and the Sociology of Knowledge" in *Continuity*, 3, (1981) pp.91-104, and Francis Dunlop, *Scheler* (London: Claridge Press, 1991).

19. Max Scheler, *Man's Place in Nature* trans. Hans Meyerhoff (Boston: Beacon Press, 1961).

20. See note 3.

21. Robert P. Erickson, *Theologians under Hitler* (New Haven, Conn.:Yale University Press, 1985).

22. Plessner's collected works are published, in nine volumes, by Suhrkamp Verlag, Frankfurt. For a late statement of Plessner's position see *inter alia Die Frage nach der Conditio Humana* (Frankfurt:Suhrkamp, 1976).

23. See note 11 above.

24. This theme, broached in *Order and History*, recurs throughout Voegelin's later essays.

25. Voegelin, *Order and History*, I p.1.

26. Voegelin, "Equivalences of Experience and Symbolization" in *Eternità e Storia* (Florence: Vallecchi, 1970) pp.215-23. Forthcoming in Voegelin *Late published Essays* (Baton Rouge: Louisiana State University Press, 1990).

27. In this connection, note, in particular, the highly nuanced discussion of Hegel in Volume Five of *Order and History, In Search of Order*.

28. Gadamer, *Dialogue and Dialectic: Eight Hermeneutical Studies on Plato* ed. and trans. P. Christopher Smith (New Haven, Conn.:Yale University Press, 1980) p.73.

29. See, in particular, *In Search of Order*.

30. Rudolf Otto, *The Idea of the Holy*, trans. John Harvey, (London: Oxford University Press, 1958).

31. See on this Voegelin's meditation "The Beginning and the Beyond" forthcoming in Voegelin, *Late Unpublished Essays* (Baton Rouge: Louisiana State University Press, 1990).

32. Voegelin, "Immortality: Experience and Symbol", *The Harvard Theological Review*, 60, 3, pp.235-279. See also, Hans Jonas, "Immortality and the Modern Temper" in Jonas, *The Phenomenon of Life: Toward a Philosophical Biology*, (Chicago: University of Chicago Press, 1966) pp.262-81.

3

THE LIMITS OF HISTORY
Ontology, Anthropology and Historical Understanding

My purpose in the present paper is to expound a notion of the limits of history as it emerges from a reading of certain authors who stand on what may be called the realist wing of the phenomenological movement. In particular, I want to suggest the relevance to a theory of historical understanding of the critical ontology of Nicolai Hartmann. Hartmann's thought has fallen into a degree of neglect since his death in 1950 but it seems to me to present a conception of reality and of man's place within it which is of considerable importance to certain central problems both in the philosophy of history and in philosophical anthropology. These are problems associated, above all, with the notion of 'historicity' —a term made familiar, to phenomenologists at least, by the work of Husserl and Heidegger, and which, as generally interpreted, is taken to imply that man's being, and perhaps being as such, must be conceived in essentially historical terms, as process rather than as atemporal essence or form. More often than not, the notion of the historicity of being is taken as warranting the rejection of any conception of the human condition that seems to take man's nature or place in the world as being in any sense other than the ever-changing product of the historical process itself. This view I shall call 'radical historicism'.

In a recent work, *Hegel, Heidegger and the Ground of History*, Michael Allen Gillespie has pointed out some of the problems that such a view entails both for human self-interpretation and for our conception of historical inquiry. "Whether we like it or not", Gillespie writes, "our world has come to conceive of history as the human actuality. It is thus all the more perplexing and disconcerting that we are unable to articulate a conception of history that can consistently sustain human dignity. . . . The philosophical development that occurs under the names Hegel, Savigny, Marx, Dilthey and Heidegger represents the increasing and ultimately utter historicization of Western life and thought. Moreover this process is driven forward not by the success of history in explaining human life but by its failure: just as men have sought to cure the ills of democracy with more democracy, so they have sought to cure the ills of history with more history. This cure, however, has left the patient if not fatally weakened at least thoroughly confused and frightened." [1]

In a way that calls to mind the work of Leo Strauss and his followers, Gillespie seems to suggest that the historicization of our conception of man, an intellectual development closely associated with the modern world's rejection of the claims of classical metaphysics to attain knowledge of eternal or at least supra-historical truth, leads inevitably to moral nihilism. This is an argument for which I have considerable sympathy, and yet, as Gillespie's own patient and even sympathetic readings of both Hegel and Heidegger bear out, there are indeed powerful reasons why history has come to occupy the pre-eminent position it now holds in so many interpretations of human existence. The force of these reasons is such that, whatever our other options may be, we cannot hope to overcome the implications of radical historicism by retreating to an equally radical anti-historicism based upon the denial of the significance of historical change at either the anthropological or the ontological level.

In other words, any viable answer to the challenge of radical historicism must be one that is able to incorporate, within its own arguments, a theoretically adequate account of the phenomenon of the historicity of man, and even, in a sense, of being itself, whose discovery is the motivating insight of the whole historicist project. Even the ultimately anti-historicist project of delineating what I have termed 'the limits of history', and of making sense of the structure of man's being in terms of these limits, must begin by recognizing that, in Hartmann's words: "Everything real is in flux, involved in a constant coming into, or going out of existence. Motion and becoming form the universal mode of being of the real, no matter whether it be a question of material things, living forms, or human beings. Rest and rigidity are only found in the ideal essences of the old ontology." [2]

What I wish to contend is that Hartmann's ontology, especially when it is viewed alongside the work of certain other thinkers whose philosophical conceptions derive, to a greater or lesser extent, from the phenomenological realism of Max Scheler, provides us with a way of reconciling our recognition of the historical element in man and world with a recognition, no less essential to our understanding of the human condition, of the element of trans-historical constancy or permanence in man's being. It is not only, as Hans Jonas has shown, [3] that the reality of such an element, a human nature and condition that is prior to and manifest throughout history, is essentially presupposed in any coherent theory of historical interpretation; but that it is only through ontological examination of the constitutive form of that condition — a task entailing the type of categorial analysis exemplified in Hartmann's ontology — that we will be able to make sense of the limits to which human history seems to be subject.

Philosophers today tend to be suspicious of any attempt to speak of the human condition in anything but historical terms. In particular, any reference to an element of ontological constancy in that condition arouses the suspicion that one is seeking to retreat behind the modern world's critique of metaphysics in order to re-anchor human self-understanding in the attractive but illusory realm of timeless essences or, in the Platonic sense, ideas. In phenomenological circles the main influence in this suspicion of the appeal to ontological constancy as a factor in explaining man's being in the world is that of Heidegger. Under the influence of Heidegger's 'deconstructive' reading of the history of metaphysics, modern philosophy has tended to see in the ontological notion of essence, or constant or recurrent form, a subsequent, 'metaphysical' or, more precisely, Platonic distortion of man's primordial awareness of being — one which arises out of the anxieties of *Dasein* as a temporally bounded, self-consciously finite being, and which culminates in what Heidegger calls the 'onto-theological' conception of being itself as atemporal and eternal.

Perhaps no philosopher's reputation has suffered more than Hartmann's from a too ready acceptance of what are commonly taken to be the implications of this line of argument. And this in spite of Hartmann's explicit rejection of Platonism and his insistence on separating ontological questions from the sort of onto-theological speculations which are, for example, so prominent a theme in the late works of Scheler.

Hans-Georg Gadamer, a student of Hartmann at Marburg in the 1920s and witness to the impact of Heidegger's arrival at the University, has confirmed, not least in the subsequent development of his own work, the extent to which Hartmann's brand of phenomenological realism was undermined among the rising generation of philosophers by Heidegger's novel and, as it seemed, more philosophically radical project.[4] The tension between the philosophers whom one may justly regard as the century's two greatest explorers of ontological issues, was marked, appropriately enough, in a clash not only between two modes of thinking but two styles of life; a clash vividly illustrated by Gadamer in his account of a meeting between Hartmann and Heidegger, the first formally dressed in stiff collar and black coat, the second in a skiing outfit, each on his way to or from a university lecture. "Here," Gadamer writes, "were really two antipodes: the cool reserved Balt who gave the impression of being a grand bourgeois seigneur, and the small, dark-eyed mountain farmer whose temperament repeatedly broke through despite all attempts to keep his reserve." [5]

In the battle for influence, at Marburg and beyond, Heidegger won: to the extent that many philosophers today take for granted that his work undermines the very possibility of continuing the type of ontological analysis to which Hartmann remained devoted. Such thought, it is often asserted, fails even to penetrate to the ontological level. It remains caught at the 'ontic' level, classifying and categoriszing the being of things without raising the question of what and how being is.

I cannot, in the scope of this paper, hope to answer all the questions Heidegger raises concerning the philosophical legitimacy of ontology in the sense that Hartmann gives it. In part, the intellectual worth of his analyses, especially in relation to our problem of understanding the limits of history, must be allowed to emerge from the exposition which they will receive. It is nevertheless worth making the point, emphasized especially in Eric Voegelin's analyses of the writings of the ancient philosophers, pre-Socratic as well as classical, that the experience of an element of constancy in the Greek experience of being, far from being a later Platonic distortion of the event, as Heidegger seems to suggest, may in fact be a constitutive feature of it from the beginning. Following Voegelin on this point, the duality of the experience of being, as both the flowing presence of becoming and as the intuition of abiding form, is already fully present at the beginnings of Western philosophy. And these pre-Socratic beginnings are, in turn, not to be conceived, in the retrospective image of the later development of philosophy as a theoretical discipline, as abstract exercises in thought undertaken for their own sake, but as attempts to make sense of the experienced reality of the *Lebenswelt*, in which being is experienced "not only as a stream," but as revealing "constant and recurring forms that abide in the midst of flux." [6]

If Heidegger is right, as Voegelin agrees that he is, to regard the later, Voegelin would say post-Platonic, development of propositional metaphysics as involving a distortion of the experience of being through the exclusion of the element of process or happening it primordially implies, this does not mean that the contrary factor of abiding form, whose elucidation is the subsequent goal of ontology, is not also originally present in the experience out of which philosophy arises. [7] As we shall see from our examination of Hartmann's work, recognition of this element of constancy by no means implies that we must abandon the insight that real being is, in fact, always in process. Rather, through careful analysis of what we can understand to be the structurally and temporally differentiated form of what it is that comes to presence in our experience, we may arrive at an understanding of the process of reality that far from excluding the element of abiding, ontologically identifiable form actually seems to require it.

It is a fundamental principle of phenomenological inquiry — a principle whose validity is admitted by all who call themselves 'phenomenologists' regardless of their other differences — that the validity of any theoretical construct is to be admitted only insofar as it can be understood as arising within the context of human experience. To take a couple of examples representing very different types of phenomenological project, it can be seen that, whatever else may divide them, Husserl's analysis of the origins of geometry and, more generally, of modern "Galilean" science in the experience of the life-world and Scheler's account of the givenness of the hierarchy of values in the experience of the reflective human subject share the ambition of seeking to show that even the most abstract and, in their own terms, objective truths of mathematical science and absolutist ethics can only be fully understood once we have shown how it is that such truths are discovered, or encountered, in experience itself.[8] Whatever may be the relationship of Hartmann to the phenomenological movement as a whole,[9] his ontological project requires a similar experiential grounding if it is to seem anything more than than an arbitrary, classificatory schema.

As I have suggested above, the roots of the ontological endeavour, which is to understand the nature and significance of that experience of constancy or abiding form which is an integral part of our reflective or, in Voegelin's terms, 'noetic' awareness of being, are to be found not, as Heidegger would have it, in a Platonic, proto-metaphysical denial of the original experienced reality of being as process or 'happening', but precisely as an attempt to make sense of what is an integral and irreducible element in that experience. In the context of the theme of this paper, I am suggesting that what this implies is that the elucidation of this experience of constancy, through an ontological clarification of the limits of history, is, as much as the elucidation of the experience of being as process, through the development of the notion of historicity, an essential feature of any philosophy of history capable of doing justice to the reality of man's awareness of himself as a historical being, yet, at the same time, one endowed with a given 'nature' and occupying an ontologically identifiable and enduring place in the order of things.

To carry this argument further and provide, as it were, an experiential anchorage for the exposition of Hartmann's ontology, let me provide, in what is perforce a brief and schematic form, a sketch of the elementary character of the experience in which the requirement of ontological clarification is first made manifest.

When man considers his nature and place in the cosmos he finds himself to be a free but finite being. His freedom is real but limited. Human life is lived in the tension between freedom and necessity, between what we may and what we must be and do. Though this may be true of all conscious beings, only man may be said to be aware of it, by virtue of the fact that human consciousness is, so far as we can tell, uniquely characterized by a reflective awareness of self and world.

As Scheler vividly describes in *Die Stellung des Menschen im Kosmos*, this means that while animals live 'ecstatically', outward into an environment intrinsically and exclusively structured, perceptually at least, in accordance with the survival needs of the organism, man inhabits a world of objects in which, reflectively, he perceives himself as one object among others — a being contingent to the world on which he depends and which is, within limits discovered in the course of life, subject to his manipulatory powers. The form of human subjectivity is inseparable from this discovery of contingency: and the fateful possibilities of history, and of technology as a historical phenomenon, are, in turn, opened up to the human subject by the anthropologically primordial awareness that, for man, as a self-directed object among other objects, the world is an open field of more or less estimable possibilities for action and transformation.[10]

Knowing himself to be subject to the forces that govern all things of the world, man experiences himself to be, no less, a self-directed agent — a puzzling situation which, according to Scheler, founds the possibility, the inescapability indeed, of metaphysical and religious speculation. Through the objectification of the context of his life — the primordially human reconstitution of the organism's environment, *Umwelt*, as an objective world, *Welt*[11] — man "learns to reckon ever more comprehensively with his own contingent place in the universe, with his own self and his entire physical and psychical apparatus as with something foreign to him, something that stands in relation of strict causality with other things. . . . But," Scheler continues, "the centre, whence Man performs the acts of objectification of his body and soul, and makes the world in its fullness of space and time into an object — this centre cannot itself be a 'part' of this world, cannot possess a definite location in space and time: it can only be situated in the highest ground of being itself."[12] Hence, according to Scheler, the quest to understand the origins, the *arche*, of self and world — the experiential source of cosmogonic myth, of pre-Socratic mystic philosophy, of natural theology, including, of course, the unorthodox version then expounded by Scheler himself, and of all doctrines of transcendental subjectivity from Kant to Husserl and beyond.

In the context of the present paper, it is important to note that, according to this reading, the characteristically modern, and especially post-Kantian, project of seeking the origins of the experienced world in the activity of a world-constituting subject arises out of the same eminently questionable experience of being which also lies at the source of metaphysical speculation concerning the ultimate ground and source of things. More than this, it may even be said that the two projects, epistemological and metaphysical, share, in spite of their apparent differences, a common style of questioning. Both may properly be conceived as essentially "archaeological" undertakings; in the sense that each responds to the enigma of being through development of a type of questioning that seeks to understand being, not in terms of its perceived structure in the here and now, but by reference to its *arche* or constitutive origin.

The common question, whose very different answers we find expressed respectively in propositional metaphysics and the no less propositional epistemology of post-Kantian philosophy, is: How does the world we experience as real come to be what it is? Under the impact of the work of the various writers identified by Gillespie in the passage cited above, this is the question that has, in the contemporary period, been redefined in terms of the notion of the historicity of man and being: to such an extent that it is sometimes difficult for today's students to understand how it could ever have been convincingly answered in anything but strictly historical terms. The climax of the process of the historicization of the linked questions of knowledge and being may be found, to take one influential example, in the work of Richard Rorty, in whose recent writings epistemology and metaphysics alike have ceased to have any significance except as terms that name distinct moments in the perennial "conversation" through which man comes, eventually to a recognition of the utter historicity of his being.[13]

It is not my purpose to deny the legitimacy of the archaeological question, nor, consequently, to question the notion of historicity as such. Rather, I want to show that a questioning of the experience of being in terms of its constitutive origins by no means exhausts the problem of the understanding of being which is at the source of philosophy. The same experience which provokes the archaeological question of source or origin requires, for its elucidation, a reflection upon the given and abiding ontological structure of what it is we know to be.

Thanks above all to the work of Heidegger, we have learned to rethink the philosophical experience of being as a happening or event; but, as my earlier references to Voegelin suggest, that experience, which 'happens' first among the Ionian Greeks, is not an experience of undifferentiated process or flux. The coming-into and going-out-of being of things, whose recognition is the source of the archaeological question, and hence, eventually, of the doctrine of the utter historicity of being, is, no less, the experience of the happening of what Voegelin calls 'abiding form'; and, as such, the authentic source of what modernity has come to regard as the illusory atemporalism of post-Platonic metaphysics. If, like the followers of Heidegger, we feel bound, on the basis of a new and hermeneutically enriched appreciation of the nature of the experience in which philosophy is born, to question the legitimacy of the metaphysical reduction of being to atemporal essence or substance, should we not be equally suspicious of a line of thought that rules out of account as somehow inauthentic the no less original experience of abiding form?

To carry this line of argument a little further, and so contribute something more to my claim that an ontology of Hartmann's type, is a necessary element in the clarification of man's being in the world, let me note that the puzzling experience of being in which Scheler sees the source of the metaphysical quest to understand the ground of things —a quest renewed in different, egological rather than theological, form in the great systems of German idealism —also provokes a parallel reflection on the ontological constitution of what is.

Such a reflection, which achieves its cognitive goal, I would argue, in Hartmann's ontological differentiation of the strata of being, or something very like it, is, as much as the archaeological question, entailed in the attempt of human consciousness to elucidate its enigmatic place in the order of things as a whole. As Eric Voegelin pointed out: "Human consciousness is not a process that occurs in the world side by side with other processes without contact with these processes other than cognition; rather, it is based on animalic, vegetative, and inorganic being, and only on this basis is it consciousness of a human being. Man's structure seems to be the ontic premise for man's transcending into the world, for in none of its directions of transcending does consciousness find a level of being which is not also one in which it itself is based. Speaking ontologically, consciousness finds in the world no level which it does not also experience as its own foundation. In the 'basis-experience' of consciousness man presents himself as an epitome of the cosmos, as a microcosm. Now we do not know in what this basis 'really' consists; all our finite experience is experience of levels of being in their differentiation; the nature of the cosmos is inexperienceable, whether the nexus of basis be the foundation of the vegetative on the inorganic, of the animalic on the vegetative, or of human consciousness on the animal body. There is no doubt, however, that this basis exists. Even though the levels of being are clearly distinguishable in their respective structures, there must be something common which makes possible the continuum of all of them in human existence. The basis-experience is further reinforced through the experience that this is not a matter of a static complex but of intimate relationships in a process. We know the phenomena of maturing and growing old with parallels in processes of the body as well as the consciousness. And we know — even though it is not transparent to us — the nexus of being by virtue of which it is possible to 'date' the succession of inner illuminations of consciousness in symbols of external time. Finally we are related to the transcendent world in the mysterious relation of objective knowledge, a relation which phenomenology has by no means illumined but rather only described from without." [14]

This text comes from the essay "On Theory of Consciousness" which Voegelin sent to Alfred Schutz in 1940 as part of their correspondence regarding the significance of Husserl's *Krisis* essay.[15] I cite it here not in order to enter into the debate over the validity of the late Husserl's attempt to integrate the problem of history within the framework of a transcendental phenomenology a project which Schutz no less than Voegelin felt was beset with ultimately insurmountable problems —but because Voegelin's dense but luminous analysis of the self-clarification of consciousness in terms of a nexus of being composed of distinct yet interrelated levels of being, present both in man and world, illustrates as well as anything the sort of elucidation of experience which founds the possibility, nay the necessity, of ontology as Hartmann understands the term. What we find in Voegelin's text is a phenomenological description of the experiential ground of Hartmann's view that: "The nature of man can be adequately understood only as the integrated whole of combining strata and, furthermore, as placed within the totality of the same order of strata which, outside of man, determines the structure of the real world." [16]

In relation to the complex of problems this raises, my thesis is that, at least as it is commonly understood, the notion of the historicity of being, no less than the metaphysical denial of the ontological significance of temporality —the false opposition of being to becoming —distorts the content of our experience of reality by exalting one aspect of it to the point at which the other is excluded. It is in the context of our need to overcome this problem in the interests of human self-understanding — which is of course also an understanding of man's place in the order of things — that the significance of Hartmann's ontology is to be understood. For Hartmann's is an ontology which, while profoundly aware of the identity of real being with becoming, provides, within its account of this process, a critically tenable notion of the being of abiding form as an authentic feature of reality itself.

More specifically, in relation to the problem of the philosophy of history and of man as a historical being, I want to suggest that only such an ontology allows us to understand the process of human history for what it is: that is, as the record and adventure of an ontologically finite being striving to realize his no less finite potential upon a cosmic stage whose limits, though always incompletely known, constitute the absolute frontiers of possible human achievement and thus of what we commonly mean by *history*.

Hartmann's is, in an important sense, a limited ontology —one that seeks, so far as is possible, to divorce ontological analysis of reality as we experience it from metaphysical speculation on questions of the ultimate source and destiny of man and being. He talks of his work as a 'new ontology', thereby opposing it to older ontologies which he, a neo-Kantian as much as a phenomenologist, regarded as flawed by their obsession with critically untenable questions that fall outside the range of positive knowledge. Hartmann follows Kant in rejecting the philosophical legitimacy of all attempts to provide metaphysical answers to such questions. In ontology, as elsewhere, we must, he insists, respect the *aporias*, the impassable perplexities bounding the field of human knowledge — perplexities which represent, as Scheler's late work had so recently illustrated, an irresistible temptation to the metaphysical imagination but from whose exploration, in Hartmann's view, there flows, all too readily, the metaphysician's typical confusion between plausibility and truth.

The limits of Hartmann's ontology rest on the recognition that the overall field of what has, since St.Thomas Aquinas, been called metaphysics is divisible. Hartmann, unconsciously so far as I know, accepts the distinction drawn by Francisco Suarez between general and special metaphysics. The former is the study of all possible being: the latter of actual being. It is the second alone that constitutes the legitimate field of ontology. Ontology, in this sense, is empirically based in our experience of the world both as the foundation of our existence and as the necessary, intentional object of knowledge. Its topic is the structure of real, that is temporally and, with important exceptions, spatially existent, and ideal, that is purely intelligible, being. Its mode of investigation entails delineation of the categories which, at different levels of being, govern the behaviour of items encountered in experience. Its purpose is the attainment of an admittedly provisional but well-corroborated account of the stage on which human life is set.

It has been rightly stressed by many authors that the human world is historically constituted by actions which are meaningful to those who carry them out. To understand social reality we must, therefore, seek to grasp the meanings in terms of which social actors understand their actions. Such understanding is necessarily indirect and mediated by interpretation of the symbols through which meaning is expressed.[17]

In other words, the human sciences are necessarily hermeneutic disciplines whose proper form of inquiry owes more to the logic of textual interpretation than to the commonly accepted models of natural science. But hermeneutics, conceived in its narrower, pre-Heideggerian sense as the interpretation of meaning, has its own horizon, as Hartmann implies when he writes: "The activity of man, spiritual life and historical actuality, can by no means be adequately grasped by an understanding of meaning. With this concept we are still in the air, with no firm ground under our feet. We shall have to return to comprehension based on knowledge of laws. For the firm ground on which spirit rests is not itself spirit, nor even anything of its kind, but just what is opposite and foreign to it, the wide realm of nature, in the first place organic nature, but indirectly also inorganic nature." [18] A philosophical hermeneutics which, like Gadamer's for instance, recognizes the centrality of the experience of finitude as a clue to meaning and a limit to understanding, requires, Hartmann would have argued, as its complement, an elucidation of the context of man's activities — the cosmological as well as the cultural-historical context — in terms of whatever we may discover to be its ontological structure. Ontology, we may admit, is itself a work of interpretation, but its specific object is not the works of man but the structure of the stage on which, at all moments of history, these works are realized.

How then does Hartmann envisage the structure of the stage — a structure which is also, as we shall see, the key to understanding the specific composition of man? We may, he claims, distinguish four strata of 'real being' — inorganic nature, organic nature, consciousness and spirit. Consciousness and spirit, a term which Hartmann, following Dilthey, identifies with the man-made but supra-individual reality of culture, depend for their very existence upon the lower strata, and are, in their turn, the bearers of ideal beings, such as numbers and values. The latter exist only in the media of consciousness and spirit, but are autonomous in essence. This view corresponds to Husserl's distinction between *noesis* and *noema*, the act of thinking and the self-determining object of thought; but in Hartmann's philosophy the ideal being of such thought-objects is given a characteristically ontological significance. Ideal beings are thought-objects, but they are essentially identifiable, autonomous beings nonetheless — possessing defining features of their own, and subsisting within a total structure of being whose lower strata allow for their emergence but do not determine their essential contents.

Being must be understood as a hierarchical structure in which the higher levels depend upon the lower without being essentially determined by them. Thus organic life, for example, depends upon the existence between inorganic atoms and molecules, just as psychic life depends on the being of the organism, and spirit upon psyche, but "such a dependency in no way excludes autonomy. . . . It must only be granted that the *conditio sine qua non* of the higher forms of being is always provided by the lower forms and, in the last analysis, by the entire sequence of lower forms." [19]

The phrase *sine qua non* draws our attention to the fact that when we are talking of the ontology of human existence, we are speaking about the conditions necessary to the emergence of man's being and to its subsequent enduring, but not sufficient to explain the achieved forms of cultural and political order. The ontological order is the precondition of human history and thus of the polities that are formed within it. It forms, at every time, a frontier of human possibility; but this determines only the limits of action and never the content of human achievement.

Emergence is a notoriously vague term; and frustration at our inability to pin down any general and universally valid conditions which would explain how distinct entities, whether species or historically constituted societies, come to appear in the history of the universe, combines with what Hartmann calls a prejudice in favour of simplicity to recommend a determinist conception of ontological dependence, for which we have, in experience, very little evidence. The notion of dependence is all too often construed in a determinist sense. But this, Hartmann claims, is only because, at first sight, determinism seems more coherent than alternative views and not because it corresponds to anything in our experience of the world — an experience in which the distinctiveness of particular beings and the subject's sense of his own freedom seem to fly in the face of all conceptions of the world as a univocally determined unity.

However, since we can hardly doubt that inorganic and organic nature provide the foundations and context of all such experience, and since the modern scientific understanding of these strata is couched in terms of causal laws that relate initial conditions to necessary consequences, it seems an act of intellectual and even moral weakness to cut the chain of necessary causes at just the point at which it threatens our prized sense of autonomy. It is one of the virtues of Hartmann's conception of the world as a unity of heterogeneous strata, each governed by its own categorial systems — systems which cannot without close examination be transferred to other strata — that it allows us to reconcile the apparently conflicting experiences of causal dependence and ontological freedom without any sacrifice of intellectual rigour.

There are three major problem areas in this ontology. First, it must develop a non-determinist conception of ontological dependence between strata. Second, it must delineate the categories that are specific to particular strata, as well as those which connect them. Third, it must, in consequence of what such investigations may discover, show how the various strata are related not only in the broad world picture but within the higher beings which emerge *within* it. For it is characteristic of the four ontologically distinguishable strata of real being that: ". . . they not only do not coincide with the levels of actual structures inanimate object, organism, man, and so on but rather cut across them. They are not only strata of the real world as a totality, but also strata of the actual structures themselves. Man, for example, is not only a spirit; he has a spiritless psychic life too. He is also an organism and is even a material structure of the same nature as other inanimate things. He reacts to certain stimuli instinctively like an animal, and like an animal, too, he propagates his species; just as he experiences thrust and counter-thrust like a material object. The organism, for its part, possesses, beside the quality of being animate, also the general character of physical materiality. Indeed, only thus is it possible that the organism's life process should consist essentially in a change of materials. Nevertheless, looked at ontologically, the organism consists of only two strata, while man embraces all four strata. In the higher reaches of the animal kingdom the threefold division already begins to manifest itself inasmuch as the emergence of consciousness adds another level to organic life. . . . The tiers of reality form a stratified order not only within the unity of the world but also in the actual structures of the higher layers, in such a fashion that the lower strata are always included in the higher ones. And this relation obviously cannot be reversed. The organism cannot exist without atoms and molecules, but these can exist without the organism." [20]

The identification of the characteristic categories of each stratum is an empirical, analytical task based upon experience of the structures of real beings. Thus, for example, we find that the categories of animate nature — organic structure, adaptation and purposiveness, metabolism, self-regulation, self-restoration, the life of the species, the constancy of the species and variation — are not to be found in the inorganic layer whose existence that of the organism presupposes. They do, on the other hand, recur, in modified form, in higher beings possessed of psychic and of spiritual life. Generally then, the pattern governing the occurrence of ontologically specific categories is that, while the categories of the lower strata play their part in constituting the form of the higher, the reverse does not happen. In the failure to recognize this Hartmann sees the abiding fault of every metaphysical theory which purports to interpret all reality in terms of psychic categories such as intention and purpose.

Time, process and causality, the most universal of the categories which we initially find present at the level of inorganic being, penetrate all the higher strata. Space, in contrast, is not a feature of psychic and spiritual being. The typical categories of ontologically lower strata tend to recur in the higher strata that rest upon them; but this is not a universal law of reality and, insofar as categories *do* recur at higher levels, they do so in the context of an ontologically distinct complex.

In Hartmann's words: "The difference in the behaviour of the various categories prevents recurrence from becoming a general law. It is confined to a limited number of categories. Yet there is no complete lack of rules. On the basis of a sequence of strata it can be shown that the breaking off of certain groups of pervasive categories takes place only at certain levels. Such a level is the borderline between the organic and the psychic. Here the situation is different from the one prevailing at the frontier between inanimate nature and the organism. The categories of the inorganic all penetrate into the realm of the organic, although some of them play only a very insignificant role there. The reason for this is that the organism includes as integral parts the dynamic structures of masses ordered to one another, superinforming these structures by virtue of its own more elevated structures. Along with these inferior structures it also appropriates their categories. . . . This relation of 'superinformation' is, however, not typical of the 'distance' between strata. The psychic life is no superinformation of corporeal life. It does not integrate the organic processes and does not use them as integral parts. It is supported by these organic processes and influenced by them. But they continue below it. There may be consciousness of metabolism or growth, but only in the sense in which there is consciousness of external objects and processes. These, as objects of the consciousness, are located outside the consciousness. Neither as acts nor as content do they become part of its existence. . . . Act and content are of categorially different kind. They possess neither spatiality, nor even substantiality. The 'inner world' which is built out of them — the world of experience, feeling, perception, thinking — is an ontological region 'above' organic structure, but it only rests 'upon' it as on its ontological basis. It does not consist 'of it' as of its material. In contradistinction to superinformation, this relation of one stratum put on top of another may be styled 'superimposition'." [21]

It is in terms of superimposition rather than of superinformation that Hartmann conceives the relationship between psychic and spiritual being — a relationship which he identifies with that between personal consciousness and the supra-individual, cultural realm of 'objective spirit', "The historical life of the objective spirit," he writes, "does not consist of psychic acts but only 'rests' on them. . . . Speech, legal order, custom, morality and science are more than parts of a consciousness. The individual receives them from the common spiritual sphere of which he becomes a participant, and then hands them on. He contributes his share to their total historical process, but he does not create for himself his own speech, morality or science. Correspondingly, the spiritual world does not form the content of a superpersonal consciousness, as is believed in some metaphysical theories. Consciousness exists only as the consciousness of the individual, but this is no adequate consciousness of the objective spirit. Beside their common racial origin, the individuals are tied together only by their common spiritual world. Every human being has his psychic life incontestably for himself. Nobody else can act or suffer for him. Consciousness divides; the spirit unites." [22]

Even lengthy quotation can do only scant justice to the subtlety of Hartmann's analysis, which depends so much upon the sustained argument and the anticipation of objections which his book contains. In general terms, it seems to me that the ontology he proposes allows us to resolve many of the problems posed by man's simultaneous awareness of his freedom from and dependence upon the world. It gives precise content to the notion of relative autonomy, or finite freedom — a notion necessary to the accurate registration of our experience as human beings but which, without ontological clarification, seems intellectually evasive and even unintelligible. More than this, it offers us a convincing account of the synthetic nature of man as a unity of heterogeneous strata, a microcosm, and of the relationships of the historically formed world of culture to the acts and conditions which support and sustain it. It gives us a way to conceive the freedom of a finite, contingent being who not only realizes himself in historically accomplished forms, achieved within the context of a pre-existing cosmos, but does so by making use of mental and material resources which are, as much as the cosmic context, given elements of his inheritance.

Hartmann's conception of the relative autonomy of psyche and spirit — levels of being that emerge as distinctive, differentiated elements within and upon the stratified structure of reality which founds their possibility — is the clue to understanding the ontological status of an historically accomplished, cultural, spiritual and, as I have argued elsewhere, political order which is, at best, dimly suggested by the biological inheritance we share as members of the human race.[23] If the possibility of historically formed cultures is a function of our specific, biological identity as organisms of a particular, in some ways unprecedented type, its actualization is a matter of the cohering or drawing together of individual, historically situated, psyches in the shared traditions which constitute the identity of each culture. Each such tradition, every humanly constituted order, must, in its turn, be understood as a particular creative response to the common ontological situation in which man finds himself — a situation which is not to be understood as the consequence of human history but, rather, as its precondition.

Recognition of this defining fact of human life, which is, in Scheler's work, still obscured by the ambition of rendering the mystery of human distinctiveness intelligible within an all-encompassing general metaphysics,[24] is not only the founding insight for the developments in philosophical anthropologies associated with the names of Helmut Plessner, Arnold Gehlen and, more recently, Hans Blumenberg — for all of whom the historical existence of man is only comprehensible as a perennial creative response to an initial, ontologically given situation in which biological deficiency and cultural creativity and ingenuity seem to be mutually entailed: it is also, as Gadamer has recently reemphasised, the necessary presupposition of a historically oriented hermeneutics which takes as its object the totality of what is distinctive in and definitive of man's historical existence.[25] As this last example suggests, the

very notion of man's historicity, his existence as a self-interpreting, historically constituted being, only becomes intelligible in so far as we conceive
history itself as the history of a particular, ontologically identifiable sort of
being inhabiting a particular, equally ontologically identifiable, sort of world.

In other words, the process of history, and of man's historical self-
constitution, is only intelligible if we recognise it as the adventure of a finite
being fated to realise his potential within ontological limits which are
constitutive of the being of self and world alike. The element of constancy, or
abiding form, present *ab origine* in human experience, is, as much as the
experience of process, a feature of what we know as history. As Hartmann's
delineation of the complex categorial anatomy of man's being makes plain, it
is one that does not require explanation in terms of any notion of timeless
essences or ideas, but may be conceived as the structural result of the
increasingly differentiated becoming of the world.

The becoming of the world is a process of differentiation in which what is
differentiated achieves existence in the multiplicity of abiding forms which
traditional metaphysics sought to classify in terms of genera and species. If
there was a fault in this classificatory project, it did not lie in the idea that
reality was composed of essentially distinct beings but in the tendency to
suppose that the essences of real, as opposed to ideal, beings were, in some
sense, timeless and eternal, whereas, in fact, they are only relatively constant
structures, emerging within the differentiating process and dependent for their
continued existence on the continuing subsistence of the conditions which first
made their existence possible.

The being of the world is, at any point in this process, characterised by a
relatively stable ontological structure which is understandable as a nexus of
relations of dependence and emergence subsisting between ontologically
distinctive strata, whose presence is identifiable both within the structure of
the world as a whole and within the natures of the increasingly complex beings
that have, thus far, emerged within it. The climax of this process, at least in
terms of complexity, is found in the historical being of man, in whose specific
formation we find present the fourfold differentiation of real being —
inorganic and organic nature, psyche and spirit — and through whose
spiritual, cultural life such ideal beings as values become present in the world.

The fact that being achieves its most complete differentiation in the being
of man in no way implies that man is removed from dependence upon the
abiding structure of the world which first made his existence possible. Quite
the reverse. "Organic nature," Hartmann writes, "rises above inorganic
nature —not freely and independently, however, but on the basis of the laws
and circumstances of the world of matter, even though these laws and
circumstances are far from sufficient in themselves to constitute life. Likewise

spiritual life and consciousness have as their prequisite an organism in which and with which they come into the world. In like manner the great historical moments in cultural, spiritual life are carried by the conscious life of the individuals involved. From stratum to stratum, passing across the successive divisions, we find everywhere the principle of dependence upon the stratum below, yet at the same time the autonomy of the superimposed stratum with its own structures and laws. This relationship constitutes the real unity of the actual world. For all its variety and heterogeneity, the world is still an entity. It has the unity of a system — a system of differentiated strata. The vital point is not that the differences between these levels are unbridgeable — indeed, it may only be to us that they appear to be unbridgeable — but that new laws and categories are established which, though dependent on those of the strata below, have their own character and assert their own autonomy." [26]

Let us now, by way of conclusion, seek to explicate the significance of this for our conception of the limits of history, and to do so in terms of the three notions that appear in our subtitle — ontology, anthropology and historical understanding.

The sense in which the term ontology is being used should, by now, be clear enough. Ontology describes the effort to delineate, so far as may be possible, the structure of the reality in which man finds himself to be a participant and which is, at the same time, experienced as constitutive of his being. Reality is experienced as a process but one in which distinct and abiding elements can be differentiated. To make sense of the real being of the world we must, on the one hand, distinguish, within the overall process, between the separable, but never mutually isolated, items and events of which the world, as we experience it, is composed; and, on the other, between the categorially distinct ontological strata out of whose interplay or enmeshment the real being of things, the actual being of beings — including the being of man — is constituted.

For all the apparent abstraction of Hartmann's analysis it must be understood as founded in the attempt to clarify, or render transparent, man's primordial experience of himself as an ontologically complex being, whose formative elements and processes are also, in large part, to be found in the world he inhabits. Anthropology designates the attempt to describe the real structure that man discovers to be constitutive of what he is.

Seen thus, anthropology and ontology are mutually entailing. This must be taken in a strong sense to mean, not only that man is always, as a matter of fact, enmeshed in the nexus of the world, but that the strata composing the world of inorganic and organic nature also enter, as formative factors, into his own being and thus into the substance of history. In this sense at least, man must be conceived as something more than a self-constituting being. Only recognition of this makes historical understanding possible.

To illustrate this, consider the problems faced by a teacher trying to explain the story of Napoleon's retreat from Moscow to a class composed of beings from another planet — beings who derive sustenance directly from the atmosphere, who are impervious to changes of temperature, and who can fly at will across the surface of their planet. In such a situation the teacher would need explicitly to draw attention to the physical features of the human organism which, if left out of account, would render the story of the Russian campaign unintelligible. These features are not the products of human history, still less phantasms of man's self interpretation. They are ontologically given constants which set, at all times, the limits within which history unfolds.

To put matters another way, the intelligibility of historical narrative depends upon the more or less assumed presence, within history itself, of what we may call meta-historical features of being. These features, let us stress again, need not be conceived as in any way eternal or atemporal. They are products, or results, of the meta-historical, self-differentiating process of reality which, at a certain point of its becoming, renders human being and human history possible.

It seems to me that the notion of historicity, and the associated conception of man as a uniquely self-constituting being, while cer-tainly drawing our attention to a striking aspect of man's being, fails to elucidate the whole complex picture. Human existence is indeed historical existence but Hartmann's ontology reminds us that the adventure of history unfolds, however freely and creatively, only within the ontological 'space' in which man's specific form of being remains possible. We should not understimate the degree of free, self-constitutive activity which is possible within this space, but nor should we ignore the limits to which it is subject. If, as so many modern writers insist, we are indeed self-constituting beings who make ourselves what in fact we are through a perennial process of creative activity and self-interpretation, it is equally important to point out that activity is always activity within and upon a preexisting world, with an autonomous structure of its own, and that self-interpretation is not an arbitrary matter but involves reflection upon what we are already and iremediably constituted as being. *Ecce Homo*.

Notes

1. Michael Allen Gillespie, *Hegel, Heidegger and the Ground of History* (Chicago: University of Chicago Press, 1984), p. 13.

2. Nicolai Hartmann, *New Ways of Ontology* transl. R.C. Kuhn, (Chicago: Regnery 1952), pp.28-29.

3. Hans Jonas, "Change and Permanence: On the Possibility of Understanding

History", in Jonas: *Philosophical Essays: From Ancient Creed to Technological Man* (Chicago: University of Chicago Press, 1974), pp.237-260.

4. Hans-Georg Gadamer, *Philosophical Apprenticeships* transl. R.R.Sullivan (Cambridge, Mass.: MIT Press 1985).

5. *Ibid*, p.48-9.

6. Eric Voegelin, *Anamnesis* trans. Gerhart Niemeyer, (University of Notre Dame Press, 1978) p. 76.

7. *Ibid*.

8. Edmund Husserl, *The Crisis of European Sciences and Transcendental Phenomenology* trans. David Carr, (Evanston, Northwestern University Press, 1970), Max Scheler: *Formalism in Ethics* trans. Manfred S. Frings and Roger L. Funk, (Evanston, Northwestern University Press, 1973).

9. See the discussion of Hartmann's relationship to phenomenology in Volume I of Herbert Spiegelberg: *The Phenomenological Movement* (The Hague, Nijhoff, 1978), pp. 358-360.

10. Hans Jonas, *The Imperative of Responsibility: In Search of an Ethics for the Technological Age* (Chicago: University of Chicago Press, 1984), Arnold Gehlen: *Man in the Age of Technology* trans. P. Lipscombe, (New York: Columbia University Press, 1980).

11. The terms *welt* and *umwelt* are used here in the sense given them by Jakob von Uexkull.

12. Max Scheler, *Man's Place in Nature* trans. Hans Meyerhoff, (Boston: Beacon Press, 1961).

13. Richard Rorty, *Philosophy and the Mirror of Nature* (Princeton: Princeton University Press, 1980).

14. Eric Voegelin, *Anamnesis* loc.cit. pp.27-8.

15. On the relationship between Voegelin and Schutz see Helmut R. Wagner "Agreement in Discord: Alfred Schutz and Eric Voegelin," in P.J. Opitz and Gregor Sebba, *The Philosophy of Order: Essays on History, Consciousness and Politics* Stuttgart, Klett-Cotta, 1981 pp.74-90. Voegelin and Schutz had read Husserl's essay *"Die Krisis der europaischen Wissenschaften und die transzendentale Phanomenologie"* which appeared in *Philosophia* Belgrade, 1936 pp.77-176.

16. Nicolai Hartmann, *New Ways of Ontology*, p.121-2.

17. David J. Levy, *Realism: An Essay in Interpretation and Social Reality* Manchester, Carcanet, 1981.

18. Hartmann op.cit. p.34.

19. *Ibid*, p.36.

20. *Ibid*, p.48.

21. *Ibid*, pp.78-9.

22. *Ibid*, p.80.

23. Levy, "Politics, Nature and Freedom: On the Natural Foundation of the Political Condition", *Journal of the British Society for Phenomenology*, Vol.15, No.3, October 1984, pp. 286-300.

24. Scheler, *Man's Place in Nature*, loc.cit.

25. Hans-Georg Gadamer, *The Relevance of the Beautiful* trans. N. Walker

(Cambridge: Cambridge University Press 1987), p.46.

26. Hartmann, *Der Aufbau der realen Welt* 3rd edition, Berlin, De Gruyter, 1964, cited by Konrad Lorenz in *Behind the Mirror: A Search for a Natural History of Human Knowledge* trans. R. Taylor, (London: Methuen, 1977), p.38.

[The exposition of the ontology of Nicolai Hartmann in the present paper overlaps considerably but is not identical with the discussion of the philosopher's work in Chapter Two of David J. Levy: *Political Order: Philosophical Anthropology, Modernity and the Challenge of Ideology* Baton Rouge and London, Louisiana State University Press, 1987 pp. 19-37.]

4

THE POLITICS OF DISENCHANTMENT

Hans Freyer, Sociology and the Deradicalization of German Conservatism

1. Remembering Things Past

Some fifty years have passed since Arthur Koestler and a number of other prominent ex-communist intellectuals disowned their former ideological commitments in the famous anthology *The God that Failed*.[1] This public recantation of the totalitarian creed that had once exclusively defined the authors' hopes and fears, though not unprecedented, created a great impression on a Western public still attuned to seeing the Soviet Union in terms of our wartime alliance. The phrase that gave the book its title passed into the language as a lasting emblem of ideological disenchantment; and with the passage of years further revelations of the horrors of Soviet communism, by Solzhenitsyn, Bukovsky and others, amply confirmed the justice of Koestler's apostacy. In addition to this and, over the same period, a considerable body of philosophical literature, devoted to the critical analysis of Marxism, increasingly undermined the intellectual and moral credentials of what had once been the preferred faith of some of the best minds in the Western world.

Even today neither communism nor the Marxist sophistry that gave it its intellectual *raison d'être* is yet altogether dead. The first, though battered by the events of recent years, remains embodied in the still threatening political reality of a number of more or less disagreeable regimes. The second endures as a diffuse yet still pervasive presence in certain quarters of the intellectual world. Yet neither as political movement nor as intellectual orientation can contemporary Marxism face the world with the confidence in its scientific status and future triumph that once gave it, to some at least, a seemingly compelling appeal.

The implacable march of history faltered. And, ironically, it was at the very moment of the Soviet Union's greatest military and political successes that the communist dream began to go sour. On the one hand, with the defeat of Nazi Germany, the intellectuals' favourite excuse, that it had been necessary to choose between Stalin and Hitler, communism or fascism, lost whatever credibility it may once have had. On the other, the discovery of the extent of the crimes committed in the name of National Socialism, far from confirming the rightness of attachment to its great ideological rival, served, above all, to educate people to the dangers of all totalitarian political commitments. "After Hitler and Stalin," wrote W. H. Auden, himself once a Communist, "we know all things are possible." All things, that is, except the stuff of which the dreams of utopian politics are made.

And what of the other side? What of those intellectuals, in Germany in particular, who had invested their political hopes in the Third Reich? Here the situation was more complicated and, potentially at least, more personally painful. Not only had the physical evidence of political criminality been exposed to the eyes of the world in a way that is only now beginning to happen in the Soviet case, but the crimes in question had been committed not for the sake of a universalist ideology that could later be discarded as a youthful and, in a certain sense, generous error of judgement, but in the name of an exclusivist and admittedly perverted attachment to nationhood.

By the very terms of their public commitment to its creed the devotees of National Socialism had, as it were, turned their backs on the fundamental decencies not merely of the modern world but, arguably, of Western civilization as such. Admittedly, few German intellectuals had accepted National Socialism because they had been convinced by its pseudo-scientific claims. But many had seen in the movement an authentic if flawed expression of the will to power and even a privileged means of survival for their nation in a situation that seemed otherwise hopeless. If we are truly to understand this, as we surely should, we cannot afford merely to dismiss it as an aberration rooted in some rationally inexplicable national neurosis. Rather, we must see that the sense of threatened national and personal identity, made manifest in commitment to Hitler's Reich, was an existential reality rooted in a community of fate whose past could hardly be disowned without in some way calling into question the very traditions which had, from childhood, made each of them the man he was.

Those I have in mind were not the party ideologues like Alfred Rosenberg, nor the intellectually insignificant functionaries who manned the institutes of racial science set up under the auspices of the SS, but the major intellectual figures who, putting aside their misgivings, gave, initially at least, their enthusiastic support to the Nazi regime. These included many figures of enduring intellectual and scholarly significance; among them the philosopher

Martin Heidegger, the jurist Carl Schmitt, the poet Gottfried Benn, the Old Testament scholar Gerhard Kittel, the theologian Emmanuel Hirsch and the sociologists Arnold Gehlen and Hans Freyer. All these men survived the war, and among them only Hirsch, at one time the close friend and colleague of the Christian socialist Paul Tillich, seems never to have regretted his commitment to Hitler and his cause.[2]

Much has been written, not least by those who experienced it themselves, about the process of intellectual disenchantment with communism: rather less about the equivalent, though significantly different, process of disenchantment with National Socialism. There are several reasons for this. On the one hand, those who have written about it from the outside have taken so much for granted the moral evil of the Third Reich and the intellectual untenability of its legitimating ideology that they have tended to assume that only moral blindness and/or political opportunism could explain even a short-lived allegiance to National Socialism. On the other, those who lived through the successive stages of enthusiasm and disenchantment either tended, like Heidegger, to remain, as near as possible, silent about it or, like Schmitt, to provide more or less self-serving apologias which often seemed to explain rather less than they concealed.

Both attitudes, silence and dissimulation, are understandable. The retrospective eye of historian and participant alike cannot but view the events of 1933 through the smoke of the chimneys of Auschwitz and Treblinka. However, by the same token, we who live now ought also to recognize that though opportunism and cowardice, moral blindness and political ambition were indeed real factors in-fluencing, to various degrees, the attitudes of the new Reich's intellectual supporters, they were not the only ones. Passionate and even generous hopes and fears, for the future of the nation as much as or more than for the individual self, marked the mood of many German intellectuals at the time; and, among the majority of these who were neither left-wing nor Jewish, hope was, for a while at least, very much in the ascendent.

In this regard Ernst Jünger, for many the foremost literary voice of the intellectual right, was quite exceptional in maintaining, from the beginning, his distance from Hitler and the new regime. While other nationalist and radical conservative writers sought at the time to play down the differences that separated them from the world-view of National Socialism, Jünger seems to have taken a keen delight in emphasizing, discreetly but unmistakably, that Hitler's revolution was not the one for which he had hoped.

By the time Jünger published his famous allegorical novel *On the Marble Cliffs* in 1939, disenchantment with the regime was, to varying degrees, already widespread among intellectuals who had originally been enthusiastic about its promises and prospects. Jünger's fable is, perhaps, the single undoubted masterpiece of the "Aesopian" literature of what came to be called the "inner emigration". As a thinly veiled diagnosis of the evil that had come upon Germany, it can, with some justice, be seen as prophetically representative of a much more widespread attitude of disquiet and even hostility that was to develop among German nationalists — the attitude to the regime which was, eventually, to culminate in the 1944 attempt on Hitler's life. At the same time historical evidence compels us to recognize that, if Jünger's terrifying tale was in some sense a representative, even a prophetic work, its author was thoroughly atypical of those with whom he is usually associated. In contrast to men like Schmitt, Freyer and even the expressionist poet Benn, whose political disaffection was, in large part, the result of the regime's ideologically motivated rejection of what they had initially offered to its service, Jünger was, among nationalist intellectuals, almost alone in having, after 1933 as before, consistently rejected the temptations of conformity to the party line.

Here, however, we should note that even among those who did fall into line in 1933 no single pattern was typical. Schmitt, for example, was already an established public figure who had been an outspoken opponent of the Nazi movement under the Weimar Republic. And, when he decided to join the National Socialist party three months after Hitler took office, he seems to have been motivated, in part at least, by a quite genuine fear of arrest and perhaps worse.[3] Gehlen, by contrast, was a recently qualified lecturer, who used party membership to advance his career in a spectacular fashion. His subsequent academic progress shows what could be achieved. First named as a temporary replacement for Paul Tillich at the University of Frankfurt, the young sociologist was, within months, promoted to the chair of philosophy at Leipzig left vacant by the enforced retirement of his former teacher, the politically liberal Hans Driesch. By 1938 the ambitious young philosopher already occupied Kant's old chair at Königsberg, before moving on, yet again, to Vienna in 1940.

It can, of course, be argued that these two cases were exceptional: Schmitt's because of his previous political associations with Hitler's defeated opponents, and Gehlen's because of his previously insecure academic status and driving ambition. But that would be to miss the point. For, leaving aside the party ideologues and the theorists of race who were to provide the "scientific" legitimation for the only political decisions about which Hitler really cared, which of the intellectuals who rallied to the new regime was the typical case? Each found his own distinctive way to initial conformity; and, if their processes of disenchantment had rather more in common, that had as much to do with the regime they experienced together as with any original identity of outlook or motivation.

2. The Case of Freyer

Among the intellectuals who initially welcomed Hitler's triumph, one of the most influential at the time was the Leipzig sociologist, Hans Freyer, the subject of a recent study by Jerry Z. Muller.[4] Unlike Heidegger, now, as George Steiner somewhat uncomfortably avows, an inescapable presence on the philosophical scene, or Carl Schmitt, in recent years the subject of renewed critical interest not least among scholars on the political left,[5] Freyer is almost unknown in the English-speaking world. Nor is this surprising. For, even more than the work of his one-time ideological *confrères*, both the manner and matter of Freyer's writings are rooted in just those traditions of German thought to which English and American readers have proved most resistant. Furthermore, the exceptional degree to which many of Freyer's most significant writings were tailored to the politically specific situation of Germany in defeat makes it particularly difficult for the contemporary reader to grasp the true measure of his thought.

Freyer's obvious and passionate commitments, his fateful enmeshment in the struggles of his time, make him an historically fascinating figure, but also one whose long-term intellectual importance is especially hard to judge. The very vocabulary he used, the key symbols of his discourse, which were so transparent to his immediate audience, including the Nazis who eventually chose to reject it as a vehicle of their ideology, have, as it were, become opaque in the shadow of their historical associations. A terminology and style of discourse that once served all too effectively to evoke the spontaneous sympathy and enthusiasm of a wide audience may now only convince the reader of Freyer's irrelevance as anything but a warning against the potential derailments of the politically motivated academic.

However, even if this were all we could learn from Freyer, it would not make him unworthy of attention. For though no more than any other was Freyer the concrete embodiment of that historical abstraction, the "typical" German right-wing intellectual, he was, as Muller convincingly shows, in many ways an exceptionally representative figure of his generation. Consideration of his life and work may therefore be expected to throw light on a number of important historical issues. And so it does.

In the first place, Freyer's easy transition from a position of radical hostility to the Weimar Republic to active support of the Third Reich, his subsequent disaffection from the regime and his post-war turn to what must seem to us a more conventionally conservative suspicion of all forms of revolutionary, ideological politics, exemplify what Muller, in the sub-title of his book, terms the "deradicalization of German conservatism." Though not unparalleled in other continental European traditions, and even, recalling the political evolution of such writers as T. S. Eliot and Wyndham Lewis, one not entirely foreign to our own, this process of deradicalization was, in the degree of political reversal it entailed, a phenomenon inseparable from the unique history of Germany. And yet, as a particularly dramatic version of a more general twentieth-century experience of ideological disenchantment, the story of Freyer's political development can also be seen as representative of a number of related processes and events symptomatic of the ambivalent attitudes of intellectuals to the modern world.

Leaving aside for the moment the quite separate question of the intrinsic merits of Freyer's work, Muller's study therefore invites us to focus on an individual in whose career certain dynamics of ideological temptation and disenchantment, characteristic of the lives and careers of many other twentieth-century intellectuals, are unusually clearly defined. In Freyer's retreat, from the revolutionary activism advocated in his widely read *Revolution from the Right* (1931) to his post-war endorsement of the Federal Republic, we can recognise the outlines of an odyssey of initial disillusion and ultimate conciliation with what have become the dominant political forms of modernity that is shared not only with many of his conservative German contemporaries but, in form at least, with all those intellectuals, of the left as well as of the right, who, in the first half of this century, were tempted by the appeal of totalitarian solutions to the problems of modern industrial society.

In this connection, as Muller notes, there are illuminating comparisons to be made between Freyer and certain of his left-wing contemporaries. Perhaps the most striking of these is with the Hungarian Marxist Georg Lukács, author of *History and Class Consciousness*, whose early work, like Freyer's, was influenced by the pessimistic *Lebensphilosophie* of Georg Simmel, and who also found refuge from his existential pessimism in political engagement. Another, hardly less interesting, comparison could be made with the Frankfurt philosopher Max Horkheimer who, in a timely preface to the 1968 reissue of some of his pre-war essays warned against any attempt to utilize their arguments in a renewed assault on the political order of Western society.[6] Such parallels deserve attention, not in order to blur distinctions crucial to our understanding of the factors that influenced each individual's initial choice of his ideological com-mitments, but because they attest the presence of recurrent patterns of discontent, patterns of illusion and disillusion about and with modernity, which are part and parcel of the intellectuals' political and cultural experience of and response to the modern world.

In many ways, the consistently political focus of Freyer's writings makes them a peculiarly transparent object in which to discern the dynamics of a process, typical for many European intellectuals, of original disenchantment and ultimate reconciliation with what, to use a shorthand term, we may call the liberal-democratic order. By this I mean the process in which the characteristic institutions of "bourgeois" liberal democracy came, over time and then generally only as a result of historical catastrophe, to be seen by many of their former cultured despisers as the necessary supports of whatever remained of value in the heritage of European civilization.

But consideration of Freyer's career invites reflection on issues other than the troubled relationship of intellectuals to the industrialiszing and democratising tendencies of modernity, and their consequent inclination to seek total, ideological and politically revolutionary solutions to the problems of modern life. As the story of a notable conservative sociologist, it also raises two other important issues. The first of these is the ambiguous, simultaneously intellectual and ideological, status of sociology as a purportedly scientific discipline that was, as Robert Nisbet in particular has noted, conceived from its beginnings not so much as a neutral instrument of analysis as a form of therapeutic reaction to what its founding fathers perceived as pathological developments in contemporary society.

The second issue I have in mind here is what may well be the central dilemma of intellectual conservatism, as it has developed in the two centuries since the French Revolution. That is, the inherent problem of conservatism as a political creed that, while intellectually engaged in the struggle for the modern mind, remains in its heart notably out of sympathy with many of modernity's defining ambitions. In this dilemma we find the roots of the moral and political problems posed not only by Freyer's work but by all parallel attempts to formulate and act upon a programme of what has been called "radical" and even "revolutionary conservatism." For these are programmes which, despite their considerable appeal for those unhappy with the prevailing trends of the time, have typically tended to "succeed" politically only at the cost of destroying the remains of what culturally they want most to sustain.

To attempt to draw these themes together within the scope of a single essay may seem foolhardy. Yet just as the life of a single man can attain representative status by virtue of his engagement in the dominant issues of his day, so the issues themselves, however distinct they may have seemed at the time, will usually appear to the intellectual historian to share a common period flavour or, as Karl Mannheim puts it, an 'historical style'. The connection between the issues raised by consideration of Hans Freyer is thus not, in any narrow sense, a function of the distinctive, individualising features of his biography. Although, no doubt, the accidents of his life determined the particular emphases given at various times to the recurring themes of his work, the themes themselves are rooted in the shared historical horizon of his age. And this may be characterized as an age of disenchantment: a time marked by a widespread and deeply felt loss of religious faith, by an ever-increasing sense of the apparent meaninglessness of the historical process and, by way of reaction, by a deep desire to recover a sense of purpose and meaning in a world from which the old certainties had all too notably vanished.

3. The Sociological Path

It was Max Weber, the greatest of sociologists and one of Freyer's acknowledged mentors, who described the experience of modernity in terms of what he called the "disenchantment of the world." By this Weber meant the process whereby modern man, though increasingly adept at the 'rational' technical control of his environment, loses touch with any overall sense of the meaning of his existence.

In contrast to an earlier generation of social theorists —the generation of Comte, Spencer and Marx — Weber argued, in the wake of Nietzsche, that the understanding of the world afforded by modern natural science could never provide a substitute for the sense of being at home in the cosmos afforded by older religious and metaphysical conceptions of the universe. The experience of modernity, he suggested, is thus, at once, liberating and uncomfortable. It is liberating because of all the practical possibilities it opens up, but uncomfortable because even the optimal realization of these possibilities can never answer the essentially religious, or at least metaphysical, question of the meaning of human life. While Comte and Marx had, in their different ways, sought to suppress the problem of ultimate, religious meaning by ruling out the questions that might raise it as scientifically illegitimate and thus in a 'scientific' —positivist or materialist—age humanly irrelevant,[7] less troubled or acute minds had simply assumed that the advance of scientific knowledge would, of itself, provide adequate answers to questions of existential meaning. This current of complacency was exemplified in nineteenth-century Germany in the materialist philosophies of Büchner and Moleschott and, more generally in Europe and America, in the nineteenth-century cult of automatic and necessary Progress.

In the 1920s, Freyer's contemporaries, the logical positivists of the Vienna Circle — in reality merely one of many overlapping intellectual discussion groups that met and worked in that city between the wars —would attempt to bypass the problem of existential meaning altogether by defining what most people conceived to be its fundamental questions as themselves linguistically meaningless; on the grounds that any answers such questions evinced were empirically unverifiable and so without any real reference. This purely technical and, as Karl Popper was to show, logically untenable "solution" to the problem of meaning, while highly influential in the English speaking world, found few resonances in continental Europe.[8]

Indeed it is ironic that those who have passed into history as *the* Vienna Circle were as atypical of the intellectual life of Vienna as they were of German-speaking culture as a whole.[9] For within this culture the problem of meaning, as posed by Weber and his contemporaries and as subsequently taken up with fateful results by the succeeding generation, was a problem not of logic but of life — a substantial question of spiritual orientation whose significance for the conduct of life was such as to render not so much wrong as simply irrelevant any attempt to answer it, as the logical positivists attempted to do, in merely technical or linguistic terms. Thus, even leaving aside the ultimately self-refuting nature of its epistemological claims, a philosophy like logical positivism that could, as a matter of definition, describe as 'meaningless' such a question as whether or not God exists, was bound to seem to readers of Nietzsche and Weber, not only frivolous and, in the worst sense, abstract, but wilfully blind to the living context in which the real and painfully experienced problem of life's meaning arose.

There are parallels to Weber's notion of the disenchantment of the world, and with it the threat to existential meaning, to be found in the work of his great contemporaries, Georg Simmel and Ferdinand Tönnies. Between them these men, born in the 1850s and 1860s, and each in his own right an important influence on Freyer, articulated what Kurt Lenk has described as "the tragic consciousness of German sociology."[10] The phrase *disenchantment of the world* is Weber's own, but the experience that underlies it, the ambivalent but predominantly negative experience of the consequences of what the nineteenth-century had complacently termed "progress", is no less pervasive in the work of his fellow sociologists. We find it in Simmel's characteristically subtle discussion of what he calls 'the tragedy of culture', as well as in Tönnies's seminal account of the historical transition from traditional, organically based community, *Gemeinschaft*, to the atomized, interest-based order of modern society, *Gesellschaft*. When, after the Second World War, critics of Freyer's *Theorie des gegenwärtigen Zeitalters (Theory of the Present Age*, 1955) pointed to what they saw as his continuing one-sided emphasis on the negative aspects of social and economic modernization, they were drawing attention not only to the endurance of the theme of disenchantment, Lenk's 'tragic consciousness', in German social thought, but also to its return, after the catastrophe of the Third Reich, to the original Weberian key of stoical acceptance.

In 1934 Hermann Broch had entitled his metaphorical novel about Hitler's impact on the German people *Die Verzauberung (The Spell)*.[11] Already spiritually estranged from the world about them, Freyer and his contemporaries had been ripe for the enchanter's magic. The experience of its terrible effects gave new dimensions to the politics of disenchantment in a generation once tempted to hope that what Weber might have termed 'the re-enchantment of the world' was both possible and desirable.

4. A Pattern of Response

Hans Freyer was born in 1887 in Plagwitz, a suburb of Leipzig. Both sides of his family came of devoutly Protestant stock; and when Freyer entered the university it was, as with so many German thinkers before him, with the intention of becoming a Lutheran theologian. However, after two semesters in the theology faculty, first at the small University of Greifswald and then at Leipzig, he transferred to the faculty of philosophy. Freyer's abandonment of theological studies reflected a break with his ancestral faith and, with it, the beginnings of his quest for some form of secular substitute for the religious orientation he had lost. As Muller notes, in a case like Freyer's, secularization, consequent upon loss of faith, does not mean "simply the attenuation of traditional religion but a process in which objects outside the sphere of traditional religion are endowed with the emotional significance previously accorded to the divine." Much later, in describing the sort of intellectual most susceptible to the appeal of totalitarian ideologies, Freyer himself was to speak of him, and so of his younger self, in similar terms; as one whose "religious organs are highly developed but have lost their function." [12]

This is a pattern familiar from the lives of numerous early twentieth-century intellectuals, of the Left as well as the Right—men of deeply religious background, who sought in politics or science, but most characteristically in a potent combination of the two, a substitute for the hopes formerly vested in messianic religious faith. This type of secularization consists, not in the abandonment of religiously founded expectations, but, rather, in their transposition into an apparently secular, philosophical or political-ideological key. Karl Löwith and others have taught us to recognize it as one of the most significant feature in the intellectual culture of the nineteenth and early twentieth centuries. [13]

Freyer is very much a case in point. In his writings we find a characteristically strong sense of the illegitimacy or meaninglessness of the modern, secularized world combined with the clear desire to recover a sense of overall meaning, quasi-religious in scope, by means of the construction and willed espousal of a scientifically oriented political myth. Seeing through the pretensions of science itself to provide a substitute for religious meaning, yet unable to forgo the quest for metaphysical security —a sense of oneness with the world — Freyer exemplifies the type of secularized intellectual who attempts to assuage his lingering religious needs by seeking, through the creation of a subjectively compelling political mythology, to sacralize the secular field of human action.[14] In this way he hopes to create a state of renewed integration between the individual and the political world about him.

Knowing the mind to be moved and stabilized by myth, he sets himself to find or forge forms of belief attuned to the times. In Freyer's work, the will to believe becomes, in an avowedly, de-rationalized and emphatically post-Nietzschean parody of what Cardinal Newman had once termed the "grammar of assent", the condition of belief itself, and so the prelude to a secular faith in a world from which the possibility of re-acquiring confidence in the objective existence of a world-transcendent order had, apparently and for whatever reason, disappeared beyond the would-be believer's horizon.

As part of this endeavour, the secular sources of man's being, symbolized for Freyer, above all, by his membership of the German *Volk*, come to be endowed with a quasi-sacral significance equivalent to that once attributed to membership in the *corpus mysticum* of the Church. Drawing explicitly on Löwith's work, Freyer himself was later to accept just such an analysis of the sources of ideological disaffection with what he had, through harsh experience, by then come to accept as the inevitable tensions of modern life.

In order to identify more precisely the nature of Freyer's original response to his feelings of disenchantment with the modern world let us note that the term *secularization* does not designate any one simple or historically undifferentiated phenomenon. In the title of his great work *From Hegel to Nietzsche*[15] Löwith names the two major thinkers who represent, respectively, what, for heuristic purposes, we shall call the 'objectivist' and the 'subjectivist' forms of response to the modern world's loss of the religious sense of an ultimate world-meaning sustained by faith. By this I mean that the 'objectivist', Hegel, still sees the world, or, more particularly, world history, as possessing an objective, inherent and discoverable, meaning, equivalent in structure to divine providence. In contrast, Nietzsche sees meaning as something that can only be wrested out of primal chaos by an act of human, or perhaps super-human, will. Thus, while for Hegel the meaning of things is a cosmic-historical reality discoverable by reason, for Nietzsche it can be made real, if at all, only by the creative exercise of the inherently human will to power.

In his remarkable examination of the historical transition from Hegel's world-view to Nietzsche's, Löwith delineates a crucial chapter in what we may, in Weber's terms, recognize as the story of the progressive disenchantment of the world which occurred through the nineteenth century. And yet the figures of Hegel and Nietzsche cannot be seen in any simple chronological sense as representing successive stages of a process in which one form of response simply replaced the one before. For Freyer's generation each still represented a viable option; and, among his contemporaries, varieties of what I have called the 'objectivist', non-Nietzschean, response can be found both among those, like Lukács, who adopted the Marxist version of Hegel's theory of historical development — the secularized theodicy of the dialectic — and, if rather more equivocally, in the philosophy of those, like Nicolai Hartmann, who sought to uphold the possibility of an objective system of ethics even in an ultimately meaningless universe.

While Freyer himself is often described as a neo-Hegelian, on this issue at least he is closer to Nietzsche than to Hegel. For the educational experience that deprived him of his original Lutheran faith not only precluded his subsequent acceptance of any Hegelian notion of objectively given historical meaning: at the same time, it undermined his belief in the possibility of establishing, in place of either Christian or rationalist universalism, any alternative universally valid ethical code.

5. Sociology and Modernity: The German Case

The spiritual uncertainty of the young Freyer goes a long way toward explaining his attraction to the field of sociology. For, even more than elsewhere in Europe, sociology in Germany at the turn of the century was not conceived as an exclusively analytical discipline. Rather, its chief purpose was seen by many of its established exponents and prospective students alike as providing the rising generation with the intellectual means to orient themselves in the religiously and morally uncertain world they were destined to inhabit. In a word, sociology was, as the neo-Kantian philosopher Wilhelm Windelband put it, an *Orientierungswissenschaft* — not so much a quest for objective knowledge as a preparation for life in a world in which the very grounds of objectivity have become obscure.

Sociology is a single word but how far it can be said to refer to any single area of scientific interest or corresponding style of inquiry is quite another matter. The circumstances in which the discipline originally developed in the various nations of Europe and North America are sufficiently varied to make it seem at times that in each case we are dealing with a very different phenomenon. Robert Nisbet's characterization of the rise of what he calls "the sociological tradition" in terms of a general European response to the historical pressures unleashed in the wake of the French and the industrial revolutions is fair enough so far as it goes[16]; but, as Freyer himself noted, in each country these pressures were encountered at different times and under very different cultural and political circumstances. In consequence, what came to be termed "sociology" reflected in each case the particularities of national history and culture as much as the universal need to comprehend and control economic, political and cultural changes that seemed to threaten as much as they promised.

In Germany the initial encounter with the French Revolution — an uncomfortable historical experience in which the original bearers of what claimed to be universalist values had been the conquering soldiers of a foreign army — had given rise to a hitherto unprecedented sense of German national distinctiveness. Increasingly through the nineteenth century, this sense of particularity tended to find its most powerful political expression in the aspiration to create a potent and unified German state. Culturally, the same experience encouraged among Germans a particularistic conception of their culture as something apart from and spiritually superior to the rationalism and pretended universalism of Western civilization as it had emerged from the Enlightenment. In their turn these attitudes were given powerful philosophical justification in terms of what came to be the prevailing German idealist philosophy of culture and history. For this was a philosophy that saw in each national, cultural formation, past and present, not the necessary product of an anthropologically universal process of evolution, but a unique creative achievement of a no less particular people or *Volk*.

Inheriting the assumptions of this tradition, German sociology was thus, unlike its Western equivalents, profoundly sceptical of the possibility of constructing a universalising science of society after the model of the natural sciences. Instead, it saw its task not as the discovery of universal laws of history or social development but in terms of the need to develop a subjective understanding, *verstehen*, of the multiplicity of unique happenings and events in which history consists.

We can explain a further element in the specifically German conception of sociology — its suspicion of modernity — when we relate the emergence of the discipline itself to Germany's no less distinctive experience of industrialization. In contrast to her early experience of political revolution brought in with the baggage of a foreign army and ultimately rejected as "un-German", Germany's industrial revolution came late — in great part only after Bismark's unification of the Reich under the Prussian crown in 1871. The socially disruptive effects of industrialization, and especially the rapid urbanization of a great part of the German population, were thus contemporary with Germany's rise to world political power, of which they seemed both a consequence and a condition. As such, German industrialization, as both a condition of political power and an element disruptive of the culture it was meant to serve, could not but provoke ambiguous feelings among Freyer's contemporaries. These ranged from the romantic rejection of industrial society exemplified in the influential writings of Ludwig Klages, to the equally romantic idealisation of the disciplined, permanently mobilized, life of the industrial worker found in Ernst Jünger's *Der Arbeiter* 1932. The real ambivalence that lurks beneath such apparently clear and opposed attitudes among men who were, politically speaking, both nationalists and conservatives, arose from the more or less overt recognition that the very political and economic forces that had originally ensured Germany's rise to the status of a world power, and which, after 1918, seemed to offer the best chances for her recovery from defeat, were also widely perceived as endangering the spiritual heritage of the nation. Alongside Weber's notion of the disenchantment of the world, it was Tönnies's famous contrast between organically united, traditional *Gemeinschaft*, community, and the contractually bound, modern world of *Gesellschaft*, association, that best captured the essence of a widespread image of modernity as a process in which worldly success, on both the individual and national level, had been bought at the cost of spiritual integrity and the sense of participation in a living community of meaning.

First published in 1887, when the self-confidence of the new German Empire was at its height, Tönnies' discomforting book *Gemeinschaft und Gesellschaft* had initally found few readers. However by the time Freyer came to study it, in his student years at Leipzig, its argument and, more important still, its imagery, had become a powerful element in rendering articulate a sense of disenchantment with the established order already deeply ingrained in the rising generation. In his study, Muller cites a lecture delivered in 1910 by Windelband in which he speaks of the younger generation's "hunger for an integrated view of the world" and its quasi-religious "yearning for a comprehensive meaning of reality." [17] Typically the catchword of this generation was Tönnies' term community, *Gemeinschaft* — a word which, as Raymond Aron noted in the introduction to German sociology that he wrote in the 1930s, evoked a quasi-mystical resonance in the German consciousness that a Frenchman, or any other foreigner for that matter, would find difficult to understand.[18] The concept of *Gemeinschaft*, which had, for Tönnies himself, served to characterise, in ideal typical fashion, the morally integrated form of life of pre-industrial man as contrasted with the contractually based order of modernity, became for Freyer's generation a political symbol evoking not only the reality of the past but also a potential future state of being in which the individual could, once again, feel himself at home in a world suffused with shared meaning and purpose.

The question of generation is of great importance in explaining Freyer's attraction to and subsequent place in German sociology. The preceding generation of sociologists, Tönnies himself, Simmel and Weber, had been drawn to sociology primarily as a way of analysing the ambiguous process of Germany's modernization. The task of sociology, Weber had pronounced, was, above all, the task of "explaining how we have become what we now are." Weber and his contemporaries had stressed the spiritual costs of this historical process but had also, at the same time, drawn attention both to its economic and political benefits and to its apparent irreversibility. Sceptical of the possibility of establishing an objectively valid and universally shared ethical orientation under the conditions of modernity, they had, in the spirit of neo-Kantianism, emphasized the abiding importance of personal commitment to self-chosen values and, in Weber's case in particular, to the need to measure such commitments against the real political possibilities afforded by the contemporary world.

As a sociologist Freyer was heir to this tradition. However, in accord with the mood of his generation, his response to the prevailing sense of existential disenchantment differed markedly from the attitude of stoical acceptance cultivated by the older masters. Under the influence of the pre-war German youth movement, with whose increasingly strident nationalist wing he retained close associations well into middle age, Freyer sought, from the beginnings of his career, not simply a way of understanding the surrounding world but a way of overcoming disenchantment itself through the creation of a renewed spirit of community and common purpose.

The seeds of Freyer's future work, already sown in his student years before 1914, germinated in the course of the war, in which he served with considerable distinction on the Western Front. For if it was the ideological atmosphere of the youth movement that originally inspired his quest for community as a solution to the problem of existential disenchantment, it was specifically the experience of the trenches that convinced Freyer, like others, that such a community could become a reality for contemporary man precisely, and perhaps only, under the most extreme pressures that modern life could offer.

Today, when we think back to the literature generated by the Great War, we tend to think, above all, of the poems of Wilfred Owen and Siegfried Sassoon and, in the case of Germany, of Erich Maria Remarque's great anti-war novel *All Quiet on the Western Front*. But this literature of regret for lost lives and horror at the experience of modern warfare was only one side of the coin. Against it we must set such works as Ernst Jünger's no less remarkable epic *Storm of Steel*: a novel in which the same terrible experience is seen as the crucible in which a new man and a new form of community, the 'community of the trenches', has been forged.

The war which brought many Germans of Freyer's generation their first experience of real community founded in unquestioned common purpose ended, of course, in the trauma of national defeat. And if before 1914 Freyer and those who thought like him had already felt estranged from what they saw as the vulgarity and spiritual emptiness of the economically prosperous and politically triumphalist *Kaiserreich*, they regarded the new republic, born out of defeat, with undiscriminating abhorrence. An older man, like Max Weber, might see in the stabilization of republican government a means of renewing, at least in the long term, Germany's military and political power; but for Freyer and his kind it merely represented an institutionalization of national divisions, and the triumph in defeat of the very elements in German society, liberals, social democrats and capitalists, who seemed to embody, in their beliefs and actions, the spirit of the disenchantment of the world.

6. Freyer and Weber

Here comparison of Freyer's attitude with that of Weber is worthy of further pursuit. For what such a comparison brings to light are two very different possibilities that may be encompassed under the heading of the politics of disenchantment. By this I mean that neither for Weber nor for Freyer did the experience of modernity as disenchantment leave room for espousal of any ideology, Marxist or otherwise, that claimed to base its political programme in supposed knowledge of a necessary and ultimately rational movement of history. Rejection of all such metaphysical claims, as much as the nature of his own anti-socialist preferences, explains Weber's life-long opposition to the claim of Marxism to represent a uniquely scientific understanding of politics. A similar scepticism regarding the possibility of a purportedly scientific politics — in this case a politics based on a 'scientific', bio-racial, rather than cultural and historical, notion of the *Volk* — was eventually, and despite his own best or worst efforts, to exclude Freyer from the ranks of approved spokesmen for the ideology of National Socialism. For neither Weber nor Freyer could political commitment be considered a mere function of scientific conviction. Rather, it had always to remain a matter of personal, if historically conditioned, decision.

Weber, as much as Freyer, was concerned in 1918 to create the political conditions for a restoration of Germany's fortunes. But if, unlike the younger man, he accepted the necessity and even the desirability of the republic, this was not only a matter of the generational gap separating him from those who had fought in the war, to which we have already drawn attention. Perhaps just as important is the fact that, as a student of law, Weber's professional sensitivity to the political significance for Germany of the existence of a securely defined legal order, whatever might be its historical origins, encouraged him to see in the provisions of the Weimar constitution, not the irredeemable detritus of defeat, but an institutional framework within which the recovery of power might be made possible. In this context, it is, I think, significant that Freyer's close contemporary Carl Schmitt, whose academic background was, like Weber's own, in law rather than in sociology or philosophy, was to adopt an attitude toward the constitution akin to Weber's throughout the Weimar period, despite the otherwise close affinity between his political outlook and that of Freyer.

In pursuing the more strictly philosophical differences between Weber's notion of sociology and Freyer's, Muller describes the older man as a post-Nietzschean Kantian and the younger as a post-Nietzschean Hegelian. By this he means that both took as their starting-point an acceptance of Nietzsche's claim that the values espoused by an individual as the guiding principles of his life were always matters of personal choice and commitment not susceptible to any ultimate rational justification. But while Weber, in accord with the neo-Kantian conception of science, conceived social reality as an infinitely complex sphere that could be conceptualized from an equally infinite number of perspectives, whose choice would depend, not only on personal values, but upon the particular problem one wished to study, Freyer, influenced here by his reading of Hegel, believed that societies could be grasped as essentially distinct totalities possessing inherent formative structures and objectively given historical tendencies.

From this angle, Weber may be described as the archetypal sociological nominalist and Freyer as an uncompromising sociological realist. This is a crucial distinction which manifests itself not so much in the terms through which each pursues his inquiries, which are often the same, but in the significance that each attaches to the general concepts — capitalism, revolution, etc. — which he employs.

Weber's Kantianism and nominalism showed themselves in his ascetic conception of sociology as a science that could, at best, establish clear conceptual models, 'ideal types', in terms of which the shifting realities of historical existence could be categorised, and so compared and understood. In contrast, Freyer's Hegelian notion of social science, exemplified, despite the reference to Weber embodied in the title, in his *Soziologie als Wirklichkeitswissenschaft (Sociology as a Science of Reality*, 1929), embodied the claim that sociology was not limited to the creation of heuristically useful models, as Weber's notion of ideal types suggested, but was a science capable of identifying the essential, underlying nature of the realities it sought to comprehend. Thus, for example, while Weber conceived the term *capitalism* as an abstract, scientifically constructed model to which the organization of certain historically real modern economies more or less, but never completely, conformed, Freyer, as much as the equally Hegelian Karl Marx, defined capitalism in ontologically essentialist terms as designating the real, formative principle, or essence, of a particular type of historically concrete society.

Such socially ontological essentialism, which identifies a potentially alterable structural principle, a removable linchpin as it were, at the heart of every society, is a key ingredient in what Kenneth Minogue has recently described as the distinctively ideological vision of political life. According to Minogue, the ideological vision of politics is characterized by the belief that every form of social order has its own identifiable structural principle, and consequently that, if we want to transform the quality of human life and so dispose of the 'alien powers' that the ideological mind conceives as distorting man's being, we have only to abolish the informing but historically contingent structure, capitalism for instance, which makes things as they are.[19] Read in such an ideological perspective, Simmel's account of what he called 'the tragedy of culture', according to which the creations of the human spirit necessarily escape from and attain an existence alien to their original purposes, became for Freyer and his contemporaries, like so much else in the inherited literature of social disenchantment, not so much a reflection on the general imperfection of the human condition and the particular troubles of the time, as a provocation to revolutionary action and an invitation to identify and destroy the offending principle.

7. The Reality of Decision

But Muller's contrast between the post-Nietzschean Kantian, Weber, and the post-Nietzschean Hegelian, Freyer, can carry us yet further than this. For while Muller adequately stresses the distinction between the two men's epistemologies, Kantian and Hegelian respectively, and notes the consequences of this distinction for their respective conceptions of the proper role, not least the proper political role, of sociology, there is another more directly ethical *cum* political side to the distinction between Kantian and Hegelian philosophies, which we would do well to note.

To put matters as simply as we may, while Kantians, like Weber, tend to treat the question of moral and political commitment in strictly individual, ahistorical terms, Hegelians usually stress the collective and historical side of the issue. Thus while the Kantian tradition describes the moral life in terms of the individual's duty to live in personally chosen conformity with the universal categorical imperative to treat other persons not as means but as ends in themselves, Hegel always situated discussion of morality within an overall philosophy of history in which the individual's highest duty is conceived in terms of the requirement to act in rational conformity with the demands of the historically given situation.

It may, as Hegel observes, be the case that "the owl of Minerva flies only at twilight"; but the fact, regrettable though it undoubtedly is, that consequently only in retrospect can the truth or error of any judgement be finally determined must, according to the philosopher, be accepted as an ineluctable element of the human, historical, condition. As such it is beyond argument, and therefore it remained true, for Hegel, as once it seemed to the young Auden, who wrote, in a line he was later to regret, that "history, to the defeated, may say 'Alas' but cannot help or pardon."

For those who had felt the impact of Nietzsche, neither Kant's position nor Hegel's could be accepted in its original form. And yet, even in the post-Nietzschean environment of Freyer's youth, the distinction between Kantian and Hegelian conceptions of moral and political philosophy remained a vital one. Thus a post-Nietzschean Kantian like Weber, though rejecting the universality of Kant's categorical imperative, continued to conceive the moral life in essentially individualist terms as a life lived in allegiance to the individual's self-chosen, if admittedly rationally unjustifiable, values. In contrast, a post-Nietzschean neo-Hegelian like Freyer, while rejecting Hegel's own belief in the ultimate rationality of history, tended, in conformity with the mainstream of what, following Dilthey, the Germans called *Lebensphilosophie*, to see the individual's commitments as somehow fated by his given place in the rationally unfathomable process of life.

Here, yet another word of clarification is in order. *Fated*, in the sense I am using the term, is not to be conceived as identical with the notion of being causally determined. Fate, we may say, makes a man what he is. Consequently, it makes certain possibilities of action more or less probable but, at least in Freyer's opinion, it never *compels* any individual to act in one way rather than another. That is, and must always remain, a matter not of fate but of will. It demands not passive obedience but decision. While sharing with Weber the view that the historical circumstances in which the individual finds himself makes some options more likely to be taken up than others, Freyer, at the same time, goes well beyond his mentor in maintaining that such circumstances not only factually influence the choices made but are, beyond this, a factor to be considered in determining whether or not the choice made is morally valid for oneself. For the self in question while morally autonomous is not existentially so. He must choose to act as he decides, but it is not his to choose, either historically or ontologically, who it is who makes the choice. The self that chooses is never self-chosen.

By this I mean that, like Weber, Freyer did not believe that a man's moral and political choices are fixed for him, or caused, by such factors as nationality or generation, race or class. His view of the relationship between personal commitment and fate was more subtle than that, more tinged with a sense of the risky and potentially tragic course of life, and, I dare say, more true. For Freyer, unchosen fate, embodied in the time and place of a man's birth, in his ancestry and in the morally formative cultural environment, the Volk, into which he is cast, is not an alternative to choice or decision in human life. Rather, as the inescapable condition of whatever choice the individual is to make, as well as the formative power within the very self who chooses, it plays, and must play, a much more positive, even decisive role in the process of personal commitment than Weber would have allowed. Fate, in this view, signifies something more than the sum of the external circumstances, the historical context, within which every individual moral choice necessarily takes place. Rather, as something already embodied in the reality of a man's culturally and biologically formed identity —his inmost being which makes him the person he is —it enters actively and, in Freyer's view, quite properly as the decisive factor in the casuistry of moral decision itself.

As Muller puts it, Freyer's view was that, through the process of moral decision, "birth into a particular *Volk* was to be elevated into a consciously affirmed fate." [20] Formed by the accidents of birth and inherited culture, a man, especially in conditions of perceived crisis, is bound in the course of his life to find himself faced with the choice between acting to uphold or restore the conditions that have made him what he is or choosing to disown them. In Weber's perspective the choice would seem to be, in principle, an even one; whose outcome should depend, for the man who is moral in the pure Kantian sense, only on the direction indicated by his personally chosen values. But for Freyer, with his neo-Hegelian sensitivity to the anchorage of individual moral identity in the historical reality of the *Volk*, the decision, though freely made, must always tend to fall on the side of national, political and cultural conservation.

However, and here in contrast to Hegel, the name of the moral game which man is called upon to play is no longer the realization of universal reason in the world. It is the brute survival of the one's own group, one's *Volk* and one's *Staat*, on a field of play where conflict between elements is not so much the means whereby the historical process proceeds to an ultimate resolution —the final synthetic reconciliation of all contradictions that is the projected end of the Hegelian dialectic —but a permanent condition of human existence and political endurance.

Where Hegel had once seen the covert yet ultimately discernible hand of historical reason as justifying one choice against another, Freyer felt the no less compelling urgings of ineluctable circumstance. Thus modernity, which Freyer describes as a "critical era" — one that imposes on the individual the imperative of making choices of a type generally unprecedented in previous, more stable, times — also indicates our enduring responsibility to decide our life's course, not in accord with what must necessarily seem an imagined reason, personal-moral or historical as the case may be, but, rather, in conformity with what we currently perceive to be the factually given requirements of individual and group survival. It is this conviction, above all, that explains the constancy that, despite appearances, underlies Freyer's lifelong stance toward the world. It is the source of his espousal of Hitler's regime in the 1930s as well as of his endorsement, no less sincere but also no less beset with reservations, of the post-war Federal Republic. Both are, in the end, no more than projects of endurance. One has failed, let us therefore choose another; and among the possibilities, not that which promises most, but that which threatens least the sustaining realities of our lives.

What then are we to say? Perhaps only this, that the man of moral and intellectual scruples who takes seriously and is convinced by the major premise that underlies the post-Kantian view of man as a moral being at large in a world ungoverned by any variety of the principle of sufficient reason — and Freyer was surely such a man — cannot always act or, if Shadia Drury's analysis of the apparent anti-modernism of Freyer's younger contemporary Leo Strauss is taken seriously, even theorize in a way that will seem either consistent to others or fully satisfactory to himself.[21] The honestly accepted intellectual complexities and consequent moral confusions of modernity, some of which we have sought to indicate above, will hardly permit the luxury or comfort of such an option. Whether, under the conditions of modern times, there is any alternative possibility is another question. Examination of the problems raised by the thought and career of Hans Freyer suggests, at the least, that, in order to attain it, we would have to question anew the assumptions of a world-view that, regretfully but decisively, set the limits to the possibilities that Freyer's mind could entertain.

Notes

1. Ed. by Richard Crossman (London, 1949).
2. On the case of Hirsch see Robert P. Erickson, *Theologians under Hitler* (New Haven and London, 1985) pp.120-97.
3. Joseph W. Bendersky, *Carl Schmitt: Theorist for the Reich* (Princeton, N.J.

Princeton University Press, 1983).

4. Jerry Z. Muller, *The Other God that Failed, Hans Freyer and the Deradicalization of German Conservatism* (Princeton, N.J.: Princeton University Press, 1987).

5. George Steiner, *Heidegger* (London, 1978). On Schmitt see, for example, recent issues of the journal *Telos*.

6. See Horkheimer's "Preface" to Max Horkheimer, *Critical Theory: Selected Essays* (New York, 1972). For a discussion of this, and the political development of the early Frankfurt School in general, see David J. Levy, *Realism: An Essay in Interpretation and Social Reality*, (Manchester and Atlantic Highlands N.J. 1981) pp. 72-101.

7. On this process of forbidding the asking of certain types of question in Comte and Marx see Eric Voegelin, *From Enlightenment to Revolution* (Durham, N.C. 1975).

8. Karl Popper, *The Logic of Scientific Discovery* (London, 1959).

9. See, inter alia, Alan Janik and Stephen Toulmin, *Wittgenstein's Vienna*, New York, 1973.

10. Kurt Lenk, "The Tragic Consciousness of German Sociology", in *Modern German Sociology,* ed by Voker Meja, Dieter Misgeld and Nico Stehr (New York, 1986).

11. London, Penguin Books.

12. Cited in Muller op.cit.

13. Karl Löwith, *Meaning in History*, (Chicago, 1949).

14. Stephen A. McKnight, *Sacralizing the Secular: The Renaissance Origins of Modernity*, (Baton Rouge and London: Louisiana State University Press, 1989).

15. New York, 1967.

16. Robert Nisbet, *The Sociological Tradition* (London, 1967).

17. Muller op.cit., p.35.

18. Raymond Aron, *German Sociology*, (1937).

19. Kenneth Minogue, *Alien Powers: The Pure Theory of Ideology*, (London, 1986).

20. Muller, op.cit.

21. Shadia Drury, *The Political Philosophy of Leo Strauss*.

5

LIBERALISM, POLITICS AND ANTI-POLITICS

On the Political Ethic of Liberal Democracy

As the twentieth century enters its final decade the political culture of liberalism, and the political theory or theories that seek to justify it, find themselves in a paradoxical situation. The great mid-century crisis—the *furor ideologicus* — which once seemed to threaten the very survival of liberal, constitutional order, even in its Western, European and North American heartlands, has passed. The radically anti-liberal, messianic political creeds, which once enchanted the intellectuals and activated the masses in a destructive fury directed against the institutional heritage of nineteenth-century constitutionalism and individualism, have lost much though not yet all their appeal. The burden of the historical legacy of murder and destruction has proved too much for fascist and now, it would seem, for communist faith. Western socialists, once sold on the supposed benefits of "rational" state control of economy and society, now define their critical positions in what are, historically speaking, typically liberal terms. They talk of the need to defend "civil society" against the encroachments of the state, of the sacredness of individual rights, the dangers of revolutionary change, and of the need constantly to improve the human condition by what John Gray calls "the judicious exercise of critical reason." [1]

Alongside these political and ideological factors we must set the overwhelming fact of twentieth-century economic history: the fact that far from representing, as Marxists supposed, an irrational obstacle to the furtherance of economic advance, whether measured in terms of productive innovation, wealth creation or general economic well-being, the mechanism of the competitive market, embodying primarily if not exclusively the principle of private ownership of the means of production, has alone proved capable of providing mass populations with a reasonable and, generally speaking, improving standard of living. In view of the apparent historical affinity between liberal, constitutional politics, based on the priority of the value of individual liberty, and capitalist economics, founded in the privileged status accorded to private enterprise, this too must be counted as a considerable plus for the supporters of a liberal political order —even if the association between economic success and political liberalism is by no means as invariable as the neo-conservative, *de jure liberal*, advocates of the benefits of "global democracy" would like us to suppose.

The widespread invocation of the name and work of F. A. Hayek, a theorist who to a unique extent combines the achievements of an original contributor to liberal constitutional thought and market oriented economics alike, testifies to the unaccustomed spirit of confidence with which the public spokesmen of liberal political order now face the future. Yet here we should take pause: for Hayek himself seems by no means to share the historical optimism of those who most commonly invoke his name. The advocate of spontaneous order seems to have little faith in the spontaneous self-correction of the historical process of modernity. The new Marx of the bourgeoisie is no representative of what the Tory editor of London's *Sunday Telegraph* has termed "bourgeois triumphalism". In the contemporary world, Hayek is the pre-eminent author of a liberal rather than a socialist account of the *theoretical*, but not spontaneously practical, identity between the ethically desirable and the economically necessary in the order of what he calls the 'Great Society'. But he is certainly no advocate of the "let rip" *credo* of the global democrats, still less the stateless fantasies of the anarcho-capitalists. Instead, he advocates the installation of a complex system of authoritative institutions —a machinery of state and a rationally constructed one at that —designed not to facilitate but to curb the consuming dynamism of democratic desire.

Then again, consider the state of liberal political theory. Without entering territory I cannot hope to cover in the space of this essay, I refer to the recent and, I assume, regretful analysis of the incoherence of classical liberal theory offered recently by John Gray.[2] Gray characterizes what he calls a 'post-liberal political theory' —a now needful theory capable of legitimating continuing liberal practice without recourse to untenable beliefs about the nature of man and the dangerously libertarian programmes they engender —in terms of an arranged marriage between a modified version of the Hobbesian imperative of coercion and the Humean doctrine of the authority of convention.

Thus an influential theorist, who was, until recently, rightly regarded as the most judicious of contemporary liberal political philosophers, now seeks the security of a maximally free political order not, like his liberal mentors, in a doctrine of freedom but in the anthropologically necessary restraints of sovereign power, Hobbes, and customary cultural practice, Hume. If nothing else, this line of argument testifies to the tension that now subsists between the established political order of the free world and the libertarian, quasi-anarchist rhetoric with which many of its less thoughtful supporters still urge its claims upon our allegiance.

1. Politics and Anthropology

In the pages that follow I want to examine certain aspects of this tension as it affects liberal political theories and the polities they seek to inform. In doing this I shall orient myself primarily to the work of Hayek and to a recent work, *The Self, the Individual and the Community*, whose author, Brian Lee Crowley, seeks to show that there are surprising affinities between the anthropological assumptions of the liberal Hayek and the early twentieth-century British socialists, Beatrice and Sidney Webb.[3]

However, before proceeding further it is worth considering a little more deeply the nature of Gray's 'post-liberal' turn and its relationship to Hayek's grand theoretical enterprise. For at the centre of Crowley's provocative thesis is an argument concerning the inade-quacy of the concept of man which he finds embedded equally in the apparently opposed practical philosophies of the liberal individualist Hayek and the utilitarian collectivists, Sidney and Beatrice Webb. For all the differences in the outcome of their thought, it is Crowley's claim that both Hayek and the Webbs start from the inadequate anthropologi-cal premises which he identifies with a typically liberal view of man, knowledge and society. Reference to Gray's post-liberalism will help us both to understand the force of Crowley's criticism of Hayek and what, more broadly, he regards as the 'anti-political' nature of liberal thought, as well as the limits of Crowley's own, modern neo-Aristotelian, alternative.

In posing the problem in terms of the relationship between politics and anthropology I mean to draw attention to the continuing significance of Aristotle's definition of man as an essentially *political* animal. That is, the view that the human being is a form of life destined by his biologically given nature to live and find fulfilment only in a politically constituted society in whose composition the economic dimension is only one, and by no means the most important, part. Underlying both Crowley's turn to Aristotle — an Aristotle significantly modified in an humanitarian and democratic direction by such "moderns" as Hannah Arendt and Ronald Beiner — and Gray's invocation of Hume and, more particularly, Hobbes is a shared recognition that the classical liberal image of man, as we find it in both Hayek and the Webbs, privileges one dimension of human activity, the economic, without allowing due emphasis to the sustaining political and cultural conditions which render ordered economic activity, as well as every other element of the good life, possible.

A viable polity is not only an economy, as both Crowley and Hayek clearly recognize. But, I shall claim, neither Hayek's emphasis on the significance of the authority of legal order, the rule of law, nor Crowley's supplementation of this with an account of community in terms of a sphere of discussion and persuasion oriented toward the achievement of the common good, fully embraces the problem of political order. Each is important, but, as Gray's reference to Hobbes —even a Hobbes "freed from the crudities of Hobbes's [own] anthropology and psychology" [4] —reminds us, the field of politics is, whatever else it may be, also a field of power and force: a domain of ever-potential violence in which, to use terms borrowed with some misgivings from Carl Schmitt, the 'normal' state of political affairs, characterized by debate and respect for legality, is always open to "the challenge of the exception." [5] Where debate and law cease to be respected, as may, not so very exceptionally, happen, only the decisive exercise of sovereign power can renew their sway. As we know all too well, such power can never be trusted to do what is required for the restoration of normal political life, but in the state of exception we have no other recourse than to the decisions of an effective sovereign prepared, where necessary, to authorize the use of force.

In linking with Humean conventionalism the Hobbesian vision of politics as a humanly founded order forced on us, and more or less willingly accepted, in consequence of the murderous disorder of an anthropologically primordial 'state of nature', Gray's suggested form of 'post-liberal theorizing' resumes at a stroke the hard insight of Weberian, and Schmittian, political anthropology: that while debate is to politics as contract is to economics, the normal medium of beneficial communication, neither is self-grounding. The foundation of each rests in the possibility of enforcing the norm by recourse to abnormal but perennially necessary physical power. That is a fact of life which no modern sentimentalizing of the Aristotelian ideal of political community can ultimately avoid. The citizen of the *polis*, whom modern Aristotelians like to picture as primarily a partner in unconstrained yet orderly debate, was also a soldier, who could be summoned to arms to repress internal disorder as readily as to repel a foreign enemy from the borders of his state.

This unfashionable point needs making but not, I stress, to the exclusion of the other, Humean, element in Gray's position. For the lesson of Humean conventionalism, and the position of respect for traditional ways it implies, is that the deeper such respect is embedded, as a matter of habit, in the culture of a society, the less likely becomes the chance that we will need recourse to physical force. This is something that Hayek, a traditionalist even if, in his own terms, no conservative, well recognizes. And yet, at the same time, Hayek's over-juridical conception of sovereign order as embodied in law, which is, without force, no more than a body of words, leads him to overestimate the efficacy of the formal institutions of justice and underplay the decisive role played by covert but widely spread perceptions of legitimacy in rendering the formal judgements of the law practically effective in the life of society.

This, as Crowley might say, is, in part, a function of Hayek's politically deficient anthropology, his failure to recognize the beneficent function of sentiments of community and his rejection of the notion of the common good: but it also, in my view, reflects his historical background as an Austrian, the child of a multinational empire whose unifying political culture was, to an extent perhaps unique, identified with the supra-national, decisively non-communitarian, juridical and administrative institutions of a dynastic state.

2. Hayek the Austrian

This question of Hayek's background —his formative identity as an Austrian, by which I mean much more than that he is an economist in the Austrian tradition of Menger and von Mises —bears further consideration. It is, I think, not only a point too much neglected in discussions of Hayek's work but one which goes far to explain the reasons why his political anthropology takes the form it does. What Crowley regards as a neglect of the issue of community in Hayek's liberal, *Rechtstaatlich*, vision of economy, state and society is based, not on an underestimation of the political significance of community, *Gemeinschaft*, but on a conscious rejection of what it seems, or seemed at least in Hayek's youth, to imply.

When Hayek, in his characterization of the 'Great Society', goes out of his way to emphasize its origins in the overcoming of primitive community sentiment by the individualist ethos of self-seeking enterprise, his argument must be understood in the historical context of the ideological debate set in motion by the publication of Ferdinand Tönnies's celebrated work *Gemeinschaft und Gesellschaft (Community and Society)*, in 1887. Whatever may have been Tönnies's original intention, his typology of social forms in terms of the contrast between traditional *Gemeinschaft*, based on communitarian ties of kinship and locality, and modern *Gesellschaft*, based on mobility, competition and self-interest, provided, for the next generation of Germans and German-

Austrians, in the notion of *Gemeinschaft* itself, a powerful ideological symbol. The call for the renewal of *gemeinschaftlich*, communitarian values, became a rallying point, for all who felt uneasy with what they saw as the dehumaniszing effects of the development of industrial, capitalist society. *Gemeinschaft*, community, provided a watchword for all those who opposed and sought, through the recreation of community, to overcome the liberal capitalist state which was, from the beginning, Hayek's ideal.

In the specific context of the multinational Habsburg Empire the call to renewed community meant, for most of its advocates, the community of a self-consciously distinct nation, a *Volksgemeinschaft*, and thus the disruption of an imperial, supra-national state which, at least in theory, ruled its subjects in a spirit of obedience to a legal order that paid no regard to nation, race or creed. Emptied of its historically accidental features as the inherited territories of a particular dynasty, this monarchical state, Austria in its older sense, provides, in many ways, the constitutional model for Hayek's preferred form of polity—a *Rechtstaat* which generally confines itself to matters of law, order and defence; which guarantees, through the enforcement of law, the framework in which a free economy can operate effectively. While claiming the allegiance of its subjects, such a state emphatically disavows the ambition to express or incarnate the communal spirit, real or imagined, of the nation or any fraction of it.

In the old Austria of Hayek's youth, the politics of community were thus perceived as being decisively opposed to the politics of universal law and individual, in contrast to national or communal, liberty. The anthropology of community, whether conceived in nationalist or socialist terms, defined itself in opposition to the politically liberal, Hayekian anthropology of the self-dependent individual who is what he is by reason of individual achievement rather than birth or ascription. The appeal to community, which signifies to Crowley, as to so many of our contemporaries, merely the limitation of the effects of individualism and the market — the mitigation of the harsher consequences of liberalism by care — meant for the young Hayek, as much as for his anti-liberal contemporaries, not the qualification of the liberal and capitalist order but its destruction.

3. The Crowley Thesis

Without subscribing to the historicist myth of the determination of a man's political vision by his historical situation, it is, I think, astonishing how far the differences between Crowley's vision and that of Hayek can be elucidated by reference to the historical factor. The Austria of the early 1900s is sufficiently different from the London School of Economics in the 1980s, where Crowley's critique of Hayekian liberalism originated as a doctoral thesis, to explain, to a great extent, the nature of the criticisms advanced in the work. For Hayek's thought originates in a context in which the very point that Crowley, like so many of our generous-hearted contemporaries, takes most profoundly for granted, the compatibility of a liberal *economic* order with a renewal of communitarian, participatory politics, seemed an impossibility.

What Crowley at one point astutely terms the 'authoritarian nature' of Hayek's dedication to liberty, embodied in his simultaneous endorsement of the free market and his advocacy of a state whose fundamental political and legal institutions are taken to be beyond the effective scope of mass-democratic debate, is a function of the historical position described above. Hayek's combination of what is, covertly at least, a legally limited political authoritarianism with a form of economic and social libertarianism, so puzzling to many of his current admirers, is no mystery when set against the background of a situation, that of Austria-Hungary, in which what his great contemporary Eric Voegelin termed political 'like-mindedness', *homonoia*, was notable by its absence. For the life of debate and ordered dispute, which is central to Crowley's neo-Aristotelian image of political life, can only be a recipe for order rather than chaos when, beneath the surface of argument, there exists a fundamental consensus as to what constitutes both the real, politically relevant community and the good life. Where *homonoia* is absent the *de facto* authoritarian state is, like it or not, the necessary correlate of the maintenance of economic freedom and individual liberties alike.

The starting point for Crowley's argument is what he takes to be a significant identity of view underlying the apparently opposed political theories of Hayek and the Webbs. Both Hayek and the Webbs "see the justification of society and politics as lying solely in the direction of society as an engine of material want satisfaction." [6] Compared with this, the distinction between the Webbs' endorsement of "rational" socialist planning and Hayek's advocacy of the universal competence of the market is a secondary matter. While differing on the means of achieving the desired goal, the two, or rather three, are in full agreement on the purpose of politics.

Crowley attributes this identity to a shared intellectual inheritance, an abstract, ahistorical view of man or, as I would put it, an anthropology, which he identifies as that of liberalism. According to this view, at its core liberalism presents us with a significantly de-politicized vision of man. In liberal thought, the Aristotelian conception of man as an essentially political being, one destined to achieve his proper ends through participation in the ordering activities of public life, in active citizenship, is displaced by a 'shallow' notion of the human person. One aspect of this shallowness is to be found in the liberal's over-identification of the human good with economic well-being which is, for Aristotle, merely a precondition for the good life. But another, more significant dimension of the shallowness of liberal anthropology is to be found in its diminution of the scope of political reasoning — its reduction of reasoning about the ends of human existence — to a mere matter of instrumental calculation concerning a good, material well-being, that is already known.

This, in turn, is connected with the liberal's over-individualized view of man. The liberal tends to abstract what is supposed to be the essence of the human person, the core of his humanity, from the particular historical and cultural frameworks in which, as a matter of fact, the historically real individual always finds himself; and then seeks to present the bloodless residue that remains as the essence of man as such. Against this, Crowley urges that we need a richer view of the human self—one which recognizes the apparently paradoxical truth that it is precisely the *accidental*, historical and cultural features of a man's being that make him what *essentially* he is.[7]

I cannot, in the space of this essay, enter further into the details of Crowley's analyses of the politics, or rather anti-politics, either of Hayek or of the Webbs, which are generally astute and well-expressed. It is however important to note that, while recognising the deep affinities between them, at least at the anthropological level, Crowley is quite clear that in juxtaposing the two visions, we are not, in qualitative terms, comparing like with like. He well recognizes not only that Hayek is, in every relevant sense, much the greater, more subtle and imaginative, thinker, but also that, despite the inadequacy of its theory of politics, the social vision, or ideal, of Hayekian liberalism is infinitely preferable to that of the Webbs' managerial socialism.

With neither judgement do I disagree; even though, as already suggested, I feel that Crowley would have understood the logic of Hayek's position rather better, and even shown it a bit more sympathy, if he had taken account of the historical background against which it first took shape. When all is said and done, there is nothing arbitrary or irrational about Hayek's resistance to the siren call of the apostles of community. That said, I turn to Crowley's alternative political vision. For there we will find a rather different aspect of the tension between contemporary, *bien-pensant*, political thought and the nature of contemporary political reality. That is, the continuing tension between the fashionable concept of politics as purely a matter of debate and discourse, and the enduring political requirement, both within states and between them, of potential recourse to physical force or at least the credible threat of such action when circumstances so demand.

4. Anarcho-Aristotelianism

As indicated above, the spirit of Crowley's work places him full square in the line of the current Aristotelian revival. The recent renewal of interest in the Aristotelian conception of politics, conceived, above all, as a politics centred on the concept of active, participatory citizenship, must, I think, be understood, in large part, as simply a reaction to the failure of the ultimately anti-political ideologies of liberalism and socialism to provide, either in theory or in practice, satisfactory answers to the problem of the triadic relationship of man, state and society.

In describing these ideologies as 'anti-political' I mean that each aims, in the last resort, to make politics, in the traditional sense, redundant by so ordering society that men are freed both from the challenge of substantive political choice and from the burden of rulership by anything, or anyone, but the self-directing, yet somehow convergent, dictates of individual calculation and desire.

Thus, in the utopias of socialism and liberalism alike, men are conceived as living non-conflictually alongside each other; each freely pursuing his well-being, yet, by virtue of the prevailing social, but primarily economic arrangements, without prejudice to the well-being of others. Where the liberal and the socialist visions differ is not in their endorsement of this ideal of an essentially non-political, or historically post-political, existence but in their judgements of the sort of socio-economic arrangements that would make the ideal attainable —for one a rationally planned system of socialized pro-duction and distribution, for the other the more or less spontaneous play and interplay of the market.

Crowley's critique of the anti-political anthropology of liberalism, in terms of its exaltation of the significance of the economic over other aspects of man's being, certainly brings to light some of the sources of this shared vision. And it is, I agree, a vision whose ultimately dehumanizing aspect is well diagnosed in a passage by J. G. A. Pocock which serves as an epigraph to Crowley's second chapter. "The paradigm of commerce," Pocock observes, "presented the movement of history as being toward the indefinite multiplication of goods and brought the whole progress of material, cultural and moral civilization under this head. But so long as it did not contain any equivalent to the concept of the *zoon politikon*, of the individual as an autonomous, morally and politically choosing being, progress must appear to move away from something essential to human personality. And this corruption was self-generating; society as an engine for the production and multiplication of goods was inherently hostile to society as the moral foundation of the personality."

The reference here to the *zoon politikon*, the animal that is political by nature, is crucial. For contemporary Aristotelianism, like the equivalent revival of interest in the Hegelian notion of 'Civil Society' that has occurred in sections of the political Left, is motivated above all by the sensed need to recover an appreciation of the essentially political, as opposed to the economic, facet of human life —to revive the sense of politics as a creative dimension of human self-realization, the art of life *par excellence*, rather than as a more or less dispensable obstacle to the human good, as it appears in most traditional forms of liberal and socialist theory.

I say "most" because, *pace* Crowley's blanket condemnation of the liberal tradition as inherently anti-political, there is, in the so-called New Liberalism of certain late nineteenth-century thinkers, notably Bernard Bosanquet, a profound appreciation of the positive human significance of politics and, with it, of the state as a centre of authoritative power.[8] Indeed in its neo-Hegelian emphasis on the positive role of the State as a focus of allegiance and an ordering principle in the life of all but the smallest societies, a theory such as Bosanquet's may prove a valuable counterweight to a purported vindication of politics which, like Crowley's, recalls Aristotle's *polis* but somehow, like the new enthusiasts for Civil Society, forgets the place of Hegel's state in the political universe of modernity.

What I am getting at here is what I take to be a significant shortcoming in the project of a renewing of our sense of the human significance of politics as this is currently being pursued by neo-Aristotelians and neo-Hegelians alike. In opposition to the anti-politics of classical liberalism and socialism, both schools aim to restore to political activity its central role in the constitution of the good life. But at the same time, they both tend to fight shy of facing the problem of rulership. They both tend systematically to underestimate the enduring significance of the dimension of coercive power — the political function of a form of direction which is necessarily more than self-direction — that is, just as much as the determination of political policy by informed debate, an inevitable aspect of the political as such. The question here is whether such an evasion does not testify, alongside the legacy of what Crowley terms 'liberalism', to only another variety of anti-politics —a variety which, in the present context, we might justly term 'anarcho-Aristotelian'. By this I mean a position which, in the name of vindicating the value of politics as a form of creative human activity more or less subtly defines out of the political field its other fundamental feature as the domain of institutionalised force and power.

5. Polis and State

Let me explain my point further by reference to two of the terms already juxtaposed above, Aristotle's *polis* and Hegel's *Staat*.

Both *polis* and *Staat*, *polity* and *state*, belong to the vocabulary of what most people would recognize as authentically political visions of the human condition. And both are terms that refer to what may be called the essential element of governance, of authoritative but reasonable political direction, in the conduct of social life. However, while recognizing this common element in the overlapping concepts of polity, Aristotle's *polis*, and state, Hegel's *Staat*, it is important to note that they do not refer to this element in precisely the same way. For, while the Aristotelian concept of the *polis* evokes the undifferentiated image of a polity of self-governing citizens in which, almost by definition, there is no distinction between rulers and ruled — truly a "government of the people, by the people, for the people" to recall a celebrated but nonetheless obfuscating modern formulation of the ideal — the Hegelian notion of the state suggests an institutional form in which rule and self-rule neither are nor can be identical.

Indeed Hegel's argument for the central role of the state as a source of rational political direction in the modern world is couched precisely in terms of the impossibility, in Aristotle's own terms, of maintaining the undifferentiated order of the classical *polis* in the historical and demographic conditions of modernity.

In contrast, Crowley's recourse to what claims to be a more purely Aristotelian vision of politics is, like that of many other contemporary neo-Aristotelians, based on the conviction that the principle of political rule as the unconstrained self-rule of a free citizenry is as applicable in the conditions of the present day as it was, however briefly, in ancient Athens. While recognizing that the matter of population size, if nothing else, renders impractical the revival of the forms of direct participation that characterized the classical *polis*, modern Aristotelians tend to believe that the contemporary, post-Burkean, principle of representation is capable of making good the deficiency. On both points, however, I think that Aristotle, let alone Hegel, would have had considerable doubts.

Here we should recall that, while Aristotle may be read as positing the *polis* as a universal ideal, in the sense that it is and remains the anthropologically most desirable form of political life, he neither believed that it was everywhere attainable nor even thought that every type of man was capable of achieving or maintaining it. The universality of the ideal, and its undoubted continuing attractiveness, should not blind us to the very particular pre-political conditions, including demographic conditions concerning both the size and the composition of the population, which Aristotle, no less than Hegel, considered essential to its actualization. Whether these conditions can ever be met in the conditions of modernity is highly questionable; and, where they are not, it is doubtful how far the theory of the *polis*, conceived as a model of participatory citizenship and not, as the Greek city-state also was, one among other historically given forms of ultimately coercive rule, can provide us with an adequate understanding of what is at stake in political life.

In modern Cosmopolis, where the Greek ideal of the political identity between *ethnos* and *ethos* — between a single self-consciously distinct people and its self-constitutive way of being in the world — is notable by its absence, both from our teeming cities and from the pluralist discourse of polite liberal or post-liberal society, the appeal to community can hardly be expected to produce the sort of like-mindedness presupposed by the model of the *polis*. If this is so, we are fated to inhabit a world in which the polity is, in Hegelian terms, differentiated into the mutually sustaining realms of State and Civil Society; and where something rather like Hayek's strict institutional separation between the two may, despite its anthropological shortcomings, be the best we can hope to achieve.

Notes

1. John Gray, "Mill's and Other Liberalisms", *Critical Review* 2, 2 and 3, 12-35.
2. *Ibid.*
3. Brian Lee Crowley, *The Self, the Individual and the Community: Liberalism in the Political Thought of F. A. Hayek and Sidney Webb* (Oxford: Oxford University Press, 1987.
4. Gray, op. cit.
5. Carl Schmitt, *Political Theology: Four Chapters on the Concept of Sovereignty*, trans by George Schwab, (Cambridge, Mass.: MIT Press, 1985).
6. Crowley, op. cit. p.13.
7. See on this David J. Levy, "The Politics of the Self", originally published in the *Salisbury Review*, reprinted in *Conservative Thoughts*, ed by Roger Scruton (London: Claridge Press, 1988) 81-90.
8. Gerald F. Gauss, *The Modern Liberal Theory of Man*, (London: Croom Helm, 1983).

6

CARL SCHMITT AS A CONSERVATIVE THINKER

When Carl Schmitt died in April 1985 he was approaching his ninety-seventh birthday. The man who has sometimes been described as the Hobbes of the twentieth-century certainly shared his predecessor's gift of a long life; but this was not the only thing he had in common with the great seventeenth-century English political philosopher. There is, I believe, a Chinese prayer which runs: "May I be spared from living in interesting times." Schmitt, like Thomas Hobbes, was not so blessed. Both were fated to live in times made "interest-ing" by war and revolution, by political collapse and the displacement of regimes. Hobbes's life, which began in 1588, the year of the Spanish Armada, encompassed the reigns of James I and Charles I, the English Civil War and Cromwell's Protectorate. By the time he died, in 1679, Charles II had been seated on the restored throne of England for nearly twenty years but the foundations of the monarchical order had been shaken in a way from which they were never wholly to recover. Schmitt too was to live through a series of historical crises in which the possibility of individual survival and the bases of civilized existence were called together into question. To that fact, above all, we owe the character of their works — bodies of closely argued and coldly impassioned writings which revolve obsessively around what their authors conceive to be the fundamental questions of political order and disorder.

Reading Hobbes it has often seemed to me that while he has every claim to be considered the greatest political thinker produced by the English-speaking world, he is also the one who appears most foreign to the mainstream of the English and American traditions. This is because, since Hobbes's day, our countries have, in general, been spared the experience of the utter breakdown of legitimate order which is the normal consequence of revolution, civil war or foreign conquest. With the possible exceptions of Sweden and Switzerland, no other country has been so fortunate. We are lucky to have escaped the circumstances that might have thrown up another Hobbes, and, as a consequence, the implacable dialectic of fear and power which he developed as the foundation of his political theory has generally remained a topic of purely academic, rather than practical, political concern.

In England the perceived unity between legality and legitimacy, between accepted procedure and acceptable power, has been the norm for so long that the Englishman finds it difficult to recognize how rare it is in the modern world and, even perhaps, how fragile it may have become in his own homeland. In the United States the extraordinary endurance of a constitution that enshrines a division of powers that Hobbes would have considered impossible, has produced the miracle of a liberal-democratic *sacrum imperium* — a work of constitutional artifice which, through its embeddedness in the reality of American history, has achieved in the public mind a sacrosanct quality and hence an institutional security unmatched by any other national constitution.

Enjoying such political good fortune, we tend all too readily to take this state of affairs for granted; even though the terrible and unforgettable history of the twentieth century ought to remind us of how exceptional it is. With the historical complacency of the politically privileged we imagine the model of liberal democracy to be some sort of universal norm of political life, a goal to which all peoples should aspire and which every nation is desirous and capable of achieving. We conveniently forget the historical and geographical accidents which have saved us thus far from the worst the world can offer — factors without which even the greatest heroism might not have protected us during the wars of this century.

The closer we are to the heart of liberal democracy the more it is worth recalling that it is a relative rarity even in the contemporary world. Nor can we comfort ourselves with the thought that this is merely a problem of "under-development" — a transient stage on the way to universal democracy. Less than fifty years ago it seemed that liberal democracy was finished in the continent of Europe; and even today half that continent remains subject to an imperial power from whose traditions the political ideals that have come to define the West are almost wholly absent. It is with this sense of the fragility of constitutional order in mind that we should seek to come to grips with the work of Carl Schmitt, a man whose reputation has been indelibly tainted by his brief period as a prominent intellectual supporter of Hitler's Third Reich, but whose numerous writings contain some of the most searching analyses of the conditions of order in the modern world.

Though the subject of increasing attention in recent years, Schmitt is not a widely read author in either Britain or America. Until recently hardly any of his work had appeared in translation; and, when he was referred to at all, it was usually in the context of the history of Nazi Germany, of which he was assumed to have been both a prophet and an enthusiastic apostle. This alone seemed to render his work unworthy of serious attention; and, as a result, all too often historians and political thinkers failed examine to either what Schmitt actually wrote or whether his reputation as a theorist of Nazism was really justified.

Yet the first English translation of one of Schmitt's works appeared as long ago as 1931 when the Catholic historian Christopher Dawson published a version of his 1923 essay "Romischer Katholizismus und Politische Form" under the title of "The Necessity of Politics" as one of a series of seven "Essays in Order". After that, however, there was a readily comprehensible break until 1976, when *The Concept of the Political* was published in a translation by George Schwab together with Leo Strauss's contemporary commentary on the text dating from 1932. Schwab was already the author of *The Challenge of the Exception* 1970, the first book-length study of Schmitt's political ideas to appear in English; and a second extremely valuable book, Joseph W. Bendersky's *Carl Schmitt: Theorist for the Reich*, was published by Princeton in 1983. Since then the MIT Press has published well-edited translations of three of Schmitt's works dating from the early 1920s as part of its series of "Studies in Contemporary German Social Thought". These are *Political Theology: Four Chapters on the Concept of Sovereignty, The Crisis of Parliamentary Democracy*, and *Political Romanticism*. The appearance of these books, and the articles and reviews which they have engendered, indicates a new level of interest in Schmitt's thought — an interest which seems to be not merely historical, still less apologetic, but bound up with an appreciation, new in the English-speaking world, of the relevance of Schmitt's analyses to some at least of our present political problems.

The publication in English of a considerable portion of Schmitt's work dating from the years of the Weimar Republic will allow readers to judge for themselves how far his reputation as a precursor and ideological lantern bearer of the Third Reich is justified. For even now, insofar as the image of Schmitt enters our historical memory at all, it is as the "Crown Jurist" of Hitler's regime, the legal and political theorist who sought to legitimate the morally and politically unacceptable. For the period between 1933 and 1936 there is just enough truth in this image to ensure that Schmitt is and will remain a controversial figure whose works must be approached with particular tact and caution.

The historical reality of the Third Reich casts a long shadow over our times. In relation to Carl Schmitt it has led some commentators to read his pre-1933 writings solely in the sinister light of what was to happen after Hitler came to power. Given the moral enormity of the Nazi experience, this is understandable, and yet, in Schmitt's case, it is more than a little misleading. Historical knowledge is, by definition, knowledge with hindsight; but the events we seek to know, though understood always in retrospect, are experienced by those who make and endure them as a present process leading on to an unknown future. The historical actor is subject to pressures and influences which condition actions whose outcome he cannot foresee. In 1933 Schmitt was such an actor, compelled, albeit reluctantly, to make choices in circumstances he had sought to forestall. That he chose wrongly is a judgement with which few would now disagree; but that is not the main issue for the reader who seeks to learn from his work. The relationship between the disreputable period of Schmitt's career under the Third Reich and the earlier stages of his life and thought is complex; and in the case of so intelligent a theorist of political existence, it is one we should try to make intelligible. This cannot be done by reading writings of the 1920s and early 1930s through the distorting lens of our knowledge of subsequent events. Nor, by the same token, and from the constitutional security of the Anglophone democracies, should we take the unthinking acceptance of liberal democratic ideals as the perennial mark of the civilized mind. Schmitt's life and work must be understood against the historical background out of which they emerged.

Schmitt was born in July 1888 in the small Westphalian town of Plettenberg in the Western part of what was then the German Empire. The majority of the town's population was Protestant but Schmitt's family were, like many other Rhinelanders, devout Catholics. Three of his great uncles were priests and for some time Carl also was expected to enter the priesthood. In the years immediately after the establishment of German political unity, following the Franco-Prussian War of 1870/71, Bismark had made a major though ultimately unsuccessful effort to destroy the influence of the Catholic Church; and though by the time Schmitt was born this pressure had eased, many German Catholics, especially those who lived within the state boundaries of Prussia, still felt themselves to be, in some ways, members of a potentially threatened minority in a predominantly Protestant empire.

Schmitt's religious background was to exercise a considerable influence on his intellectual and political development. He grew up in the cultural orbit of Rhineland Catholicism, the most Westward-looking element within Imperial Germany. Years later he was to tell Ernst Niekisch: "I am Roman by origin, tradition and right"; and this sense of affinity with the Catholic, Latin world was to endure throughout his life, finding expression in a continuing interest, unusual among his contemporaries, in Western, non-German, thought. One particularly significant aspect of this was Schmitt's life long concern with the writings of the nineteenth-century, Catholic counter-revolutionary thinkers, Joseph de Maistre, Louis de Bonald, and, especially, the Spaniard Donoso Cortes, to whose works he was to return again and again in the course of his long career. While the origin of this interest may have lain in his sense of religious affinity with a prominent tradition of Catholic political thought, its persistence over the years reflects Schmitt's sense of living in an age of radical political uncertainty—one in which the inherited foundations of order had all but vanished and which required a total reorientation of political thought and action to cope with the situation. Schmitt considered that the writers of the counter-revolution had, like Hobbes and Machiavelli before them, faced parallel problems, and turned to their writings as a source of political insights for the crisis of his own age.

In the years of Schmitt's youth, however, this crisis lay in the future. Schmitt grew up before the First World War at a time when Germany was confident and strong. In 1900, after a period of education in a Catholic school, he became a pupil at the public *Gymnasium* in Attendorn, where he was exposed to other, non-Catholic currents in German intellectual life. At Attendorn, and later at university in Berlin, Munich and Strassburg, he encountered, in particular, the influence of German nationalism which was, alongside his original Catholicism, to form his future political outlook.

Largely by chance, Schmitt chose to study law, and, in 1910, he graduated with distinction from the University of Strassburg. Still a devout Catholic, Schmitt found himself drawn to the neo-Kantian school of jurisprudence, which emphasized the validity of the authority of state-created norms, while simultaneously claiming that such norms were subject to a 'higher law' knowable to reason. In Bendersky's words: "neo-Kantianism offered Schmitt a means of synthesizing the dichotomous principles he felt as a German nationalist and as a Catholic. The dictates of universal moral principles could be reconciled with the authority of the state; morality and power, religious conviction and nationalism, could be harmoniously integrated. . . . On the eve of World War I he wrote that the incontestable value of the state emanated, not from power, but from its relationship to a 'higher law'. It was the function of the state to transform this higher law into a worldly phenomenon." [1]

Bendersky entitles his account of Schmitt's early years, up to 1921, "From Apolitical Scholar to Political Theorist." The term *apolitical* is apt but requires some clarification. Before the war Schmitt, in common with most German academics and intellectuals, took for granted the political structure of the monarchical state of which he was a subject. Schmitt's pre-war outlook, though distinctively marked by his Catholic inheritance, was in many ways typical of that of the vast majority of his similarly placed contemporaries. What Bendersky calls the "apoliticism" of the young legal theorist, destined as he thought for a career in the Prussian civil service, was itself a characteristically German political outlook. It was one in which contempt for the partial and sectional struggles of party politics and a deeply rooted distrust of the social forces that might be unleashed by the advance of democracy went hand in hand with profound patriotism and a steady reliance on and faith in the guiding, leading hand of the monarchical state.

This was the politics of the "unpolitical man" to which Thomas Mann was to give expression when he wrote, in his *Reflections of an Unpolitical Man*: "I want the monarchy, I want a passionately independent government, because only it offers protection for freedom in the intellectual as well as the economic sphere. . . . I don't want this parliament and party business that will sour the whole life of the nation with its politics. . . . I don't want politics. I want competence, order and decency." [2] The tone of desperation evident in Mann's words reflects what many Germans felt and feared in 1918. For the novelist it was a moment of personal anxiety and uncertainty as well as of national disaster. For the young Schmitt it was also to prove a moment of challenge and opportunity.

The crisis that Germany faced in 1918 was deep and complex. Defeat brought with it not only the fall of the Kaiser but the collapse of the monarchical houses in the states that composed the German *Reich*. Only a year earlier, the Bolsheviks had seized power in Russia and the threat of a communist revolution in Germany seemed real enough. In Bavaria the Communist Kurt Eisner actually succeeded in seizing power, briefly establishing a Soviet regime in the most Catholic and, in some ways, most conservative of the German states. At the other end of the political spectrum right-wing nationalists, many of them organized in military bands, the so-called *Freikorps*, were calling for the restoration of the monarchy, the rejection of the peace imposed by the Western allies, and the trial for treason of those who had accepted the allied terms. In the middle, politicians of various hues, ranging from the moderate Left of the Social Democratic Party to the German Peoples Party of Gustav Stresemann, strove to create a constitutional framework which would preserve the unity of the German state and maintain the fabric of German society against threats of revolution from Left or Right. One essential element in this disparate coalition, from whose efforts the Weimar Republic was to emerge, was the Catholic Centre Party with which Schmitt was, at this stage, closely associated.

Within its ranks the Centre encompassed a wide spectrum of Catholic political opinion. While Schmitt, unlike his father, was never a Centre Party member, he wrote widely for its publications and participated in conferences organized under its auspices. In terms of its political spread he stood, from the beginning, somewhat to the right of the party; and like such other, older, intellectuals as the historian Friedrich Meinecke and the sociologist Max Weber, he accepted the republic without much enthusiasm — seeing in it, not the realization of a cherished ideal, but merely the historically necessary means for preserving the political integrity of the German nation.

Something of Schmitt's attitude to the republic is brought out in the following passage from his book on constitutional law, published in 1928: "By accepting the Weimar constitution", he wrote, "the German nation does not want to disavow its identity with the German nation of the constitution of 1871; it wants to renew its *Reich*. . . but not establish a new *Reich*. Just because it is a democratic constitution, the new constitution does not establish a new German state. It only signifies that a people, which until now believed in. . . monarchical principles. . . has decided to continue its existence on the basis of a constitution which it has granted itself." [3]

Politically speaking, therefore, Schmitt emphasized above all the continuity between the republican and the monarchical state. Whatever its form, he argued, the German state continued to command the allegiance of its citizens as the custodian and sovereign authority of the nation — a position which set him apart from the overt anti-republicanism of most of the radical conservative intellectuals with whom he is sometimes associated. As a constitutional lawyer, Schmitt strove, throughout the period of the republic, to strengthen those institutions, especially the Presidency, which represented and acted on behalf of national unity. From the beginning he supported a strong interpretation of the scope of the famous Article 48 of the Weimar constitution — an article in whose drafting Max Weber was a crucial influence — which authorized the *Reichspräsident* to use force in the case of rebellion or "when public security and order are seriously disturbed or endangered". [4]

Schmitt's interpretation of the constitution as authorizing the temporary institution of a "commissarial dictatorship" by the president in the event of national emergency provoked considerable dispute from the moment it was first put forward at a conference of constitutional lawyers in 1924. In the final years of the Weimar Republic, after 1929, it was to provide justification for the rule by decree practised by the executive branch of government, the President and Chancellor, in the face of the numerical domination of parliament, the *Reichstag*, by parties, especially the Nazi and the Communist parties, dedicated to the overthrow of the Republic.

Schmitt's attitudes throughout this period were governed by one overriding purpose; to prevent the destruction of the established order by the extremist parties of right or left. As early as 1923, in the first edition of *The Crisis of Parliamentary Democracy* [5], he had pointed to the existence of a potentially irresolvable tension between the liberal-parliamentary and the democratic principles in the Weimar constitution: and though hardly a democrat by conviction, he saw the democratic institution of a directly elected president, authorized to rule by decree in situations of national emergency, as the sole possible guarantee of the integrity of the state in conditions in which there existed no national consensus supporting the legitimacy of the established form of government. After 1929, the composition of the *Reichstag* bore out his worst fears. The parliamentary body was dominated by the representatives of parties whose prime purpose was to cripple government and so destroy the existing state.

In the aftermath of the War, the threat to the state, and hence to the integrity of the nation, had seemed to come from the possibility of armed revolution. By the end of the twenties the main danger came from within the parliamentary system. Extremist parties could bring down any government by a vote of no confidence, so provoking new elections and eventually forcing the President to appoint a Chancellor and government from among their own ranks. Schmitt's answer to this problem, put forward in *Legalitat und Legitimitat* 1932, was to argue that, since no constitution could provide the legal means for its own destruction, the powers of the president, laid out in the second part of the Weimar constitution, could and must be used to stop the anti-constitutional parties from gaining power. This would, Schmitt recognized, eventually require revision of the constitution in order to restrict the principle of "equal chance" to parties that accepted the constitutional system. But since he believed that such constitutional revision could not take place before political stability had been restored, presidential rule, as authorised by Article 48, must continue until that point had been reached.

Schmitt hoped that the combined efforts of President Hindenburg and the political circle surrounding Kurt von Schleicher would bring this about. Unfortunately not only was Hindenburg unhappy with the quasi-dictatorial role that was being forced upon him, but the political manoeuvres of Schleicher and his associates were not enough to prevent a growing deterioration in the government's position. The economic state of the country favoured the growth of the anti-constitutional parties; and though, between the elections of July and November 1932, the Nazis lost two million votes, they remained, at the end of the year, the largest party in the *Reichstag*. This was the background to Hindenburg's appointment of Hitler as Chancellor in January 1933.

Schmitt's immediate reaction was, predictably, one of disappointment and distaste. Unlike many other conservative-minded Germans he had little faith in the ability of the other rightist politicians to "tame" the National Socialist government. But events moved swiftly as Hitler strengthened his grip upon power; and, increasingly, Schmitt, conscious of his vulnerable position as a prominent figure in the lost struggle to prevent Hitler's appointment, felt that he had better accept the *fait accompli*.

In late April he received a letter from the philosopher Martin Heidegger urging him to reconcile himself to the new regime, and, on the 1st May 1933, he joined the Nazi Party. Over the next three years Schmitt made great efforts to ingratiate himself with the Nazi Party and government; but in spite of the patronage of Goering and Hans Frank, he was unsuccessful in overcoming the suspicion with which he was regarded by the party ideologues. At the same time, his revisions of his work to fit in with the ideology of the regime, his disowning of his Jewish former associates, his highly publicized initiative to rid German legal thinking of what he now called pernicious Jewish influences, and his development of new theoretical justifications for German expansion, gave him a reputation he was never to lose, as a leading intellectual ornament and theorist of the Third Reich.

The complexity of the events in the period that led up to Hitler's acquisition of power through constitutional means is only slightly greater than the complexity of Schmitt's motivation in the months and years that followed. Detailed examination of both is beyond the scope of this essay; but in order to understand the true significance of Schmitt's theoretical work before 1933 it is necessary to make a few points about the latter.

In a review of Bendersky's book on Schmitt, Daniel Johnson has made the point that "unlike the romantics, who suffered from many illusions about National Socialism, Schmitt fell victim to one only: that he could prove his disingenuous loyalty useful by theorising." [6] In Schmitt's acceptance of and active engagement with the Nazi regime we may recognize various factors: among them, a streak of opportunism in his character; a fear that he might pay, perhaps with his life, for his former opposition to the Nazi quest for power; a vanity that was flattered by the thought that he might indeed become the Crown Jurist of the new German Empire; and an ingrained unwillingness, rooted in his political outlook, to place himself in a position of opposition to politically established power. Of these only the last is important in judging the significance of his pre-1933 writings.

It is notable that every one of Schmitt's works to have appeared in English translation was written in the decade following the end of the First World War. *Political Romanticism, Political Theology, The Crisis of Parliamentary Democracy* and *The Necessity of Politics*, as well as the untranslated but important book on dictatorship, *Die Dictatur*, all appeared between 1919 and 1923. *The Concept of the Political* followed five years later in 1928. The books are short, never much more than pamphlet length, but packed with interesting and provocative ideas. Unlike most of his German contemporaries, Schmitt put clarity and brevity at a premium. It has been said that he wrote German as though it were Latin; and, though something of the character of his prose is inevitably lost in translation, the quality of his mind shines through clearly enough. Schmitt's writings are marked by the rigour of the arguments they deploy and a sure instinct for identifying the fundamental points at issue.

Faced with a number of brief books, produced in quick succession at a time of widely perceived political crisis, it is tempting to regard them as merely occasional works —bound pamphlets written in response to particular events whose significance is tied to the circumstances in which they were composed.

And so at one level they are. Whatever the richness of their theoretical content, Schmitt's purpose in writing them was eminently practical. In conditions of defeat and potential political disintegration, Schmitt found himself engaged in the business of political theorizing in order to discover the roots of and the possible solutions to Germany's all too practical political problems. The fundamental character of his considerations, which extends to an analysis of the foundations of political order, is a reflection of the depth of the problems which Germany's new republic faced.

The question that such works inevitably raise in the mind of the contemporary English or American reader is: How far were such problems peculiar to the situation of Germany in the aftermath of war? Or, putting matters differently, to what extent are they problems shared by other, more deeply rooted, liberal democracies? To these questions there can be no simple answer. Whether he is writing about the shortcomings of the apolitical tradition of German romanticism — a tradition marked both by the cult of the politically disengaged individual and the cultivation of a nationalist political vision — or the problems of reconciling presidential authority with liberal representative institutions in a viable nation state, Schmitt's starting point is the German political reality of which he is part. At the same time, the radical nature of his reflections, his refusal to rest content with a depiction of the surface of events, pulls him always in the direction of a deeper anatomy of the conditions of order.

He searches his own and his nation's past and present in order to arrive at knowledge of what is essential to politics as such. But this essence of politics, whose core is perhaps to be found in *The Concept of the Political,* is not a timeless thing divorced from the changes brought about by history. Schmitt's outlook is clearly rooted in the nationalist and Catholic traditions which formed him. But, unlike more sentimental or romantic representatives of these traditions, he is aware that the development of the modern world has changed the nature of the political. Not for him the dreams of reviving the political forms of medieval Christendom or the ethnically homogeneous *Volksgemeinschaft* beloved of German nationalism. Schmitt's political thought is not simply a creature of its author's present concerns, but an attempt to cope with the changes which the passage to modernity has introduced into the political picture.

Schmitt's attitudes to the political culture of modernity are those of a man conservative both by instinct and intellectual formation. Central to his thought is the insistence that politics is a fundamental dimension of human existence — a sphere of activity concerned with the organization of a human community for action in a world that is always potentially threatening to the survival of individual and group alike. Man is a being at risk in the world. His nature is such that conflict and war are ever-present possibilities.

In contrast to his friend, the writer Ernst Jünger, Schmitt neither glorifies this situation nor claims that war provides a unique opportunity for the expression of what is highest in human nature. The possibility of human conflict and, at the limit, war is, in Schmitt's view, simply a fact of life; and one whose recognition is fundamental to political considerations. The desire for a world without war is perfectly understandable, and, unlike some of his contemporaries, Schmitt sees the prevention of war as a political imperative of the highest order. His point is not that we should not seek to preserve peace between nations but that such an end is not served by the utopian pretence that the *risk* of war can ever be definitively overcome.

At a time when, in Western Europe in particular, there are many who have fooled themselves into believing that the Soviet Union entertains no aggressive designs against them, and that, consequently, some measure of unilateral, one-sided disarmament could contribute to the diminution of the chances of nuclear war, Schmitt's words are as pertinent as when they were first written more than fifty years ago. "It would", he writes, "be a mistake to believe that a nation could eliminate the distinction between friend and enemy by declaring its friendship for the entire world or by voluntarily disarming itself. The world will not thereby become depoliticized, and it will not be transplanted into a condition of pure morality, pure justice, or pure economics. If a people is afraid of the trials and risks implied by existing in the sphere of politics, then another people will appear which will assume these trials by protecting it against foreign enemies and thereby taking over political rule. . . . It would be a deranged calculation to suppose that the enemy could perhaps be touched by the absence of a resistance. . . . If a people no longer possesses the energy or the will to maintain itself in the sphere of politics, the latter will not thereby vanish from the world. Only a weak people will disappear." [7]

While fully supporting his nation's cause in the First World War, Schmitt, unlike many other German intellectuals, never interpreted the conflict as a necessary and desirable spiritual struggle between idealistic German *Kultur* and the liberal materialist civilization of the West. As a Catholic, he was too conscious of his affinities with the traditions of Western civilization and of the ambiguities of the Bismarkian Reich to interpret the struggle in such simplistic moral terms. The same factors account for the gulf, never overcome even in his post-1933 writings, between Schmitt's state-centred political vision and the *volkisch* glorification of a racially conceived German nation. In Schmitt's thinking the state is conceived not as an instrument of an ethnically based and hence biologically united nation, but as the guarantor of order within politically defined borders and the central institution responsible for the preservation of national, territorial integrity. This important distinction, so often ignored by those who condemn Schmitt as a prophet of the Third Reich, was readily apparent to the Nazi ideologues who dismissed his reconciliation with the new regime as a fraud and who, by 1937, had driven him out of the public life of the new Germany.

In contrast to the ideological exponents of nationalist or socialist dictatorship as well as to liberal advocates of parliamentary democracy as an end in itself, Schmitt's attitude to the form of the state is essentially pragmatic. What is important about a state is not its institutional form, republican or monarchical, but its effectiveness in carrying out its essential functions. Schmitt's increasing impatience with the Weimar Republic was not the result of a principled rejection of republicanism as such but of frustration at the inability of Germany's republican politicians to maintain the authority of the state and the apparent impossibility of reconciling necessary executive power with a legislature increasingly dominated by anti-constitutional parties. Faced, as he saw it, with the choice between supporting executive authority or the principle of parliamentary government, Schmitt consistently opted for the former. Far from expressing an ingrained hostility to the constitutional form of the post-war German republic, this attitude reflected Schmitt's desire to make the new constitution work. That this entailed the consistent assertion of the executive sovereignty of the president over and eventually against the legislature was a function of the fundamental ideological divisions within the German electorate.

The reflection of these divisions in the *Reichstag*, the domination of parliament after 1929 by deputies belonging to the anti-constitutional parties, the Communists and the German Nationalist Party as well as Hitler's National Socialists, made parliamentary government un-workable. Schmitt's support for rule by presidential decree in the final years of the Weimar Republic was intended, not to prepare the way for the institution of a permanent dictatorship, but to provide the constitutional forces with the time and political space to overcome what he hoped would be a temporary crisis. Throughout this period Schmitt argued that the measures adopted by the executive were consistent with the provisions of the constitution and in accord with the emergency powers reserved to the president in Article 48.

The position Schmitt maintained had, of course, a particular significance in the political circumstances of the time, in which he was seen as the main academic supporter of presidential rule by decree; but the considerations underlying his attitude have a more general relevance. Schmitt's arguments are based on recognition that the possibilities of maintaining liberal democratic institutions and the rule of law depend upon the effectiveness of executive power no less than in any other political dispensation. No ideological formulation of the democratic principle in terms of popular self-government can negate the fact that every viable political entity requires that there be an effective sovereign power. No viable theory of the rule of law can blind itself to the reality that, in the last resort, law itself requires the guarantee that only such a sovereign can provide.

Schmitt had argued this point in his *Political Theology*, first published in 1922, where he developed his celebrated and still controversial "decisionistic" theory of sovereignty. Liberal legal and political theorists had argued that in the modern constitutional state ultimate authority resides in the rule of law itself. In Schmitt's view this ignored the basic political fact that the operation of normal, and hence norm-governed, legal order presupposes a continuing general conformity with the very norms the law is meant to ensure. The authority that undergirds the rule of law is not, and cannot be, simply that of law itself.

Politically speaking, the rule of law is not self-grounding; for if the legal order is called into question — if, as is always possible, "law and order" breaks down — its maintenance or restoration is seen to depend upon the existence of a sovereign endowed with the authority and, ultimately, the power to renew it. The normative order of law rests on the absolute, if final, authority of the political sovereign. According to Schmitt, the essence of sovereignty lies precisely in possession of the authority to decide when the normal conditions presupposed by the rule of law obtain and when they cannot; or as he tersely formulates it in the first sentence of *Political Theology*, "Sovereign is he who decides on the exception".

Schmitt's point is that whether or not such an eventuality is foreseen and explicitly provided for in constitutional law, the decision as to when it has been reached, as well as subsequent decisions as to how to resolve it, cannot be settled by reference to legal norms but are, and must necessarily be, matters of political decision by the sovereign. In the circumstances of what he calls "a state of exception", a constitutional sovereign is bound, not by norms of the legal code, rendered ineffective by the breakdown of respect for lawful obligations, but by his constitutional duty as *sovereign* to take such political measures as may be necessary to restore a situation in which legal norms may, once more, be made effective. Schmitt's argument is, now as ever, a timely reminder of the political foundation on which the rule of law rests and which is its final, if still imperfect, guarantee.

In the third chapter of *Political Theology*, Schmitt argues that sovereignty, like other major concepts of political thought, represents the secularized form of what was originally a theological concept. This interpretation has been challenged by Hans Blumenberg in *The Legitimacy of the Modern Age* MIT Press, 1983 as part of his massive assault on the validity of all theories which interpret modernity in terms of the category of secularization. In contrast, Schmitt's fellow Catholic, Jacques Maritain, accepts the theological derivation of the concept of sovereignty, but only in order to argue that the use of the term in political discourse is both theoretically misleading and practically dangerous.

The issues raised on this point by Schmitt's various critics are complex and important and certainly cannot be settled here. The question of sovereignty —what it is, where in any given state it resides, whether it can ever in fact be limited —has been at the centre of political-theoretical discussion for some three to four hundred years. It has occupied this place ever since the religious disputes of the Reformation and the subsequent assertion of the priority of secular political authority as an unequivocal answer to the problem of political order in religiously divided societies. The liberal democratic ideology of our time, with its assertion of the conceptual identity of rulers and ruled —government of the people, by the people, for the people —can scarcely be said to have clarified the issue, whatever its undoubted symbolic value. The idea of popular sovereignty, as much as the neo-Kantian identification of legitimate sovereignty with the rule of law, tends to mystify a state of affairs in which effective rulership, involving personal decisions informed by the criteria of political effectiveness and authoritative for the citizenry as a whole, has lost none of its importance in the life of nations.

Schmitt's assertion of the continuity between the republican state and the *Kaiserreich*, which it had replaced, reflects not merely his personal political preferences as a conservative and a nationalist, but an awareness, unclouded by liberal sentiments hostile to the very recognition of the reality of political power, of the continuing significance of effective sovereignty in the modern democratic state.

No less interesting is his chapter, again in *Political Theology*, "On the Counterrevolutionary Philosophy of the State." Here Schmitt traces the path between Joseph de Maistre's self-doubting project of restoring the traditional legitimacy of the monarchical state and Donoso Cortes's assertion of the inevitability of choice between anarchy and dictatorship in a world which no longer recognizes the sovereign's authority as legitimate. This is not only a fascinating excursion into a neglected but important area of the history of ideas, but, in my view, illumines the troubling logic of Schmitt's own political development. More generally, the examination of the path that lead Cortes, the great Spanish conservative, to endorse absolute dictatorship as an answer, though hardly a solution, to what he perceived as a new "fall" into a no less absolute disorder, throws light on the complex and often equivocal attitudes of continental European conservatives to the rise of fascism in the inter-war years.

The weakness of parliamentary democratic institutions in most European countries between the wars, the perceived threat of communist revolution combined with an apparent atrophy of executive power, made many

conservatives receptive to the appeal of authoritarian political movements —
many of which adopted the ideological and organizational trappings made
fashionable by Mussolini's Italy. During the Weimar years Schmitt was, if
anything, unusually immune to this temptation. At the same time he considered
that the political system of parliamentary democracy embodied a dangerous
contradiction between its liberal and its democratic elements. Thus, in *The
Crisis of Parliamentary Democracy*, he argues that the rise of mass politics,
a politics characterized by the predominant influence of extra-parliamentary
pressure groups representing special interests, has undermined the legitimacy
of parliamentary government.

According to Schmitt, this legitimacy rests, or rather rested, on a belief in
parliamentary debate as a quest for true, disinterested judgement in matters of
public concern and on a Burkean notion of representation. According to
Burke, the representative is not the deputy and spokesman of any particular
interest group but a figure elected in order to exercise his independent
judgement on behalf of all his constituents in accordance with what he believes
to be the general, national, political interest. The democratization of politics
threatens both these foundations. The representative comes to be conceived as
the mandated deputy of an ideologically founded party, perceiving itself and
perceived as the collective representative of a particular element in society.
Parliamentary debate ceases to be regarded as a means of achieving objective
judgement and becomes an arena of struggle between competing and potentially incompatible ideologies and interest groups.

The history of the Weimar Republic illustrated only too well the political
impasse to which this situation can lead, at least where no historically formed
consensus underpins national, political institutions. In such circumstances the
executive can only act effectively to the extent that it is able, and constitution-
ally entitled, to exercise the functions of government independently of the
legislature. If parliamentary democracy today seems rather less fragile than it
did when Schmitt was writing, this is not, I think, because it has resolved the
dilemmas he so perceptively identified, but because well-justified horror at the
alternatives on offer has made us rather less demanding of its intellectually
dubious *raisons d'etre*. It is perhaps this negative experience which is the
primary source of the renewed legitimacy of parliamentary institutions in
Europe since the war.

It is still too early to judge Schmitt's work with anything approaching a
politically disinterested eye. Perhaps any political writer whose works continue to be read beyond his time must be and remain a controversial figure; for
if the issues he raises are no longer matters of debate and dispute, that means
that they are no longer politically alive. Such writers have only an antiquarian
interest. They belong to the history of ideas but not to the perennial debate of

political philosophy. In truth we do not yet know to which class Schmitt belongs; though I suspect that his discussions of sovereignty and of the nature of the political ensure him a permanent place in the great tradition of Western political thinking. Only time will tell. For the moment only this is certain: that Carl Schmitt remains essential reading for those concerned with the future of the free nation states of the West. As diagnostician and critic he is worth a score of uncritical admirers of what we take too readily for granted as our birthright of freedom.

Notes

1. Joseph W. Bendersky, *Carl Schmitt: Theorist for the Reich* (Princeton, N.J.: Princeton University Press), 1983.

2. Thomas Mann, *Betrachtungen eines Unpolitischen*, quoted by Ellen Kennedy in her introduction to Schmitt's *The Crisis of Parliamentary Democracy* (Cambridge, Mass.: MIT Press, 1985), p.xxiv.

3. Quoted by Bendersky in his study of Schmitt. See note 1.

4. On the significance of this article see the work of Bendersky and Ellen Kennedy's informative "Introduction" to *The Crisis of Parliamentary Democracy*.

5. See note 2.

6. Daniel Johnson, "The New Machiavelli: Carl Schmitt at 95" *The Salisbury Review* Winter 1984, pp.48-50.

7. Carl Schmitt, *The Concept of the Political* (New Brunswick, N.J.: Rutgers University Press), pp.51-53.

7

POLITICS, TECHNOLOGY AND THE RESPONSIBILITY OF INTELLECTUALS

1. Modernity and Technology

In the pages that follow I want to explore certain fundamental issues raised by consideration of the responsibility of intellectuals in the historically specific conditions of the contemporary world. The perspective adopted is that of an historically and ontologically oriented philosophical anthropology. By this I mean a philosophically explicit conception of man's nature and place in the world which is sensitive both to the unchanging conditions of man's specifically given form of life — the range of what Arnold Gehlen has termed 'anthropological constants'[1] — and to the historical novelties which this underdetermined and ecologically unstable life-form renders possible and which have become, in the present age, established facts of life. In this perspective, which owes much to the seminal work of Max Scheler and his more or less faithful followers in the development of a distinctive philosophical-anthropological tradition, the specific differences of man's contemporary existence, which we shall group together under the heading of 'modernity', are to be understood as *existential* novelties developed within and dependent upon an enduring *ontological* framework — a structure at once of nature and of human nature —whose persistence alone renders the continuation of human life possible.

Seen thus, modernity is to be understood as the historically unprecedented realization and continuing development of certain existential possibilities which are, for all the novelty of their outcome, implicit from the beginning in man's mode of being in the world. These possibilities, realized through history as an incremental result of human actions, tend over time to enlarge the extent to which, as a matter of fact rather than of right, man becomes, regardless of what he may intend or desire, responsible for the maintenance of the conditions which make possible not only the persistence of life but, at the limit, the very being of the planet.

Following the lead of Hans Jonas in *The Imperative of Responsibility*,[2] I want to explore the problem of the present nature and range of human responsibility. More specifically, I shall focus on the problem of what, if any, are the particular responsibilities of intel-lectuals when viewed against the background of this extension of man's power radically to alter conditions of existence on whose endurance, now subject to the tender mercies of human care, his own continues to depend.

The thesis to be maintained is that what may be termed the dialectic of dependence — an intrinsically unstable state of affairs in which the world on which man depends has become itself radically dependent on what he decides to do — imposes certain quite specific responsibilities and restraints upon intellectual activity. The need for these restraints, which can be rejected only at the cost of likely extinction, represents a definitive refutation, not of reason itself, but of the Enlightenment intellectual's self-serving dream that the world might be remade in the image of his own rationalist imagination. In terms first made familiar in Schelling's criticism of the pan-rationalism of Hegel, the dialectic of dependence represents the reassertion of the primacy of nature over reason, of actual life over the utopian dream of what can never be. And the irony of it all is that the refutation occurs not because the Enlightenment was wrong about the extent of man's freedom from any supra-human measure but precisely because it was right.

While it is the development of modern technology, or, more precisely, the extension of the range of technologically induced effects into the very structure of the supporting world, that must be regarded as the primary cause of the enlargement of the scope of human responsibility, the problem of what principles are now to guide us in the exercise of that responsibility is, in itself, nothing new. The principles in question are, as I hope to show, coeval with mankind: not in the sense that they are always known or that men are always capable of stating what they may be, but because they are imperatives of action rooted in the survival requirements of an emergent life-form, that of man as such, which is, from the beginning, uniquely responsible for its own fate.

To put it at its simplest, while other animals are organically attuned to survival in a given ecological niche, human beings are, from the mysterious moment of their emergence into the fabric of the world, uniquely responsible for the creation and maintenance of an equivalent space in nature in which their continued existence becomes possible. While other organisms survive because, and only insofar as, they are genetically adapted to their environment, the survival of human beings depends, *ab initio*, on a capacity to adapt the environment to their own ends. This is the distinctive principle of the human life-form, and represents, in its way, a break with the governing principle of animal life at least as remarkable as that which separates the mode of animal existence from that of plants. Exploration of how this break may have come about must await another occasion, as must any sort of argued refutation of those socio-biological purists who would deny its scientific reality. Our concern here is with the consequences of what I take to be a plausibly assumed human distinctiveness as they affect the issue of human, and even planetary survival, and, more narrowly, with the role of intellectuals in making the possibility that we will in fact survive a little more likely.

In relation to the articulation of the principles governing the exercise of responsibility, the problems we presently face ought not to be regarded, in deterministic fashion, as direct and necessary results of the development of technology as such. The story of that development is not only an affair of the last few centuries but, as we shall have cause to emphasize, one that arises as a primordially necessary response to the original conditions of human survival in the world. What is more, the development of technology has always been governed, though rarely without extra-technological, religious or otherwise customary restraints, by its own immanent imperatives based on the single principle of the quest for ever-greater practical effectiveness. That is, after all, the sole native principle of a purely technological rationality, and its logic guides the development of the sling and the throwing spear as much as that of the personal computer or the compact disc player.

The significant point, then, is not that technology itself is a source of problems but rather that, in the contemporary world, the magnitude of recent technological achievements tends to cloud the issue of whether there may be considerations other than those inherent in the technological project which must still be taken into account in determining the proper course of action now and for the future. The only really novel question — the question that arises now as never before — is whether, even and perhaps especially within the sphere of *techne*, we require a sort of self-denying ordinance equivalent to those humanly imposed restraints that have traditionally characterized the ethical and political spheres of life.

The matter, as we shall see, is complicated by the fact that the striking success of modern man's accomplishments in the technological sphere tends, when contrasted with his more dubious record in ethics and politics, to call into question the claim to authority of the very forms of non-technological reasoning that may now, more than ever, be required. The place of "Reason in the Age of Science", to recall the title of a recent anthology of essays by Hans-Georg Gadamer which is highly pertinent to our theme, is rendered doubly problematic by the fact that, quite apart from the justifiable prestige of a conception of natural science and a strictly instrumental reason bound up, in the public mind at least, with the experienced reality of technological achievement, what has been presented, over the last two centuries, as non-technological, political or historical reason has, all too often, turned out to be little more than a *rationale* for legalized murder.

The development of technology itself contributes directly to the novelty of the contemporary problem of responsibility only in the limited sense that it extends the sphere of being for which man is *de facto* responsible. Beyond this the problem of responsibility is not one caused by the extension of technology but, rather, by the human, psychological tendency, in the face of that development, to extend the model of a purely technological rationality to all areas of life. And this, as I shall argue, at a time when, as a result of the extended range of purely technical competence, the *logos* proper to technology —that of a technological rationality which takes account only of practical effective-ness —is no longer, alone and of itself, sufficient to order the conduct even of the most strictly technological activity.

No doubt there are other equally useful and enlightening ways to approach the problem of the responsibilities, and in particular the political responsibili-ties, of intellectuals in the world today; responsibilities which are, of course, not everywhere the same. The approach adopted here abstracts from the significant differences which derive from the variety of cultural, political and economic circumstances found on the present world scene in order to focus on the problem of this responsibility in its most universal aspect. I adopt this approach not because I underestimate the significance of the differences between the role of intellectuals in free and totalitarian regimes, nor those that separate the economically advanced from the less developed portions of the world, but because there is, beyond these differences, a universal problem of responsibility which has devolved upon mankind —one which, for the first time, involves the question of whether or not the species is to have a future at all.

The particular responsibilities of intellectuals within this state of affairs are, then, to be understood against the background of the general responsibility of man for his own future. I term this responsibility "political" because, as it has become increasingly subject to human control, nature, the perennial object and target of technological activity, and a sphere of being whose self-renewing existence could once be taken for granted, has, in consequence of the cumulative effect of that activity, acquired something of the ontological status formerly and rightly attributed exclusively to the traditional objects of political concern.

By this I mean that nature has now become what human, social and political institutions always have been — a supporting reality objectively necessary to human survival but whose own future endurance is manifestly dependent upon human ingenuity, cultivation and care. As Hans Jonas puts it with only marginal exaggeration: "The boundary between 'city' and 'nature' has been obliterated; the city of men, once an enclave in the nonhuman world, spreads over the whole of terrestial nature and usurps its place. The difference between the artificial and the natural has vanished, the natural is swallowed up in the sphere of the artificial and at the same time the total artifact the works of man that have become 'the world' and as such envelop their makers generates a 'nature' of its own, that is, a necessity with which human freedom has to cope in an entirely new sense." [3]

I shall return to Jonas later. For the moment what needs to be brought out of his words is the implication that the scope of political responsibility now extends over a level of reality, the stratum of physical, inorganic as well as organic, nature, to which it could formerly remain relatively indifferent. Many writers, particularly in the Marxist tradition, have drawn our attention to the way in which the works of man, realized in the institutional forms of society or culture, tend to form a 'second nature' — a 'reified' realm of objectively existing constraints upon the human subject from whose activities they nonetheless derive. What fewer have noticed, at least until recently, is the other side of the coin: that just as the stabilization of cultural practices in institutional form creates a new, quasi-natural, because objectively given, framework within which human life is necessarily conducted, so, primarily as a result of technological activity, nature acquires over time something of the ontological status of culture. The continuation of nature *tout court*, the ontologically given basis which renders human life possible, becomes as dependent on human activity as the 'second nature' of culture.

In this way the sphere of political responsibility, which is, broadly speaking, coextensive with the range of human life-conditions alterable by human decision, is radically enlarged by the reduction of nature to what I term a quasi-institutional status. While the origins of nature, as distinct from those of culture, are not attributable to human activity, its continuing integrity has become so. Within this process, whereby the results of action oriented by an always imperfect knowledge of its actual consequences enter ever deeper into the structure of the human environment, two elements stand out as especially relevant to consideration of what may be the particular responsibilities of those we call intellectuals.

The first refers to the status of the intellectual as holder of a distinct range of socially recognized "scientific" knowledge. That is, in his role as a "professional" or "expert" to be consulted on projects related to his specialist field. The second refers to the less "technical", more loosely "philosophical" role often attributed to and claimed by intellectuals in general. That is the role of determining, on the basis of the analytical, discursive and rhetorical skills normally associated with intellectual activities, more than on possession of a distinct professional perspective and stock of knowledge, the likely overall consequences of particular courses of action and, hence, the desirability of pursuing them.

In the first case the intellectual speaks from a position authorized by his claim to possession of specialized knowledge. In the second, actual possession of what may otherwise be recognized as a sphere of "scientific" knowledge is almost incidental. The poet or novelist will do as well as and often better than the psychologist or the economist. For what counts here is a presumed capacity, popularly supposed to be born out of engagement in intellectual activity as such, to reach significant conclusions about the long-term consequences of a multitude of originally distinct actions.

At least since the Enlightenment, this activity has tended to take one or other of the typical forms of historical prophecy. This, in all its guises, ranging from the social scientific "discovery" of necessary "laws of history" to the popular form of utopian and, more recently, anti-utopian novels, is a characteristically modern undertaking, whose source is the no less distinctively modern conviction that human existence is subject over history to the possibility, and, for some, the necessity of fundamental, ontological alteration. The real cognitive value of all such speculation is, of its nature, difficult to assess, and, given the variety of conclusions to which it leads, it is tempting to attribute its undoubted influence to rhetorical factors alone. The speculative intellectual, it may be said and often is by those engaged in the severely practical business of everyday politics, is a specialist in the use of words, and his forays outside his own specialized field of knowledge are of no more cognitive value than anyone else's. When it comes to matters of practical philosophy, judgements of value, and speculations about the future course of events, we are all more or less percipient amateurs. Such is the attitude of the "practical man"; but though there is a certain truth in it, the temptation altogether to dismiss the wider "philosophical" role of the contemporary intellectual, and hence the attribution of particular, political responsibilities attaching to his activities, ought to be resisted.

The reason for this is that though intellectual activities do not, of themselves, make those engaged in them either any wiser or more obviously practically or politically responsible —the reverse is as often the case —the nature of our civilization is such that both the specialized knowledge of the expert and the capacity to determine, even speculatively, the likely long-term risks and consequences of present, knowledge-guided action have today a practical relevance they have never had before.

In other words, the distinction between theoretical and practical knowledge, which underlies the traditional, Aristotelian, view of politics as an activity requiring no more knowledge than that we may reasonably expect of the mature citizen, is significantly undercut by developments which make specialist, pre-eminently theoretical, knowledge more relevant to our knowledge of the political environment than in previous ages. Recognition of this is an essential part of what we mean when we speak of ourselves, as we often do, as living in a uniquely "technological" age. It seems to me that this widespread but rather vague notion requires further clarification if we are to determine, more precisely, the particular nature of the political responsibility of the contemporary intellectual.

2. A Technological Age?

The phrase *technological age* is used by so many people in so many different contexts that we are inclined to take it for granted that we know what it means. And, at a certain level, we do. We inhabit a world where the effects of human technology are everywhere to be seen, and not only seen but used and relied on. As once men conceived the limits of their lives to be defined by the presence and pressures of implacable nature — a realm not made by man and ultimately beyond his control — so their descendants have come to see technology itself as representing the new and intrinsically unlimited horizon of human possibility.

On the scale of the individual and the human race alike the level of technology achieved and about to be achieved seems to expand the range of man's potentialities in hitherto unprecedented ways. This expansion of possibilities is obviously a human achievement, the result of human efforts and thus, in principle, it would seem to fall full square within the range of human control and responsibility. And yet the technologically defined world of modernity is, as much as the natural world, experienced as subject to dynamics of its own; tending to move in a fixed direction toward an unknown and uncertain end. The careful calculation of appropriate means to chosen ends, which is characteristic of each individual technological project, seems to play little or no part in the process of technology as a whole, which advances ever outwards, expanding human powers without apparent regard to what the consequences may be.

It is for this reason that we tend to think of the sphere of technology with the same ambivalence with which our ancestors once regarded nature. Technology is the pre-eminent object of both hope and terror. It promises the material for a life of happiness and ease and is, at the same time, sensed to be pregnant with apocalyptic possibilities. It is simultaneously worshipped, cultivated and feared as an inescapable and dominant reality in the life of the species. Those who claim to know its secrets are, like the magicians of old, consulted without ever really being trusted; and this is not because they are thought to be any less intrinsically trustworthy than the rest of mankind but because they are suspected of meddling with forces ultimately beyond their control in ways whose consequences cannot be forseen.

This ambivalent attitude to the power of technology is characteristic of the mood of the present day. It is an essential part of what we mean when we say that we live in a technological age; for an age tends to characterize itself, above all, by whatever it is that defines its hopes and fears. And yet the widespread self-designation of ours as an "age of technology" is in some respects thoroughly misleading, suggesting as it does that technology is a new factor on the scene, a feature that sets us apart from our human predecessors.

The classification of distinctive epochs in terms of some specific difference that separates the mode of life of their inhabitants from what went before is one of the ways we make sense of the past. As a classificatory scheme, the idea of successive, distinctive ages enables us to extend our comprehension of the human story into the shadowy realms of prehistory. When we speak of the bronze age or the iron age we are referring to moments in history in which the horizon of human possibilities was extended by the discovery of the use of a new material. Equally, when we speak of the "agrarian revolution" as marking a new epoch in human existence, the agrarian age, we are thinking of the ways in which man was able transform his way of life by bringing under his control and guidance processes that were already present in nature.

The term *technological age* is not, however, like that, if only because the development of agriculture, like the working of metals and of stone before them, is already an essentially technological achievement — the result of the development of techniques which involve not merely the manipulation but the modification to human ends of materials and processes originally found in nature. The essence of technology is not to be found in the use of such materials and forces, a capacity we share to a limited extent with tool-using animals, but precisely in their consciously creative modification to serve human purposes. But when seen in this light, the phrase *technological age* loses its distinctiveness and hence its historical usefulness. For in this, its fundamental sense, every epoch in human history has been an age of technology; and if we want to understand the real specific difference of our particular *technological age* we would do well to remind ourselves of this.

To put it another way, the use of technology and even our dependence upon it, far from setting us apart from our human ancestors, represents one of the most striking elements of continuity in the human story. Such dependence is not a mark of the uniqueness of the modern age but a feature that primordially separates the human mode of being from the life forms of the other animals.

From the beginning, the capacity for technological achievement introduces a unique dynamism into the relationship between man and the world he
is fated to inhabit; for the modification of naturally given elements by
technique always does more than simply extend the possibilities of individual
and group survival. The application of technology to the problems of organic
survival tends cumulatively to transform the world in which it is applied. This
in turn creates the opportunity and even the necessity for the development of
new technologies, and hence transforms the world still further. Thus, in
ecological terms, the dynamism of technology is, from the start, an intrinsically destabilising factor. The assurance or stabilization of human life chances
has always been won at the cost of the destabilization of the environment
which makes life possible. This makes human technology qualitatively
different from what may seem, at first sight, to be the equivalent, though
organically given, 'techniques' that ensure the survival of other species.

There are, of course, many species of animals which have proved extraor-
dinarily well able to cope with the changes that human activity has brought
about in their environments. Others have been less fortunate. But whether or
not an animal species survives always depends upon its capacity to adapt itself
to an environment over which it has no control. The human case is different;
for though man is, no less than the animal, ecologically dependent upon a
supporting world, the only world that can afford him the support he requires
is one whose elements have, to a greater or lesser extent, been modified by
human technology. The effects of such modifications are, as I have suggested,
cumulative, and tend, over the long term but with increasing rapidity, to alter
what we may term the "balance of power" between man and nature.

If today we feel ourselves to be in a unique position it is, therefore, not
because we have entered an unprecedented stage of dependence on technology,
but because the perennial development of world-transforming technique has
reached a stage at which our possibilities seem to be limited, pre-eminently
if not uniquely, by the capacities of technology itself. This has been part of the
human prospect from the beginning, even if it is only in retrospect that it can
be understood as such. In Heideggerian terms it must be seen as part of the
inherent destiny of Being — a fated moment in which, paradoxically, the
concealment of man's ontological dependence is matched by a revelation of
real and discomforting ontological possibilities. In the more modest language
of post-Schelerian anthropology, it is a situation historically entailed in a form
of life unique to man: a life-form that ensures its endurance, not by adaptation
to a given environment, but by modifying the environment to suit its own ends.
Such a project must end either in a failure which would mean extinction or,
as I have suggested, in a success whose mark is the reduction of nature to the
status of a quasi-institution — that is a level of reality necessary to survival

but no longer capable of endurance without constant human care.

It is the perception that we have now reached this point, rather than any clear idea of what, if anything, is qualitatively different about modern technology, that leads to the assertion that ours is an unprecedentedly technological age. For while it is difficult to pin down any qualitative as opposed to quantitative difference setting modern technologies apart from those we have inherited, it is impossible to ignore the extent to which the development of technique, in the widest sense, has made us responsible for the future of man and world together in a way that is indeed historically and qualitatively unprecedented. What I am suggesting is that, contrary to what may be implied by the notion that we moderns are at once the creatures and creators of a distinct "Age of Technology", it is awareness of our increased *de facto* responsibility rather than anything inherent in the nature of today's technology that characterizes the uneasy consciousness of the present time.

To put it another way, the characteristic anxiety of the technological age is based not so much on mistrust of technology itself as on man's increasingly conscious mistrust of himself. This element of self-doubt is not a function of any change in human nature but of a disturbing awareness of the growing disproportion between the powers at man's disposal and his essentially unaltered capacity to judge rightly how they are to be used. The alteration in what I have called the balance of power between man and nature gives rise to a situation in which, ever more clearly, problems of technology are bound up with ethical and political problems with which we seem peculiarly ill-prepared to deal.

Some thirty years ago Arnold Gehlen identified this crucial feature in our situation when he wrote: "What men fear are not the monstrous destructive energies of the atomic nucleus, but their own; not the H-bomb but themselves. They sense, rightly, that they cannot count on an internal constraint upon the use of a power one holds in one's hands to emerge suddenly in the final stage of a development, whose main tendency for two hundred years has been exactly to remove such constraints, to further and enhance a purely objective, rational and technical concern with effectiveness." [4] Underlying Gehlen's words is the recognition that the increasingly rapid development of man's technical powers over the last two centuries has been accompanied by a decline in the effectiveness of any spiritual or moral elements, ideas and/or institutions, that might constrain their use. Quite apart from the already mentioned factors that have undermined the authority of forms of non-technological, religious and political, rationality, the very success of technological achievement has tended to destroy man's sense of dependence on any power, natural or supernatural, greater than himself. And so at a time when we seem urgently to require some form of authoritative guidance to cope with the ethical and political issues opened up by the advance of technology, we lack both the ethics and the institutions that might provide it.

Gehlen's approach to these problems derives from his distinctive theory of man and the human condition — a naturalistic variant of philosophical anthropology that understands the political and technological dynamic of human achievement as a many-faceted response to an initial state of organic and instinctual deficiency which has no parallel in the animal world. "Ultimately," he writes, "all attainments of the human mind remain enigmatic; but the enigma would be all the more impenetrable if not seen in connection with man's organic and instinctual deficiencies; for his intellect relieves him of the necessity to undergo organic adaptations to which animals are subject, and conversely allows him to alter his original circumstances to suit himself." [5] How or why such a form of being arose is beyond the scope of our present considerations; and in a sense, it may even be irrelevant whether or not we accept its historical accuracy as a picture of man's primordial state. In heuristic terms alone, Gehlen's model of man as an organically and instinctually deficient being would retain its value as a way of making intelligible the diverse dimensions of human activity and thus of helping us to understand something about the problems we now face. For the need to respond creatively — that is through forms of activity guided by conscious reflection — while providing sufficient reason for the development of forms of political organization and of technology, also gives us a clue as to why the states of being we attain through such responses remain forever fragile and problematic.

The source of this fragility, which underlies the problem of responsibility in its broadest sense, emerges clearly when, once more, we set the life forms of man and animal alongside each other in order to discover what seems to make them distinct from one another. Man and animal alike face the problem of ensuring their survival in a potentially threatening world; but while the solutions available to the animal are entailed in its genetic inheritance, those of man must be formed and transmitted through processes entailing conscious reflection, cultural creation and the appropriation of tradition. Here we encounter a different though related dimension of responsibility — man's responsibility not merely for the creation of a space which makes his life possible but for the cultivation of those disciplined attitudes which protect him from imagining that such a space, which is, necessarily, a politically institutionalised world or culture, could ever be a free gift of nature. No organism is or can be responsible for its genetic inheritance, but responsibility, the Janus-faced concomitant of man's reflective consciousness, is inseparable from the burden and benefit of culture — the artificial nature in which alone it is man's nature to dwell.

The problem of man's responsibility for the maintenance of a humanly possible state of being is thus, like technology itself, a primordial feature of human life. They are, indeed, only the two sides of a single anthropological coin. As a problem, however, it becomes more acute the further man goes along his destined path of modifying and all but transforming his surroundings. For, throughout the course of human history, the world man comes to inhabit, his supporting environment, becomes one in which the marks of artifice are pro-gressively more deeply inscribed. At least since the agricultural revolution, through irrigation, deforestation and the selective breeding of plants and animals, the art of man has entered into the very structures of nature. As a result of this, the boundary between the ontologically given and the humanly chosen—the objects, respectively, of pure theory and of practice — has altogether lost what, perhaps deceptively, we imagine to have been its original clarity. Whatever boundary there may be has shifted, without ever quite vanishing, to the point where it has ceased to have any correspondence with the apparently related common sense distinction, beloved of the advertising industry and still so influential on the more naive forms of ecological thought, between the natural and the artificial. In consequence, almost imperceptibly at first, man's original responsibility for his own survival has tended to become a matter of responsibility for the world as a whole.

This must lead us to question the general validity of the dictionary definition of the word *artificial*, according to which it means "produced by art and not by nature" or "produced by art and not existing in nature." In the area that concerns us here, and in the light of Helmuth Plessner's convincing analysis of what he suggestively terms man's "natural artificiality", this mutually exclusive distinction is unhelpful. Adopted uncritically it may even be dangerous, encouraging, in the face of present anxieties, the development of ecological thought in the direction of a romantic primitivism as impossible as it is inhuman. For, less than ever is it possible to make a clear distinction between the works of man and the resources of nature which support him. The earth bears the inexpungeable marks of human efforts and the very fruits of the field are cultivated for consumption in forms created by centuries of selective breeding. Only the existence of such "artifical" forms of life — sub-species created by man and incapable of independent survival — allows the human race to exist in anything like its present numbers.

This, I admit, is very far from being an unmixed blessing; and it may well be that even the present size of the world's population will produce tensions that will preclude any solution of the problem, at once political and technological, of how our species is to survive in a world for whose own survival it has made itself factually responsible. On the scale of humanity as a whole there is now no safety in numbers; but any efforts we make to cope with this situation are and must be further steps along the path of artifice — measures to be politically decided and instituted by whatever means may seem technically appropriate and ethically acceptable. The point to be stressed is that, *pace* the dreams of a certain romantic ecologism, there is no self-regulating balance of nature on which we, as a species, could fall back. At this level at least, history is irreversible and with it the burden of responsibility we have assumed. Whatever the future holds, it will not be a paradisiac return to, or, as Ernst Bloch fantasized, a new arrival at a utopian state of harmony with nature. That was never man's way in the world. It is not now, and never can be.

3. Myth and Modernity

In his book *Work on Myth*,[6] Hans Blumenberg makes a fascinating case for the mutual entailment of what may be called, respectively, the hermeneutic and the anthropological aspects of this situation, drawing attention to the extent to which the truth of man's successive schemes of self-interpretation, whether mythical, religious or scientific, is always, more or less directly, bound up with his need to come to terms with the ontologically limited and yet existentially unfixed character of his nature and place in the world.

Starting from assumptions rooted in Gehlen's theory of man as an instinctually deprived or "deficient" being, Blumenberg interprets the course of human history in terms of the unceasing effort to overcome an initial situation of human being in which "man came close to not having control of the conditions of his existence and, what is more important, believed that he simply lacked control of them."[7] Man in this, his original situation, is subject to what Blumenberg calls "the absolutism of reality"; and it is the human response to this primordial state of powerlessness which is recorded in the evidence of subsequent history.

Blumenberg's evocation of this initial situation echoes Gehlen's conviction that we cannot hope to elucidate the enigmatic nature of human attainments without reference to man's organic and instinctual deficiencies; though, unlike Gehlen himself, Blumenberg does not feel it necessary to lay out the direct evidence we have for the historical, or rather pre-historical, reality of such a state. Rather, he speaks, in primarily heuristic terms, of the notion of a limit situation, that of the absolutism of reality, as playing a role in his theory equivalent to that played by the 'state of nature' in older theories of culture and the state: that is, a "concept of the limit toward which the extrapolation of tangible, historical features into the archaic tends."[8] In other words, Blumenberg presents the anthropological hypothesis of the original absolutism of reality as the conceptual key that opens the door to an intelligible hermeneutic of the full range of human culture.

Though dominated by the requirement of survival, the human response to the absolutism of reality is not, as our emphasis on technology may have suggested, merely narrowly practical, directed only toward the material modification of the world, but symbolic and cognitive as well. According to Blumenberg's reading, the world interpretations of myth, of religion and of science are, no less than tools and weapons, instruments of human survival; attempts to overcome an initially threatening world of nameless forces by reducing it to a state in which it can be comprehended and so cognitively mastered. To name is already, in a certain sense, to tame, and so to help create the existential space, the world of culture, in which man's continuing survival can be ensured. "All trust", Blumenberg writes, "begins with names in connection with which stories can be told. This state of affairs is involved in the biblical story of the beginning, with the giving of names in Paradise. But it is also involved in the faith that underlies all magic and that is still characteristic of the beginnings of science, the faith that the suitable naming of things will suspend the enmity between them and man, turning it into a relationship of pure serviceability. The fright that has found the way back to language has already been endured." [9]

At the level of symbolic achievement, man makes himself at home in the world through a process of linguistic representation, in which the given data of existence are subjected to interpretation and represented as a coherent cosmos in which he can conceive himself as having an intelligible place and destiny. Blumenberg argues that such representations, which are manifest in the typical symbolic forms of myth, religion and science, are, like tools and weapons, subject through human history to a process of quasi-natural selection — a process he suggestively terms the "Darwinism of words." The words that survive the trials of time, and therefore the patterns of words embodied in successive patterns of self-interpretation, are those which prove most effective not only in extending man's control over the world but in making sense of the changing existential situations in which he finds himself. Thus, parallel to the perennial march of technological achievement, we find an unceasing "work on myth" — an equally perennial reworking of the initial patterns of human self-interpretation to take account of man's increasing awareness of his responsibility for his own fate and, ultimately, that of the world. In his book, Blumenberg illustrates this process primarily through a detailed examination of the way in which the myth of Prometheus has been successively appropriated and reworked in the cultural history of the West.

In the context of a discussion of technology the Prometheus myth, or rather the successive "mythologies" that can be drawn from it, may seem to occupy a privileged position. The story of the theft of fire from the gods is, after all, the technological myth *par excellence* — a tale of how man acquires the means to overcome his initial state of deficiency: and it is significant that, from its first cultural appearance in the poems of Hesiod, it is fraught with ambiguous implications. Depending on the outlook of the mythologist, it can be read either as a blasphemous seizure of powers which are not man's by right or as a praiseworthy triumph of human ingenuity over the life-threatening powers that initially govern the cosmos.

The greater becomes the confidence in technological progress as the royal road to human fulfilment, the more man tends to identify himself with the figure of Prometheus as he appears in the second reading. This second Prometheus is the anthropologically beneficent and guiltless Prometheus who is the boyhood hero of Karl Marx and whose spirit imbues the predominant optimism of the nineteenth century world-view. From such a 'Prometheanism' the ambiguity of the ancient myth is significantly absent. Of course, in the case of Marx, the other aspect of the myth, Prometheus the blasphemer, the implacable enemy of divine power, is also a central ingredient of the vision of the human condition; but here blasphemy has ceased to be a crime and become a duty, a necessary precondition for a truly human existence.

This reflects Marx's anthropological or, rather, misanthropological vision in which man is imagined as only becoming fully human when no longer subject to or even constrained by any non-human, natural or supernatural power. Divine power is to be banished from a world in which man alone must be the master if he is to survive and flourish. The pursuit of unconstrained human autonomy, as the most all-embracing of the rights of man, is seen as incompatible with recognition of any divine right to order the cosmos. And this because divine right, in nature as well as in political society, is seen simply as the sanctification of given conditions which it is man's destiny to overcome.

Thus far, Marx has gone no further than the Feuerbach of *The Essence of Christianity*, whose criticism of religion is, as he avows, the necessary foundation of all further criticism. Where he does go further is in extending the Feuerbachian disavowal of the autonomy of the divine to a no less radical, anti-Feuerbachian disavowal of the autonomy of the natural. This is the step he takes in the Theses on Feuerbach, which begin with the sentence: "The chief defect of all hitherto existing materialism that of Feuerbach included is that the thing, reality, sensuousness, is conceived only in the form of the object or of contemplation, but not as sensuous human activity, practice, not subjectively", and end with the famous assertion that "the philosophers have only interpreted the world, in various ways: the point is to change it." In this way, the Prometheanism of the nineteenth century, exemplified in the work of Marx, disowns the ambivalence inherent in the original myth in an unequivocal assertion of man's right to restructure the conditions of his existence, natural as well as social and political. The relationship between man and world is indeed to be reduced to one of "pure serviceability".

Though new in its application to the socio-political realm, this 'right' to change the world is something that had always been tacitly assumed within the sphere of technique itself, in which, as we have seen, practical effectiveness is, and always was, the sole intrinsic criterion of judgement. What is more, whatever criticisms we may have to make of Marx's position, the transformatory imperative to which he appeals against what he thinks of as the passivity of Feuerbachian materialism is fully in keeping with the reality of man's historical relationship with nature. This relationship was never wholly, nor even primarily contemplative. For the primacy of contemplation is incompatible with the demands placed upon man by an original condition of deficiency in which the price of survival is precisely the moulding to human purposes of the initially given conditions of existence. What then is wrong with Marx's move?

Here let us cite, once more, the words of Blumenberg, that, while "man is always already on this side of the absolutism of reality. . . he never entirely attains the certainty that he has reached the turning-point in his history at which the relative predominance of reality over his consciousness and his fate has turned into the supremacy of the subject." [10] Nor, *pace* Marx's claim that reality, properly conceived, must be seen as "sensuous human activity, practice", can he ever attain such a certainty.

The supremacy of the human subject over reality, which Marx, in conformity with his Hegelian inheritance, seeks to vindicate, is ultimately belied by the unbreakable dependence of human survival upon respect for conditions which it is beyond man's power to alter. Reality is always more than "sensuous human activity", to which it provides both the historical, existential limit and the ontological foundation. But to see this one would have to draw a distinction that was utterly foreign to Marx's mind — a distinction, already occluded by Kant's denial of the knowability of what he called the "noumenal world of things-in-themselves" and banished from Marx's philosophical horizon by Hegel's identification of Being with the self-realization of Spirit. That is the distinction between the ontologically given conditions of man's being in the world and the ever-finite realm of existential possibilities opened up in the adventure of history. The first are encountered initially in the resistance which the world offers to human historical activity and, perhaps definitively, in the late twentieth century rediscovery of the limited resources of the earth.

Man does indeed always relate to nature in the active mode of self-realization, as creative creature, but the space of creativity is always bounded by the ontological structure of a world, a reality in itself, that makes the continuing existence of a creative being such as man possible. Beyond the proper scope of practice lies an order of things before which we can only stop to contemplate and, where possible, understand.

So long as the balance of power remained tipped in nature's favour the exclusivity of the criterion of practical effectiveness in man's dealings with the natural world posed no great existential problems. However, once nature had been reduced to dependence on man, albeit in an ontologically ambiguous fashion, once it had become what I have called a 'quasi-institution', the same criterion became a highly dubious guide to action. For in itself the technological criterion of practical, world-transforming effectiveness provides us with no way of distinguishing the point at which transformatory action, without ceasing to be apparently beneficial in the short term, begins to undermine the possibility of there continuing to be a humanly habitable world. At such a point, when considered in the light of the fundamental anthropological interest in survival, the inherent logic of technology, a logic that is itself anthropologically entailed in the primordial human need to master an initially threatening world, ceases to be sufficient unto itself. The logic of the quest for ever more effective means of transforming nature and the imperative of human survival, from which the anthropological legitimacy of that quest derives as a necessary consequence of man's original and enduring natural deficiencies, cease to coincide and even, at the limit, become mutually exclusive.

In this historically specific position, sound judgement, not least within the technical sphere, requires the application of criteria that are foreign and even opposed to the inherently transformatory dynamic of technology. The source of such criteria, which are required to provide a logic of self-limitation, are only to be found by recourse to spheres of life and thought in which, in contrast to the sphere of *techne*, human action had always been shaped by awareness that the conditions conducive to the good life, and perhaps to life itself, were themselves dependent on human conservation and care. That is, from the traditions of practical, prudential reasoning about the moral and political dimensions of human life —pre-ideological traditions that embodied an assertion of the primacy of conservation over transformation, and which recognized that, in politics at least, the fundamental imperative is not to change the world but to conserve it.

The problem here is that, in the intellectual and spiritual climate of modernity, such traditions tend to be undervalued in comparison with what is perceived as the self-evident value of a bountiful technology —a technology which can, if required, further justify itself by reference to its affiliation with the universally respected and respectable knowledge provided by the natural sciences. Thus, far from the prudential logic of practical reason finding a place in the projects of technology, as now would seem to be required, the transformatory logic of technique tends to dominate the prevailing forms of political discourse. The purpose of politics, like that of technology, comes to be conceived, in the manner typical of future-oriented ideology, as the transformation rather than the conservation of the world. At the extreme, as represented by the visionary works of Ernst Bloch, politics and technology are presented as equivalent and parallel vehicles of ontological transformation, of what Eric Voegelin terms 'metastasis', whose ultimate purpose is to raise man to a qualitatively higher level of being. In this way, mankind, the collective Prometheus, can finally be unbound from the oppressive chains of finitude.

Though Bloch is, as I say, an extreme case, his pattern of thought is revealingly representative of a crucial element in modern, ideological conceptions of politics. In Reinhart Koselleck's view, such conceptions involve a radical break between what he calls "the space of experience" and "the horizon of expectation." [11] The lessons of experience, which refer to the past, and which provide the sources of political pedagogy in all pre-ideological notions of practical, prudential reason, whether we take our preferred model of such a philosophy from Aristotle, from Machiavelli or from Hume, are, in the ideological politics of modernity, devalued as guides to present practice and dismissed from their previous role as providing limits to our expectations for the future. The reasons for this are interesting insofar as they explain both the continuing strength of the ideological conception of politics as a primarily transformatory activity, in spite of the horrifying results that regularly follow in the wake of attempts to put such transformatory politics into practice, and the difficulties that are faced by any attempt to vindicate once more the claims of an older political wisdom.

The crucial point is this: the modern devaluation of the significance of experience as a framework for expectation is not merely, nor even primarily, the result of a wilfull ignorance or forgetfulness of history — a peculiar and enigmatic conceit of modern man. Even a world-view that systematically devalues the pedagogy of the past, and dismisses as irrelevant the exemplary significance of past happenings, is no exception to the rule that all such views derive whatever power they possess over the human mind by virtue of their apparent capacity to make sense of lived experience. What Koselleck refers to as the tension between experience and expectation is, as he notes, an anthropological constant; and if the contemporary form of this tension seems to divorce the horizon of expectation from the historically knowable space of experience, that too must be understood as having an historical experiential basis. What we may condemn as the *hubris* of utopian expectations, expectations divorced from the space of experience and thus from what we know of the human condition, only becomes intelligible at all when set against certain distinctive features which are part and parcel of the experience of modernity. Without reference to this experiential foundation for the disavowal of experience the whole phenomenon is incomprehensible.

This becomes especially obvious when we consider, first, the gap between the promises and the achievements of utopian ideologies and of the political experiments that have been based on them, and, second, the enduring appeal of such ideologies despite their manifest failures in practice. For example, it is certainly not by its recorded, still less its unrecorded deeds that the advocates of Marxist socialism would want us to know it. The appeal, such as it is, is exclusively to the expectation of an imagined future whose credibility depends, precisely, upon its utter disengagement from the reality of past experience. The continuing viability of such an appeal depends in turn, not upon a collective historical amnesia, which is hardly possible, but upon an understanding of history which, at the risk of solecism, we may term the peculiarly modern experience of experience. That is, an experience of historical time as a shifting field in which expectations engendered by the past regularly prove themselves inadequate to the comprehension of the unfolding present.

To put the matter concisely, future expectation is not freed from the prognostic guidance of past experience because, in any simple sense, experience can be dismissed as irrelevant. Rather the nature of our modern experience of an ever-accelerating pace of political, technological and industrial change is such that expectations, derived from past experience, are regularly experienced as being outpaced by what actually comes to pass. In this way, under the conditions of modernity, experience itself tends to undermine whatever claims it may have had to condition future expectation.

The result of this is that, even when, as generally happens, unfolding events turn out to be inimical to what was desired, let alone expected, their unprecedented novelty is enough to seem to disqualify any return from future-oriented ideologies to a conception of practical philosophy which, like those of Aristotle, Machiavelli and Hume, rests on the presumption of the constancy of the human condition. The failure of ideological projections leads not to a restoration of pre-ideological notions of the scope of human action, but to a state of confusion and unease in which the choice seems to lie between an ever more irresponsible reassertion of utopian hopes and a qualified fatalism which distracts itself from thoughts of apocalypse with schemes of piecemeal social engineering that reproduce in miniature the failures of institutionalized utopianism, and with the creation of "ethical committees" charged with regulating areas of scientific knowledge and technological enterprise whose exponential growth they have no adequate means of controlling.

4. The Place of Ethics

In this concluding section I shall try to draw out some of the practical, ethical, consquences that flow from the situation described above; paying special attention to Hans Jonas' recent endeavours to formulate what he calls "an ethics for the technological age".

We have seen that, even in the intrinsically transformatory sphere of technology, the metastatic notion that human activity can fundamentally transform the character, and, particularly, the inherent structure of ontological dependence that is the foundation of our being, involved a grotequely exaggerated notion of what action can accomplish. For, even in becoming a sphere whose continued existence is subject to the uncertainties of human decision, and thus a human responsibility, nature retains, its original ontological primacy over the creatures who depend upon it, including man himself. In overcoming the initial form of the absolutism of reality, in which reality is experienced as a realm of forces utterly beyond human control, man does not thereby overcome the effective primacy of the real. Not only do his actions create new levels of reality which impose upon him burdens of their own; but these spheres, cultural, political and technological, remain ultimately dependent upon the subsistence of the very level, nature *tout court,* against whose threats the 'second nature' of civilization is initially created.

The dependence of nature on man, which is such a salient feature of the contemporary world, and which results from our success in learning to make use of the once incomprehensible forces which threatened our existence, cannot therefore obviate the more fundamental dependence of man on nature, nor abolish the ontological limit that this entails. The extension of human mastery over nature entails not the absolutism of freedom, as technological utopians like Bloch once imagined, but, rather, the absolute burden of responsibility for the survival of a world in which life remains possible. This, in essence, is the reality of a situation, at once novel and rooted in the primordial imperatives of human life, which underlies our current state of unease.

In itself, such existential uncertainty is nothing new. It is inseperable from the reflective life of the members of a species uniquely aware both of their own individual mortality, and of the ambiguous effects of the self-created powers at their disposal. What, however, does seem to be new about the present form of existential uncertainty is that its object is displaced from the limited perspective of the present to include all potential futures. Uncertainty has been radicalised to the extent that we have come to recognise that we are capable not only of cutting back what presently lives but of tearing life up by the roots. Unlike our remote ancestors we need no longer doubt the technical efficacy of the powers we have to hand. It is not their insufficiency that we need fear but their extraordinary potency, in comparison with which our inherited powers of judgement seem weak indeed. Existential mastery of nature sits uneasily alongside a renewed and urgent sense of ontological dependence.

In the perspective of Gehlen's anthropology, the existential uncertainty of the contemporary world can be seen to reproduce, on a cosmic scale and in response to a scientifically informed analysis of the possible conditions of existence, the same survival anxiety which has formed part of man's condition from the beginning. In the same light, it may even be that the radical uncertainty which seems uniquely to characterise our present age is also not without precedent. Paradoxically though, we seem to share it not with our immediate historical prdecessors, but with the inhabitants of those archaic societies, described by Mircea Eliade, which lived in the belief that cosmic catastrophe was always imminent and could only be held off through the careful and regular practice of rituals of world renewal.[12] In some ways we may be existentially closer to such cultures than to the optimistic world-view of that earlier stage of modernity when recognition of the dynamism of human achievement was taken to imply that the intrinsic risks and liabilities of life were about to be definitively overcome. If our's is still, in some ways, a 'Promethean' age, its Prometheanism is marked anew by awareness of the profound ambiguities that attend man's assumption of responsibility for his fate.

By this I mean that in the phase of modernity we have now entered our sense of what is at stake in the actions we undertake is closer to that imagined by the men of archaic civilizations – on whom responsibility for political and cosmic order weighed with equal force –than to the characteristic attitudes of the last two centuries, in which trust in technological advance went hand in hand with belief in a form of intellectual progress that was simultaneously scientific and ethical. If this is so, and if we are right in conceiving our future to be unprecedentedly at risk, then we may find more salutary lessons in archaic conceptions of world order and man's place within it than in the still potent legacy of Enlightenment optimism. In particular, we will find ourselves having to reformulate our ideas of ethical and political responsibility to take account of responsibility for realms of being which, in Enlightenment thought, were considered to be subject only to the automatism of a physical order beyond human disturbance. What this implies is not a revival of archaic myths of the sources of human responsibility for cosmic order, but the formulation of a practical philosophy – an ethics and a politics – that takes proper account of the reality of that responsibility in our age.

In *The Imperative of Responsibility*, Hans Jonas has given an unequalled example of the sort of rethinking required. Jonas' book takes as its starting point the situation I have sought to describe above – one in which the growth in the technological powers at man's disposal has reached a point at which the causal reach of human action extends to the question of the very survival of the world. In the past, he writes: "The presence of man in the world has been a first and unquestionable given, from which all ideas of obligation in human conduct started out. Now it has itself become an *object* of obligation: the obligation namely to ensure the very premise of obligation, that is, the *foothold* of a moral universe in the physical world – the existence of mere *candidates* for a moral order. This entails, among other things, the duty to preserve this physical world in such a state that the conditions for that presence remain intact; which in turn means protecting the world's vulnerability from what could imperil those conditions." [13]

The field of ethics remains, as ever it was, coextensive with the area of reality subject to the effect of human decisions; but since this now includes the whole natural, organic and inorganic world, an ethics appropriate to the age must bring within its scope a range of issues which previous ethics could, quite properly, ignore. Where, previously, ethics could confine itself to investigation of the conditions of right order among men and to the evaluation of the likely immediate consequences of action, it must now take account of what Jonas calls man's obligation to nature – both in itself and as the precondition for human life – and to the probable long-term effects of human activity. "We must", Jonas argues, "educate our soul to a willingness to let itself be affected by the mere thought of possible fortunes and calamities of future generations, so that the projections of futurology will not remain mere food for idle curiosity or equally idle pessimism." [14]

It is not tempermental pessimism but a carefully calculated awareness of the disproportion between the scope of technology and the finite resources of nature, including human nature, that leads Jonas to propose, in explicit opposition to Bloch's famous *Principle of Hope*, an 'heuristics of fear' as the guiding principle in our future conduct. [15] Acceptance of such a principle does not entail abstention from technological innovation but only that we give extra weight to what we can see to be reasonable and scientifically well-founded fears about the effects such innovation may have. In seeming to tip the balance of judgement in this way, an heuristics of fear actually does no more than redress the initial imbalance produced by the inherent innovatory dynamic of technology itself. Seen in this light, the heuristics of fear, which Jonas proposes, is not a recommendation of pessimism but a reassertion of the traditional – Thomist and Aristotelian as well as Humean – primacy of prudence among the virtues required in practical reasoning.

The need for such a generalised restatement is a result of what I have called the shift in the balance of power between man and nature – a shift whose most significant feature is that, under the impact of human agency, nature is seen no longer to possess the seemingly inexhaustible capacity for self-regeneration that previous generations could take for granted. This introduces a new dimension into what traditionally has been seen as the domain of practical philosophy; a dimension in which, on the one hand, consideration of complex and long-term scientific and technological projections must play a central, informing role in determining political and ethical considerations, and, on the other, where considerations of prudence, the stock in trade of practical decision making, must be introduced into a field of human activity in which previously they played little or no part at all.

Out of this situation there emerges a whole complex of problems which demand further careful investigation by philosophy and the human sciences. Many of them are raised and clarified by Jonas himself in the course of his attempt to develop the principles on which an ethics of cosmic responsibility must rest. The most significant aspect of his argument, beyond the lucidity of the way in which he describes the existential novelty of man's present situation, lies in his elaboration of a metaphysics of morals derived from the philosophy of nature enunciated in his previous work, in particular *The Phenomenon of Life*.[15] According to this philosophy, the realm of nature is permeated by teleology, not in the sense that it plays any knowable part in a Divinely ordained scheme of things, but simply because every organism is oriented in its activities toward its own survival.

The reformulation of a practical philosophy, a politics and ethics attuned to our technological age, is therefore, at root, a practical imperative derived from the orientation to survival that we share with every living being, and which is, as we have seen, also at the source of technology itself. As a moral project, a sensed obligation directed toward our survival as moral beings, it is clearly one that has no precise equivalent in the animal world. And yet, in so far as its aim is to preserve ourselves in our ontologically given state of being as moral beings, it is just as clearly derived from the guiding imperative which runs through the whole phenomenon of life. Surely there could be no more urgent philosophical task – nor any more likely to remind us of our rootedness in the wider order of a being we did not create – than the further development of a line of thinking on which our very future may depend.

Notes

1. David J. Levy *Political Order*, (Louisiana: Louisiana State University Press, 1987).

2. Hans Jonas *The Imperative of Responsibility: Towards an Ethics for the Technological Age*, (Chicago, 1984).

3. Jonas op.cit. p.10.

4. Arnold Gehlen, *Man in the Age of Technology*, (New York, 1980), p,101.

5. Gehlen op.cit p.4.

6. Hans Blumenberg, *Work on Myth*, (MIT Press, 1985).

7. Blumenberg op.cit. p.3.

8. ibid.

9. ibid. p.9

10. ibid. p.10

11. Reinhart Koselleck, *Futures Past: On the Semantics of Historical Time*, (MIT Press, 1985).

12. Mircea Eliade, *The Myth of the Eternal Return*, (Princeton University Press 1954).

13. Jonas op.cit. p.10

14. ibid p.28.

15. Chicago, 1966.

8

ISRAEL AND JUDAH

Politics and Religion in the Two Hebrew Kingdoms

In or about 930 B.C. King Solomon died in his royal city of Jerusalem. In a long and generally peaceful reign of forty years Solomon had consolidated the single Hebrew monarchy established by his father David. Under Solomon the monarchy remained what it had become under King David, the most important political and military power in the area that lies between the river Euphrates and the frontiers of Egypt. Within a year of Solomon's death this situation was transformed. Rehoboam, Solomon's son and designated heir, continued to reign in Jerusalem but his kingdom was confined to the city itself, the territory of the southern tribe of Judah and part of the lands of the tribe of Benjamin.

Even before Solomon's death, there were clear signs that all was not well within what is sometimes called, with only marginal exaggeration, the Davidic Empire. Resentment among the Northern Hebrew tribes at the burdens, in tax and forced labour, resulting from the King's ambitious military and religious building projects, had already led to an attempt at secession under the leadership of Jeroboam, son of Nabat. Solomon had suppressed the rebellion but Jeroboam had escaped to Egypt and, as events were to show, remained a potent threat to the political authority of the Davidic dynasty and the unity of the Hebrew peoples. Meanwhile two of Solomon's non-Hebrew tributaries, King Hadad of Edom and King Rezon of Damascus, had taken advantage of the situation to throw off the burden of allegiance to Jerusalem.

A politically astute successor might have saved the situation, preserved the unity of the Hebrew kingdom and restored its hegemony in the region. The new King Rehoboam was not such a man. Having agreed to meet the elders of the northern tribes at Shechem in order to hear their complaints against his father's rule, he ignored the advice of his senior advisors and, instead of righting, or even pretending to right, their grievances, he responded by boasting of his power and threatening increased burdens. The result was renewed rebellion which Rehoboam was unable to suppress. Jeroboam, already returned from exile, became effective ruler of the ten northern tribes as King of Israel while Rehoboam fled south to Jerusalem to reign as monarch of the residual Kingdom of Judah.

Throughout the reigns of Rehoboam, Jeroboam and their immediate successors there was intermittent war between the two kingdoms, as each sought to establish its power over the disputed territory of the tribe of Benjamin. The local Palestinian potentates, who had paid tribute to David and to Solomon, seized the opportunity to re-establish their independence; and, to the north, the new dynasty in Damascus consolidated its power and expanded its territory at the expense of Israel. The political primacy of the Hebrew kings in the area was over. It had lasted a mere seventy years.

For the next two hundred years the two kingdoms of Israel and Judah existed alongside each other. At times they were at war with one another: at others they were allies fighting together against some other power. The fortunes of each waxed and waned; but at no time, not even in the forty years of prosperity which coincided with the reign of Jeroboam II in Israel 786-746 and Uzziah in Judah 783-742, was either kingdom more than one among the multitude of small Western Semitic, Palestinian and Syriac states which maintained a precarious existence between Egypt and Mesopotamia.

Through most of this period Egypt was relatively quiescent, beset by internal problems which prevented it from re-establishing its authority in Western Asia. The main threat to the survival of the mutually hostile kingdoms of Syria and Palestine came from the East with the rise of the great power of Assyria. In 853 a temporary alliance between the northern Kingdom of Israel, ruled by Ahab, and the Aramaean kingdoms of Damascus and Hamath fought a bloody battle against the Assyrians under Shalmaneser III 859-824 at Qarqar in what is now western Syria. Though the Assyrians claimed victory over an army to which King Ahab had contributed the impressive force of 10,000 infantry and 2,000 chariots, the battle seems to have been indecisive. Shalmaneser withdrew from Syria only to return in 849 in the first of a series of campaigns which culminated in the unsuccessful siege of Damascus in 841. Thereafter the Assyrian challenge was not renewed for nearly forty years until Adad-Nirari attacked Damascus again in 803. After this the threat of Assyrian conquest of the West Semitic states was constant.

In the short term, permanent Assyrian pressure on the Kingdom of Damascus after 803 weakened the power of Israel's most dangerous local enemy, making possible the temporary revival of Israelite power under Jeroboam II in the middle of the eighth century B.C.. Only gradually and too late did it become apparent that an Assyrian threat to the independence of the Aramaean kingdoms must also threaten the Kingdom of Israel. At the last moment Israel and Damascus decided once more to act together. This time, unlike at Qarqar, the result was disaster. In 732 Damascus fell to the Assyrian King Tiglath-Pileser III, and ten years later his successor, Sargon II, captured Samaria, the capital of Israel, after a siege of three years. The northern Hebrew kingdom, already greatly diminished by Assyrian annexations, was destroyed.

To the south, the King of Judah, Ahaz 735-715, was by this time already a tributary of Assyria. In 734 he had wisely refused to join the anti-Assyrian coalition led by King Rezin of Damascus and King Pekah of Israel. In an effort to force Judah to join and strengthen their desperate alliance a joint Israelite/Aramaean army had invaded the southern kingdom with the intention of replacing its recalcitrant monarch with one more sympathetic to the allied cause. Ahaz had appealed to the Assyrians for help, and, with Tiglath-Pileser's attack on Damascus, relief had come, though at the price of Judah's becoming a tributary of Assyria. The invading armies had withdrawn from Judah to face the Assyrians and defeat. Rezin of Damascus was killed when his capital fell, and in the same year, 732, Pekah of Israel was deposed and replaced on the throne of a diminished Israel by an Assyrian nominee, Hoshea. When the new Israelite king, perhaps with Egyptian encouragement, refused to pay his tribute, Samaria too was destroyed and the northern kingdom wiped from the face of the world.

The Kingdom of Judah survived for a further 140 years, outlasting the Assyrian Empire itself by a quarter century, until it too fell to another Mesopotamian power, the revived Babylonian empire under Nebuchadnezzar, who finally destroyed Jerusalem in 587. Through most of this period Judah was vassal of one great power or another — at first Assyria, then, briefly, Egypt, and finally Babylon. The ultimate fall of Jerusalem came, like that of Samaria before it, when the ruler nominated by the imperial power, the unfortunate and indecisive Zedekiah, refused his required tribute and brought down upon himself and his kingdom the full might of a Mesopotamian army. With the fall of Jerusalem the great temple of Yahweh, built by Solomon, was destroyed. The monarchy was abolished and the political independence of what remained of the Hebrew kingdom of David and Solomon was brought to an end.

Even from this brief overview of political events it should be clear that the history of the kingdoms of Israel and Judah is complex, bloody and inextricably bound up with that of their immediate and more distant and powerful neighbours. We may speculate as to whether an alliance of Western Semitic kingdoms of the sort that fought the Assyrians to a standstill at Qarqar in the middle of the ninth century B.C. could have halted Assyrian expansion indefinitely; but such speculation is futile and takes no account of the political conditions of the area — marked as they were by bitter ethnic, dynastic and religious rivalries.

Three years before Assyrian power was temporarily checked at Qarqar by Israelites and Aramaeans in alliance, Ahab of Israel had been at war with King Ben-Hadad II of Damascus. Three years after the battle he was at war with him again, this time allied with King Jehoshaphat of Judah in a vain attempt to recapture the border city of Ramoth-Gilead. The mutual hatred and suspicion between the petty kingdoms of Palestine and Syria made anything but the most temporary alliances between them impossible. Assyria, though periodically distracted from her western neighbours by problems to the north and east, had only to wait in order to pick off the states one by one. This was the pattern events were to follow throughout the eighth century. No long-term alliance of minor West Asian kingdoms was ever on the cards. The only power in the area that ever had the imperial potential that could, perhaps, have provided an effective political and military barrier to the western expansion of the Mesopotamian empires had been the united Hebrew monarchy as it had existed under David and Solomon; and this, as we have seen, collapsed with the accession of Rehoboam to the Jerusalem throne.

The political history of the kingdoms of Israel and Judah between 930 and 587, while fascinating as a chronicle of intrigue, struggle and fatefully frustrated ambitions, would have seemed, then and for a long time after, of very minor importance in comparison with the rise and fall of the great imperial powers. It derives its unique, abiding significance from the religious legacy inherited from the Hebrew worshippers of Yahweh by their ethnic and spiritual descendents, the Jews, and their spiritual cousins in Christianity and Islam. It is this that today makes us think back upon Assyria as an episode in the history of Israel, and not, as appeared at the time, on Israel as yet another doomed name notched upon the loaded victory steles of the Assyrian kings.

The period of the Hebrew monarchies was the age in which what is now called the Old Testament began to take recognizable form. Many of the Psalms, it is now clear, were originally composed for use in the cultic activities in Solomon's temple. Some, such as Psalms 80 and 81, originated in the Yahwistic sanctuaries of the Northern Kingdom. The age of Ahab the warrior was also the age of Elijah, the no less warlike prophet. Elijah's successor Elisha played a part in the downfall and extermination of the Omride dynasty to which Ahab belonged. In eighth century Israel, the land so successfully governed by Jeroboam II, Amos, the first of the 'writing prohets' who left us books bearing their names, proclaimed his implacable message of condemnation and doom. Hosea preached in the Northern Kingdom in the years immediately preceding its fall. In Judah, Isaiah of Jerusalem began to preach about the same time. After the fall of Israel, the land of "Ephraim, Benjamin and Manasseh" for whose national salvation the 80th Psalm still pleads, sacred traditions which were, in all probability, hitherto peculiar to the North, spread to the Kingdom of Judah, eventually giving rise to the composite but coherent Judaeo-Israelite theology of the Deuteronomist school. This theology, whose doctrinal core is to be found in the Book of Deuteronomy, underlies the historical judgements of the men who composed, out of existing records, the Books of Samuel and of Kings. The same theology provided the inspiration for the important religious reformation carried out by King Josiah 640-609 about 621 with the approval of Jeremiah, the last great prophet of the kingdoms. Though some scholars restrict the term Judaism to the form of religion established in Palestine after the end of the Babylonian exile, the outlines of this religion are already clear by the last quarter of the seventh century.

In speaking of the history of Israel and Judah it is impossible to separate the religious and political threads. The political histories of the kingdoms, though crucially dependent on events beyond their borders, were no less influenced by their peculiar religious identities. In turn, the religious identity inherited by later Judaism, and hence Christianity, from the Kingdom of Judah only survived and took the form it did because the southern kingdom continued to exist after northern Israel had fallen, and, as I shall argue, because over a century of precarious and incomplete independence the Yahwists of the Deuteronomist school incorporated the religious traditions of both in a single canon.

The success of the work of composition begun in the seventh century was considerable. Coherent narratives were spun out of diverse and sometimes conflicting chronicles and traditions. The overwhelming threat and promise of Yahweh's judgement runs as the predominant *leitmotif* through the composition as a whole. It unifies moments in which the prospect of harmonious resolution is prepared and continually deferred, until the theme of Israel's hope is left to the solo voice of Deutero-Isaiah's "suffering servant". Thence it is passed on to the post-exilic community and the future, of which we are still part.

Inheritors of a single "Old Testament", the story of the one people of Israel and their one God, Jews and Christians alike can read the prophetic books written before the fall of the monarchies without noticing that, while the theme of Yahweh's judgement upon his people is common to all of them, the origins of the bond between God and His chosen people are diversely reported. The casual reader of the Bible is unlikely to notice that while, in the late eighth century, the northern Israelite prophet Hosea invokes the tradition of the Exodus from Egypt, his younger Judaean contemporary Isaiah says nothing of any covenant between Yahweh and His people pre-dating the royal covenant between God and the dynasty of David. Both prophets appeal to the special relationship between Yahweh and the people but the root of this relationship is seen by each in utterly distinct events. Only retrospectively can these events be read as episodes in a single story —a sacred history which may indeed recall the reality of the formation of a single people under a single god, but which, in the days of Hosea and Isaiah, was apparently insignificant or beyond contemporary historical recall.

It was the subsequent task of the Deuteronomists of seventh century Judah to weld together the diverse traditions of Yahweh's northern and southern worshippers. To this end they constructed a historical theology around the figure of Moses and the proclamation of God's law in the Sinai desert. Drawing on the memory of a figure and an event which had, hitherto, played little part in either Israelite or Judaean theology, they made the history of Yahweh's dealings with Moses the axis point of a sacred history within which the patriarchal stories, sacred to Israel, and the Davidic covenant, sacred to Judah, could both find an intelligible place. In the light of this historical theology they composed the theological history which we now know in the historical books of the Old Testament.

By the time Jerusalem fell, this work of composition was sufficiently complete and theologically coherent to enable it to serve as the theological basis for a Jewish religion capable of surviving exile and the end of statehood. The union of Israel and Judah, politically broken by Israel's rejection of the House of David 300 years before, was remade in the last years of the Judaean kingdom in a form more enduring than the state itself. The paradigmatic history of Judah-Israel, formed by the Deuteronomists from the diverse traditions of Yahweh's worshippers, created a potent symbol around which the remnent of the Hebrew tribes could reform as, at last, a single people under God. The legatees of several covenants became the people of a single book. The shadowy and perhaps half-forgotten figure of Moses was raised from the obscurity of who knows what popular memory to become, not, like Jacob/Israel, one of the patriarchal ancestors of the people, nor, like Judah's David, a maker of the state, but the founder and first prophet of the Jewish faith.

In the light of Deuteronomist history the political schism between Israel and Judah is presented as a breaking apart of a single people of God. But, as the material incorporated by the Deuteronomist historians itself makes plain, there was, politically speaking, never such a people. In saying this I do not wish to deny that the Hebrew tribes may have shared a common ethnic origin, nor that Irving Zeitlin, following the Israeli scholar Yehezkel Kaufmann, may be correct in accepting the essential historical authenticity of the account of the conquest of Canaan given in the Book of Joshua.[1] Some students of Old

Testament history have certainly gone too far in discounting the biblical account of the conquest in favour of the hypothesis of a generally peaceful infiltration by a plurality of pastoralist clans. Nevertheless, as the example of the Anglo-Saxon invasion of Britain shows, ethnically and religiously related peoples, organized in tribes, may more or less simultaneously invade and settle a land without there being any form of political unity or even alliance between them. The idea that such groups form a single people may be more apparent to their victims than to themselves. The sense of unity in a community is never greater than when that community is under threat; and only when there is a common threat to diverse and formerly rival groups, the sort of threat which the Danes posed to the Anglo-Saxons and the Philistines to the Israelites, does the sense of shared origin become the basis of shared statehood.

In pre-monarchic days the territory of what was later to become Jeroboam's Kingdom of Israel was settled by a number of tribes who recognized their kinship with one another, tracing their ancestry to the sons of the patriarch Jacob and worshipping Yahweh as their god. It is customary to speak of pre-monarchic Israel as a tribal confederation sharing in the worship of a common God at mutually recognized shrines. This is fair enough provided we recognize that the tribes did not form any sort of political unit organized for regular, common action in the world. The very early "Song of Deborah" 5 Judges provides a rare and probably contemporary glimpse of joint action undertaken by the tribes of Ephraim, Issacher, Naphtali, Zebulon, Benjamin and Machir/ Manasseh about 1125 B.C. against an alliance of Canaanite kings led by Sisera. The eastern, trans-Jordanian tribes of Gilead and Reuben, the north western tribe of Asher and the tribe of Dan are mentioned and reproached for taking no part in the war. There is, of course, no mention of Judah, whose territory was isolated from the Israelite confederacy by the line of independent Canaanite city states, including Jerusalem, which ran along Judah's northern borders.

The wars of Gideon against the Midianite nomads also brought together an incomplete alliance of Hebrew tribes against a common enemy. Once again this alliance, led by a charismatic warrior, seems not to have outlasted the emergency produced by the nomad raids. In the end it was another, more formidable foreign threat, that of the Philistines, which provoked the establishment of a more permanent, institutionalized leadership in the monarchy of Saul, a Benjaminite whose title was "King" but whose authority depended, as much as that of such "judges" as Gideon, on his charisma.

The monarchy of Saul, whose charismatic and hence institutionally vulnerable character resembles that of the Israelite "judgeship" more than the common model of near-eastern kingship, proved incapable of overcoming the Philistine threat. But during Saul's brief reign Judah was drawn into the

Israelite struggle in the form of David, son of Jesse. The circumstances surrounding the foundation of Saul's kingship, his career and stormy relationship with the young Judaean warrior, his death in battle and the subsequent events which led to David's accession to the throne of Israel would, if fully recounted, more than fill the space of this essay. For present purposes it is enough to point out a few crucial facts which influence the subsequent development of the Hebrew monarchies.

Whichever of the two biblical accounts one takes of Saul's designation as king over Israel, it is clear that his right to the throne was seen as dependent upon his being the choice of Yahweh. His anointing by the seer Samuel and his acclamation by the Israelites were both acts of recognition that he was indeed Yahweh's choice. As his charisma was seen to fade, with his increasing fits of melancholy and depression, so the authority of his kingship ebbed away, and, with it, his chances of rallying the full host of Israel against the foe. Kingship in the northern state of Israel continued to reflect the persistent, destabilizing influence of the charismatic factor already apparent in the monarchy of Saul. As a result, the dynastic principle of hereditary monarchy was never strongly established in the North.

Jeroboam, original leader of Israel's secession from the Davidic kingdom was secretly anointed as the recognized choice of Yahweh by the prophet Ahijah of Shiloh even while Solomon still reigned in Jerusalem. Later, the fanatically Yahwist general Jehu, commander of the Israelite army, was anointed in similarly secret fashion by a prophetic follower of Elisha while the house of Omri still occupied the throne in Samaria. Prophetic anointing and public acclamation were essential to the legitimacy of the Israelite monarchy, but the mandate of kingship was revocable at any time by the voice of Yahweh speaking through a prophet. This, as will be apparent, was hardly a recipe for institutional stability, since even at times when a pattern of monarchical succession seemed to be emerging, no one could tell through whom the will of God would next declare itself.

The kingdom established by David in Judah, seven years before the Israelites offered him the northern crown in desperation and despair, was of a very different type. It seems initially to have rested on David's military power as leader of a trained band of professional soldiers; and then, particularly after the conquest of Jebusite Jerusalem, on a sanctification of his kingship and that of his dynasty by its association with the Jerusalem cult of El-Elyon, God Most High, who, as 14/22 Genesis makes plain, came to be regarded as identical with Yahweh. The so-called "royal theology", built around the cult centred at the Jerusalem temple, implied, as so many of the Psalms declare, that there was now an unconditional covenant between God and his servant David. This provided lasting legitimacy for the Davidic dynasty, which maintained its rule in Judah so long as the kingdom endured and which, even after its fall, remained the focus of Jewish hopes for a religious and political revival.

In Israel David's position was different. Accepting the offer of the Israelite crown, he found that he had accepted the specific forms of legitimation which its tenure entailed. His probable desire to substitute for these the principle of heredity, by producing an heir from his marriage to Saul's daughter Michal, was frustrated by her infertility. Once the threat of Philistine conquest had been seen off, the monarchy's hold on Israel was fragile even while David reigned, as the revolts of Absolom and the Benjaminite Sheba ben Bichri show. After putting down these rebellions, David seems to have taken the fateful step of administering Israel much like the other non-Judaean parts of his empire. He levied forced labour from the northern tribes and, under Solomon, this burden was greatly increased to satisfy the new king's ambitious building schemes. It is small wonder that when Solomon's son, Rehoboam, went to meet the men of Israel at Shechem, the old cult centre of the confederacy, they asked him to remove this imposition. Rehoboam's refusal to do so precipitated the Israelite secession from the Davidic monarchy and the collapse of the Judaeo-Israelite kingdom. It is notable that the Israelite leaders' call to secession echoed exactly the slogan of Sheba's rebellion against David fifty years before: "What share have we in David? We have no inheritance in the son of Jesse. To your tents Israel! Henceforth look after your own house, David!" (1 Kings 12, 16).

The contrasting origins of monarchy and statehood in Israel and Judah go far toward explaining the differences in their political and religious histories in the two centuries following Solomon's death. Judah's stability and continuing loyalty to the Davidic dynasty provide a striking contrast to the record of rebellion and usurpation we find in Israel. In view of what we have said above, it is therefore hardly surprising that the articulation of a distinctive tradition of direct, prophetic appeal to the word and will of Yahweh, which finds expression in the books of the eighth-century prophets, Amos, Hosea, Micah and Isaiah, and, subsequently, in Jeremiah and the prophets of the exile, is prefigured in the history of Israel rather than that of Judah. This may seem odd in view of the fact that, with the exception of Hosea, all these "writing prophets" were Judaeans and not Israelites of the northern tribes. However the fact is that at least up to the point of the final crisis of the northern kingdom, what we now recognize as the characteristic activities of the prophets were, apparently, confined to Israel alone.

Thus, some years before the fall of Samaria, the Judaean Amos proclaimed his prophecies not in his native Judah but in the Israel of Jeroboam II. The prophet's message of condemnation was, not unnaturally, unwelcome to the Israelite authorities; and, after what may have been a period of a mere few months' preaching, he was deported, as a foreigner, back to Judah on the orders of the Israelite High Priest Amaziah.

The early prophecies of Isaiah, the first to be proclaimed within Judah, coincide with the period of Israel's downfall and are marked by a well-informed awareness of the extent of Assyrian power and the imminence of Assyrian conquest. Seeing the approaching destruction of Israel, Isaiah's major purpose seems to have been to warn Judah against bringing a similar disaster upon itself. In this warning political and religious themes are inextricably intertwined. Israel, Isaiah proclaims, has brought its fate upon itself both by its disloyalty to Yahweh and by placing its trust in the power of military alliances to resist the Assyrian army. Judah must return to the way of Yahweh. It must place its trust in its God and, unlike Israel, refrain from engagement in futile political and military manoeuvres directed against the overwhelming power of Assyria.

The flowering of prophecy in Judah, evident in the teachings of Isaiah, Micah and their successors, can thus be seen primarily as a response to the perceived fate of Yahweh's other people, Israel. Right down to the period of Jeremiah and the fall of Jerusalem the Judaean prophetic tradition is marked by the prophets' attempts to influence the course of Judah away from that which, as they believed, had brought doom upon the northern kingdom. In the end these efforts were unsuccessful. There is a pathetic similarity between the frantic, diplomatic manoeuvrings that mark the last years of Judah's independence and the equally understandable but vain attempts of the last kings of Israel to preserve themselves from Assyrian conquest. And yet, as we have already noted, though the 135 years that separate the fall of Samaria from that of Jerusalem are crowned with failure, both from the point of view of kingly politics and that of the prophetic call to repentance, they provided the necessary time in which the Yahwistic religion of Judah could, by the incorporation of Israelite traditions, develop to a point at which it could survive the end of Judaean statehood.

One side of this development can be seen in the Deuteronomist historians' creative blending of the Yahwistic traditions of Israel and Judah. Another aspect is to be found in the new prophetic interpretation of the relationship between Yahweh and His chosen people — an interpretation of Judah's position before God which, one suspects, could not have carried conviction except in the light of the terrible and apparently irreversible fate of the ethnically and religiously related kingdom and people of Israel.

As I see it, the position may be expressed as follows. On the one hand, only the incorporation of northern Israelite religious traditions into the temple- and monarchy-centred religion of Judah enabled Judaean religion to achieve a form that could survive the destruction of David's throne and

Solomon's temple. On the other, it was the Judaean legacy of stable religious and political institutions, the Davidic dynasty and the religious primacy of the Jerusalem priesthood and cult, which allowed the state of Judah to survive in a world dominated by Assyria and so provide the environment in which Yahwism could develop to a point at which its religious survival beyond statehood itself became a possibility. In short, it was the combination of Judaean institutions and Israelite religious traditions, which only took place after the fall of the northern kingdom, that made possible the transmission of the faith of Yahweh into a stateless future.

We know all too little about the ways in which the Israelite legacy penetrated Judah in this period. During the first half of the seventh century, after the end of Isaiah's ministry, the prophets fall silent. For most of the time, under the long reign of King Manasseh 687-642 and his son Amon 642-640, Judah was a loyal vassal of Assyria. Non-Yahwistic, pagan cults flourished, though opinions differ as to how far these reflect Assyrian religious influence and how far a spontaneous renewal of the native cults of Canaan. The revival of Yahwism came only when Josiah succeeded to the throne in 640 —a revival which culminated in the public proclamation of the Deuteronomic code in 621. We can only speculate about the processes by which, in the course of the early seventh century, Judaic Yahwism, under the pressure of what must have seemed a royal apostasy from Judah's national faith, came increasingly to be permeated by Israelite influences. That the times were ripe for such a penetration is hardly surprising when we consider the extent to which the Yahwism of Israel, in contrast to that of Judah, was not tied to the institutions of the hereditary monarchy and the Jerusalem temple.

Under Manasseh, the king most associated with the institutionalization of non-Hebrew, "pagan" cults, Judaean Yahwism became, to some extent, a religion of opposition to royal policy. Put into this position by what were no doubt the politically prudent actions of the pro-Assyrian king, the guardians of Yahwism in Judah, the local Yahwist priests and Levites, must surely have found encouragement and inspiration in the traditions of an Israelite Yahwism which had, at least from the time of Elijah and Ahab in the mid-ninth century, kept its distance from the policies and fate of Israel's kings.

Evidence for the penetration of Judaean Yahwism by Israelite influences may be found in the enthusiasm with which the people of Judah seem to have received the Deuteronomic reform of Josiah. The effect of Israelite religious influence created a fertile environment for the Yahwistic revival and the formulation of the symbolic unity of "all Israel" which King Josiah claimed as his and Judah's inheritance after 621.

In pragmatic terms the results of this claim can be seen in Josiah's attempt to impose his political rule as well as the reformed and purified religion of

Yahweh not only on Judah but on the estranged territory of what had been the Kingdon of Israel. The decline of Assyria, under the pressure of Nabopolasser's revolt in Babylon and the increasingly damaging incursions of the Medes, had led to the breakdown of Assyrian rule in the province of Samaria. Josiah took advantage of this to destroy the local shrines and high places of the various cults, Yahwist as well as pagan, within the former Northern kingdom. Deuteronomic Yahwism was to be the religion of "all Israel" and the worship of God was to be centred in the Jerusalem temple, now purged of all vestiges of foreign cults.

According to the interpretation of Albrecht Alt and his school, neatly summarized by Siegfried Herrmann,[2] the Book of Deuteronomy collects together the religious traditions of the vanished state of Israel. Alt suggests that the core of what we know as the Deuteronomic code was composed out of the ancient traditions of Israelite religion some time after the fall of Samaria, and was intended to be a religio-political programme for a restored, authentically Yahwist state in the territory of the former northern kingdom. In the political situation produced by the waning of Assyrian power, the adoption and proclamation of the book in Judaean Jerusalem perfectly served King Josiah's religious and political purposes. For Josiah aimed at nothing less than the creation of a single religiously and politically homogeneous Hebrew monarchy — the "all Israel" whose previous, pre-monarchic existence is assumed in Deuteronomy.

Deuteronomy, in Herrmann's words, first, "provided the basic principle that Yahweh might legitimately be worshipped only in one place, which Josiah recognized as being the temple in Jerusalem neither the temple nor Jerusalem is ever mentioned in Deuteronomy itself. Secondly, the demand for single-minded devotion to the one God Yahweh legitimated the removal of all foreign cults and the unrestricted circulation of all the traditions of Yahweh. Finally, the idea of a united Israel acting as a totality from the beginning of its history underlined Josiah's political intention to extend his influence also to the northern kingdom of Israel. This is what Josiah saw as a new historical perspective: a united Israel under the one God, who was prepared to accept the cultic offerings of his people at one sanctuary. At the same time these are the constitutive elements of Josiah's basic conception; the king of Jerusalem becomes the protector of the traditions of the former northern state of Israel. Jerusalem and the house of David bind themselves without qualification to the law of Israel; in short, there is a move back through David to Moses."[3] Only at this point does Moses come to be regarded as the great lawgiver. Only with the Judaean king's proclamation of the authority of Deuteronomy do the religious traditions of the north acquire their unqualified significance for Judah. At the same time, what had previously been the exclusive traditions of

Israel are, as it were, brought under the "protection" of the Judaean king in Jerusalem, whose authority is further reinforced by the enforced concentration of the cult in the single royal temple.

Seen in this light, Josiah's adoption of Deuteronomy as the foundation for the future policy of the Jerusalem monarchy was a shrewd move in his ambitious plan to re-create the unified greater Israel of David and Solomon. The renewed form of a united Hebrew kingdom was to have none of the *ad hoc* features of the original. The practice of religion and the basis of political legitimacy were, as never before, to be uniform throughout the monarchy.

However, the possibility of succeeding in his imperial enterprise depended upon factors beyond Josiah's control. David had built his empire in the tenth century at a time when there was no great imperial power capable of stopping him. In 621 Josiah could see that Assyria was in decline, but that in itself did not leave open the way of renewed empire. Nabopolasser had become an independent king in Babylon in 625. In 614 the Assyrian holy city of Asshur fell to the Medes and, in 612, the imperial capital, Nineveh, was captured by the allied armies of the Medes and the Babylonians. At the same time in Egypt there was a vigorous new dynasty which, having thrown off Assyrian rule itself in 650, had no desire to see the neighboring parts of Asia come under any new imperial influence but its own. For all Josiah's energy the international situation was not propitious for a small but ambitious kingdom like Judah.

In 609, fearing the extension of Babylonian power over what had formerly been the western provinces of the Assyrian empire, the new Pharoah Necho marched north. Nineveh had fallen three years before and Necho's intention was to redress the Asian balance of power, and thus ensure Egypt's interests, by relieving the pressure on what remained of the Assyrian state, now, under its last king Asshur-Uballit II, confined to the area of Haran, north of the Euphrates. King Josiah tried to stop the Egyptians as they advanced through what he had come to regard as his own sphere of influence but was defeated and killed at Megiddo. Necho, in his turn, failed to save what remained of Assyria. The last Assyrian stronghold fell to the Babylonians in 606 and, the next year, the Babylonian crown prince Nebuchadnezzar inflicted a crushing defeat on the Egyptians at Carchemish, forcing them back through Syria to the frontiers of Egypt.

In four eventful years Josiah's dream of restoring a greater Judaeo-Israelite state on the dual foundation of Deuteronomic Yahwism and the Jerusalem monarchy had been shattered. Egypt and then Babylon had taken control of political events in the area; and, as Jeremiah saw all too clearly, any attempt to argue with the facts of military and political power, as they now stood, would bring disaster on what remained of the Hebrew kingdom. But the legacy of Josiah's ambitions ran deep; and over the next quarter century his inadequate royal successors proved unable to resist the temptation of defying the might of Babylon. The result was the end of the kingdom of Judah.

The conquest of the Judaean state brought in its train the destruction of what had traditionally been the two central pillars of Judah's political and religious identity —the divinely ordained monarchy of the house of David and the temple of Yahweh in Jerusalem. That this dual catastrophe did not mean the end of Judaic religion is, I have suggested, attributable, in large part, to the way that the religion of Judah had developed over the previous century under the influence of northern, Israelite Yahwism. Thus far, we have emphasized one aspect of this process: the creative formulation of a Deuteronomist theology in which the Judaean symbols of the royal Davidic covenant and the Jerusalem temple came, without being devalued, to be seen as episodes in a longer history of Yahweh's dealings with the children of Israel.

This theology, with its long historical perspective reaching back to the patriarchs and its emphasis on the centrality of Moses and the revelation of God's law in the Sinai desert, allowed Judah's fall to be understood, not as evidence of Yahweh's powerlessness or disinterest in His people, but as one more theologically meaningful, because theophanically charged, chapter in a turbulent, revelatory history whose fulfilment was yet to be achieved. In addition to giving the Judaeans a way of making religious sense of politically catastrophic events, Deuteronomism gave them the foundations of a law by which they could live and preserve their identity in a condition of statelessness.

But there is another aspect to matters which, up to this point, we have only mentioned in passing. That is the role of the pre-exilic prophets in reforming Judah's faith and, more especially, the significance of prophecy as an act of witness to the continuing presence of Yahweh's intent and judgement in the unfolding of historical events.

In the traditional royal theology of Judah, the will of Yahweh was seen as manifest in the institution of the Davidic dynasty and the construction of the temple in Jerusalem. Through the temple cult and the acts of the anointed *and* hereditary monarchy God was seen as present in the world. It is sometimes claimed that the message of the prophets entailed a rejection of this theology and its cultic embodiment, but this is misleading. The prophets of Judah, though critical of particular royal policies and of what they sometimes regarded as the spiritual emptiness of the practice of the temple cult, were not the enemies of either kingship or cult. So long as the kingdom of Judah lasted, their efforts were directed to saving both, by bringing king and people back to obedience to the will of Yahweh as disclosed in prophetic experience.

With the exception of Amos, Hosea and the earliest teachings of Isaiah in Jerusalem, the story of the writing prophets, whose names are attached to books of the Bible, belongs to the history of Judah and of Judaic religion in the period after the destruction of the kingdom of Israel. Yet, as we have already seen in relation to the development of Deuteronomist theology, Judah's religious identity in this period was profoundly affected by the legacy of Israel. Israel, now politically extinct, survived spiritually and even flourished in the more institutionally stable environment of Judah. The extinct political Israel enjoyed a sort of posthumous existence as a negative example of what Yahweh might also do to His people in the southern kingdom. The living, spiritual Israel of the unextinguished, northern religious traditions was grafted on to the Judaean stem, and, over time and in the face of looming political problems, came to exert a formative and reformatory influence on the religion of the south.

The effects of the Israelite legacy on Judah were ambivalent; and nowhere more so than in the impact of the Judaean prophets, whose predecessors, as individual witnesses to the continuing revelations of Yahweh, are to be found in the north, with Elijah, Elisha and their followers. To understand the political and religious significance of these figures of the ninth century we must understand the distinct place they occupied in the history of the Israelite state and society. Once this is understood we will see why Israel's legacy to Judah was so ambivalent.

The biblical use of the term *nabi*, prophet, precedes the appearance of those to whom we now customarily apply it. The original *nebiim* were not prophets in the sense we usually understand the word. They were ecstatic visionaries, akin to the Islamic dervishes, who wandered around in groups, dancing themselves into a frenzy, and who, in times of war or celebration, could be depended upon to encourage the fervour of the people. Later, with the institutionalization of monarchy, the term *nabi* came to be applied to the circles of court prophets who attended the king, and, through the use of oracles and divination, gave divine blessing to his actions. We are told that King Ahab was attended by two hundred such prophets of Yahweh whom he consulted before going off to fight the king of Damascus at Ramoth Gilead in 850. In the last years of the Judaean monarchy, Jeremiah's formidable opponent, the prophet Hananiah, is a late example of this type of *nabi*. Jeremiah's disputes with the politically optimistic Hananiah recall, as perhaps they are meant to do, the events of 250 years before, when the solitary figure of Micaiah ben Imlah, in all probability a disciple of Elijah, had warned Israel's King Ahab against placing his faith in the encouraging oracles of the court prophets.

Within Israel, Elijah and his followers represented a current of single-minded, one might say, fanatical Yahwism which would not accept any compromise with the religious traditions of Israel's neighbours nor with the similar traditions native to Canaan. Israelites and Canaanites lived alongside each other within the boundaries of the kingdom of Ahab. Over the years there had been intermarriage between the groups, and it would be a mistake to see in the religious struggle between the exclusive Yahwism of Elijah and the Baal worship, encouraged by Ahab's Phoenician queen Jezebel, a reflection of an ethnic struggle between two distinct racial groups. Indeed, it is probably wrong to suppose that most inhabitants of Israel would even have perceived the claims of Yahweh and Baal as in any way incompatible with one another. In the old religion of Canaan Baal was essentially a fertility god, the patron of agriculture; and many, perhaps most Israelites were now settled on the land as cultivators. These people were farmers, not prophets or theologians; and the fertility cults associated with Baal, a god or gods —for there were many local Baals —whose death and resurrection reflected the cycle of the crops, must have seemed an integral part of their religion. No doubt the religion of the Israelite peasantry incorporated originally Canaanite elements in much the same way as the Christianity of the Romanian peasantry described by Mircea Eliade incorporates elements which clearly derive from the pre-Christian fertility cults of the area.

Yahwism of the exclusivist type represented by Elijah tended to draw its main support from the eastern, trans-Jordanian tribes, whose way of life remained closest to the pastoralism of the original Hebrew clans. Such people had little respect for the agriculturalists' worship of Baal, or for the considerations of state which led King Ahab, like Solomon before him, to forge political and marital alliances with worshippers of gods other than Yahweh. In consequence, their effect on the conduct of Israel's worldly affairs was socially divisive and politically disastrous.

The most dramatic illustration of this is to be found in the prophetically blessed *coup d'état* of Jehu which toppled the Omride dynasty some ten years after Ahab's death. Jehu's rebellion was launched at what was, from the national political point of view, the worst possible moment, while Israel, this time in alliance with Judah, was, yet again, at war with Damascus. Accompanied by the Yahwist fanatic Jehonadab, founder of the purist sect known as the Rechabites, Jehu, the commander of Israel's army, massacred the whole Israelite royal family, half the royal house of Judah, including King Ahaziah, and innumerable priests and worshippers of Baal. The effect of this bloodletting was to weaken Israel at a time whe she could particularly ill afford it. Not only did the new prophetically sanctified king have to pay homage to the King of Assyria, as the price for being temporarily saved from defeat by Damascus; but once the Assyrians had withdrawn from Damascene territory, Jehu proceeded to lose a large part of his kingdom to Hazael, the new and vigorous king of Damascus. Such was the political price of carrying out the prophetic programme associated with Elijah and his disciples.

A century or so later, Hosea was to condemn the massacres that had accompanied Jehu's *coup*; but even then part of the prophet's purpose seems to have been to subvert further the legitimacy of an Israelite monarchy which was desperately struggling to keep the state in being.

The later impact of prophecy in Judah is harder to evaluate in political terms. The prophets themselves were Judaeans who, in large part, accepted Judah's specific theological heritage and thus the religiously sanctioned legitimacy of the Jerusalem monarchy. The coincidence of the flowering of prophecy and the rise of great imperial powers which threatened the very existence of the kingdom makes it difficult to judge how far prophetic warnings against relying on foreign alliances were motivated by a realistic sense of political possibilities and how far by the unwarranted belief, attributed to Isaiah by Eric Voegelin, that Yahweh could be relied upon to intervene miraculously against Judah's foreign enemies.[4]

The situation is further complicated by the fact that, as we have seen, under the rule of King Josiah the Davidic dynasty associated itself with a programme of exclusive, intolerant Yahwism of a type that even the heirs of Elijah might have been expected to approve. At the same time, the utterances of the prophets, concerned as they are with the existence of injustice in society, reveal at times a seemingly inexpungeable hostility to the settled life of city and state and a nostalgia for the simpler pastoral society of the past. This tendency is particularly pronounced in the prophecy of Micah, but even the often urbane and undoubtedly sophisticated Jeremiah goes out of his way to praise the city-hating Rechabites whose spiritual forefather was the dreadful Jehonadab.

This alone should remind us that the Judaean prophets were heirs to part at least of the religious legacy of the northern kingdom; and, it would seem, to just that portion most damaging to the prospects for preserving independent statehood. Yet it would be wrong to jump to any hasty conclusions about the political intentions and impact of the prophets of Judah. On the one hand, the prophetic legacy, transplanted to Judah, was, as it were, "Judaized" and hence, to a considerable extent, integrated with the political culture of a theologically legitimated monarchical state. On the other, under Israelite influence, the theological stance of Judah's kings as well as her prophets developed in a direction, foreign to its original form, which allowed Judaean religion to become a faith capable of surviving even when the state vanished from the map of the world.

That this faith entailed political tensions, consequent upon the recognition of the absolute nature of Yahweh's demands in an iremediably imperfect world, is a fact whose consequences are with us still, wherever men consider the relationship between what seems to be demanded of us by biblical faith and the pragmatic imperatives of political survival. The history of religion and politics in the kingdoms of Israel and Judah is the original, paradigmatic history of the attempt to live in full consciousness of the tension between these two poles. It is a project to which all the West is heir. Throughout the history of the kingdoms there were kings and prophets who sought to resolve the tension in the direction of one pole or the other. None succeeded in this; and no one has succeeded since; for success could only mean the eclipse of the distinct requirements of what later tradition has identified, rather too neatly, as the separate yet mutually implicated fields of faith and nature.

In the Hebrew kingdoms both sets of requirements had ways of asserting themselves that were difficult to ignore and, once recognized, even harder to reconcile. The history of the kingdoms teaches us, at the very least, that there is no neat political-religious formula that is able to ensure either our worldly survival or our divine-transcendent salvation. What perhaps it also teaches is the need to learn to live with the reality of the tension between the two; and so to recognise that only when both are respected as inescapable features of our human condition can we be said to have discovered the truth of our being as creatures at once of God and the world.

Notes

1. Irving Zeitlin, *Ancient Israel.*
2. Siegfried Hermann, *A History of Israel in Old Testament Times* S.P.C.K., London, 1981.
3. Hermann op.cit., p.268.
4. Eric Voegelin, *Israel and Revalation* Louisiana State University Press, 1955.

9

"THE GOOD RELIGION"

Reflections on the History and Fate of Zoroastrianism

"The Good Religion" was the name given to their faith by the Zoroastrians of the second, Sassanian, Persian Empire. This was the empire, founded by Ardashir I in A.D. 226, which lasted until the Muslim conquest of Persia in A.D. 652. Under the Sassanid kings Zoroastrianism was the state religion of one of the great powers of the world. But to put matters as simply as this is to cover up many of the problems which make consideration of the long history and ultimate fate of the Zoroastrian religion so fascinating and, at times, frustrating to specialist and non-specialist alike.

We are told by the *Denkart*, one of the most important of our sources for the religious history of the period, that when Ardashir, son of Papak, overthrew his Parthian overlord, he and his high priest, Tansar, set themselves the task of establishing or, as they saw it, reviving the religion founded by the prophet Zoroaster or Zarathustra. They are depicted as the dual restorers of a national religion which had, one gathers from the tone of the text, been in eclipse for some five centuries since Alexander the Great defeated the armies of King Darius III around 330 B.C.

According to the same Zoroastrian source, the teachings of the religion were scattered and had become confused. So when the king commanded that they be gathered and regularized, Tansar had the business of constructing a consistent orthodoxy out of the conflicting traditions which survived. In the *Denkart*'s words: "Tansar set about his business, selected one version and left the rest out of the canon: and he issued this decree:'The interpretation of all the teachings from the religion of the worshippers of Mazdah is our responsibility: for now there is no lack of certain knowledge concerning them." [1]

170

The alliance of church and crown in the promotion of a not always steady religious orthodoxy, evident in the *Denkart*'s account of the restoration, is characteristic of the whole Sassanian period, and, indeed, of Zoroastrian thought in general. For, in words attributed to King Ardashir: "Religion and kingship are two brothers, and neither can dispense with the other. Religion is the foundation of kingship and kingship protects religion. For whatever lacks a foundation must perish, and whatever lacks a protector disappears." [2]

But what was the orthodoxy and where was it to be found? Certainly there exists today a body of orthodox Zoroastrian teaching. It consists in an elaborate and intellectually impressive doctrinal *corpus*, preserved in the so-called Pahlavi books. But these books, whose collective name refers to the dialect of Middle Persian in which they are written, were all composed, at least in their surviving forms, at a much later date. Even though there is general agreement that the teachings they embody represent the orthodoxy as established under King Shapur II 309-379 and associated with the name of his High Priest, Aturpat, all the books appear to have been written in the period that followed the overthrow of the Sassanian empire, and with it the Zoroastrian state church, by the Muslim Arabs in the seventh century.

Though throne and altar were allies in the promotion of orthodoxy under the Sassanid monarchs, it is clear that the achievement of a single orthodox position — one amounting to a clear definition of the true doctrine of the established religion —was a difficult task. It involved a hard choice between conflicting tendencies already present within the native Iranian tradition as well as a permanent struggle against new or foreign religions, like Christianity and Manichaeism, which pretended, as much as the "Good Religion" itself, to embody a universal truth founded in divine revelation. Throughout the Sassanian period these religions were perceived not merely as threatening the integrity of the religious truth revealed through the word of the prophet Zoroaster and preserved by the priests of his restored church but as politically disruptive elements that might undermine the stability of the empire.

It is probable that the Pahlavi books exaggerate the doctrinal confusion that existed among Zoroastrians under the Parthian kings, who were themselves ethnically Iranian monarchs and, at least according to their own lights, authentic worshippers of Mazdah. In thus exaggerating the extent of the religious problem faced by Ardashir and the priest Tansar, the Pahlavi texts reflect not only the claim of the Sassanid dynasty to be the restorer and first servant of the faith, but also the novelty of the cultural and religious situation in which Zoroastrianism found itself in the third century A.D. For if Sassanian Zoroastrianism is characterized by a concern with doctrinal definition, intellectual consistency and uniformity of religious practice, this is, in part at least, because the world which the Persian "King of Kings" aspired to rule, and within whose bounds the Good Religion was to be promoted and protected, was one marked, as never before, by the presence of rival religions, each of which aspired to universality and laid claim to a monopoly of divinely revealed truth.

Re-forming the old Iranian faith in a fashion that might enable it to triumph in such a religious and political environment was no easy matter. The priests, legatees of a confused and confusing past, faced a hermeneutic task of awful proportions and the kings, whose future was seen as bound up with the furtherance of the Zoroastrian religion as the distinctive faith of their empire, confronted a political difficulty unknown to their Iranian predecessors. The result of the attempt to meet these challenges was, on the one hand, a uniformity of purpose and, as it emerged, destiny, between church and state — the terms are neither inappropriate nor anachronistic — and, on the other, a theology and a conception of the religious legitimation of monarchical rule that, perhaps to a unique extent, reconciled the demands of worldly order with the revelations of a prophetically founded religion.

While this aspiration to reconcile the claims of religion with the imperatives of political survival sounds reasonable enough, its effects were, as any historian of religion might realise, predictable and, to the modern mind, at times distasteful. An inscription of the great High Priest Karter, the prelate who brought the self-proclaimed prophet Mani to his death in A.D. 277, mentions Jews, Christians, Manichees, Mandaeans, Buddhists and Brahmans among those persecuted in the effort to realize the unity of rule and religion to which the Zoroastrian Church aspired. And to this day Christians of the Armenian tradition still remember the martyrs Adhur-Hormizd and Anahidh who died in the reign of Yezdigerd II in the course of his endeavour to enforce conformity to his own, not altogether orthodox, form of the religion of Mazdah.

Zoroastrianism was, like its rivals, a religion with universalist claims. Its prophet spoke, perhaps more clearly even than the Hebrew prophets, to all men and not simply to the ethnic group to which he belonged. Through his mouth the truth of the Wise Lord, called Ahurah Mazdah in early Zoroastrianism but whom the Sassanians called Ohrmazd, was proclaimed to all mankind as a summons to abandon the Lie and to join the cosmic struggle against the evil of Angra Mainyu, later Ahriman, the Lord of Evil.

In every phase of its development Zoroastrianism is characterized by the belief that man's earthly activity contributes to the course of the divine struggle of Good against Evil. Some authorities believe that the pure dualism of the Pahlavi books, from which the popular conception of the teachings of the Good Religion derives, and which assert the absolute, ontological distinction of Good from Evil, Light from Darkness, was a late development.

Certainly it was never without challenge even within the Zoroastrian community. Within Zoroastrianism the main source of this challenge to dualist orthodoxy came from the Zurvanite belief that Ohrmazd and Ahriman alike derived their being from Zurvan, Fate.

Zurvanism, in one form or another, was the perennial other of dualist orthodoxy. It represented a challenge which the pure dualists found it imperative to reject yet impossible finally to banish. The rejection of Zurvanism was essential to orthodox dualists because, by deriving Ohrmazd and Ahriman alike from a single source, the Zurvanites seemed to compromise the pure goodness of the Wise Lord — born, as it were, according to Zurvanite doctrine, from a source capable of corruption. At the same time, final victory over Zurvanism was hard to achieve; for though the heretics could be seen as challenging a central feature of Zoroastrian spirituality — the belief in the absolute distinctiveness of Good from Evil — their derivation of Good and Evil alike from a single undifferentiated source had the merit of resolving the ontological enigma posed by the dualist assertion that there are, *ab origine*, two coeval and opposed divine beings.

This enigma is present in any religious system based upon absolute dualism and presents a challenge to the intellectual coherence of such a faith. But as the spokesmen of Zoroastrian orthodoxy never ceased to point out, the alternative view, characteristic not merely of Zurvanite heresy but of Judaism, Christianity and, later, Islam, which derive all creation from a single divine source, is beset by the no less grave problem of how we may explain the presence of Evil in the creation of an omnipotent and all-good God.

Whatever may have been the assumptions concerning the status of dualism in early, pre-Sassanian Zoroastrian belief, the relationship between Good and Evil, Ohrmazd and Ahriman, is unlikely to have appeared to believers in the explicitly problematic form it later assumes. For it is only when a revealed religion finds it necessary to explicate its message in the coherent form of a systematic theology that such enigmas become troubling. Belief and cult know nothing of the puzzles of metaphysics: and, even though these lurk always in the content of religion, they emerge as conscious problems, requiring authoritative settlement, only when the theologians set about the task of ensuring the integrity of the received faith by rendering the mystery of the divine in the form of an argued and, consequently arguable, dogmatics. This, in turn, only happens at the moment in a religion's history when it finds itself forced to define the content of its faith in the face of external or internal, heretical, challenge. In the history of Zoroastrianism the need for such an endeavour arose only when the religion found its pretensions to truth challenged by the disciples of alternative "world faiths" and in the face of the political demand, central to the imperial ambitions of the Sassanid kings, that there be a uniform state church within the new Iranian Empire.

What we may say with certainty is that, whatever the implicit ontological content of "original" Zoroastrianism, the explicit interpretation of the world as a battleground fought over by the opposing forces of the Truth and the Lie is part of the religion from the beginning. If religious persecution is always distasteful to the modern temper, we may at least admit that, according to their own lights, the Zoroastrians, with their passionate belief in the value of earthly existence and in the eschatological efficacy of worldly action as an essential element of the divine struggle against evil, had a better reason than most to suppress the devotees of untruth with every means available to them.

It is in the light of Zoroastrian respect for the things of this world, created by Ohrmazd as part of his battle plan against Ahriman, that we should understand the mutual implication of the Good Religion and the rule of the King of Kings, whose religious task it was to assure good order within that level of creation over which he presided. The same intimacy between church and crown, typical of the Sassanian era, contributed not a little to the long-term but relentless decline of the Zoroastrian religion after the forces of the last Sassanid king, Yezdigerd III, were defeated by the bearers of another truth revealed to another prophet deep in the Arabian peninsula. The words of King Ardashir on the mutual dependence of religion and kingship disclosed the uncomfortable aspect of their truth when kingship could no longer be the protector of the Good Religion. The ancient religion of Iran declined; and in its place there flourished another which, eventually, destroyed, in the name of religion, a monarchy which, though Muslim by faith, looked back, beyond Muhammed, to its political foundation by the Persian king Cyrus in 550 B.C.

I say this not to make any topical point about relatively recent political events, but to express my conviction that reflection on the history and fate of Zoroastrianism, and, in particular, on the Zoroastrian conception of the relationship between earthly, political order and the heavenly order—between the temporal and the transcendent good — can bring out, especially clearly, certain problems inherent in all attempts to relate these two, perhaps equally compelling, objects of the human quest. These are problems which are not confined to Zoroastrianism nor to Islam, but are perhaps inseparable from a form of existence, the human condition, which is structured both by the need to assure worldly survival and by the experienced pull of demands that seem to emanate from beyond the world.

Such problems are, I suggest, especially evident in any religious tradition that understands its origin to lie in special revelation through the prophetic word. The tension between the temporal and the transcendent—which is not identical with the familiar distinction between the profane and the sacred — may be a feature of man's religious consciousness as such, but in religions of the revealed word it has ways of asserting itself that, all too often, threaten to destroy man's communion with one pole or another. When this happens there is always the temptation either to sacrifice the requirements of earthly survival, the temporal good, in presumed obedience to divine command, or to dismiss the transcendent, the prophetically articulated call of the divine, as something irrelevant or harmful to the prospects of life. More troubling still, as the case of Zoroastrianism shows, even where the two orders seem to coexist in theologically warranted harmony, this is no guarantee of religious or political survival.

Zoroastrianism sought to establish, in its theology as well as in the practice of the faithful, the closest possible harmony between the two orders of the temporal and the transcendent: both of which it conceived as spheres in which good order battled for eventual triumph over evil. Even the stratum of animal life was regarded as divided between the beneficent creatures made by Ohrmazd, notably the cow and the dog, and the pestilential creatures of Ahriman. The signs of the divine/human struggle between good and evil were everywhere to be seen; and this was not conceived as a struggle between man and god, nor, as Christianity taught, as an inner conflict between the pull of the earthly and the divine within human nature. Rather, Zoroastrianism held that there were both men and gods engaged on each side of the battle.

Between the forces of good and evil there was, as it were, a state of ontological equality. And the eventual triumph of Good, in which the Zoroastrian was nonetheless bound to believe, was therefore seen not, as in Christianity, as the result of the infinite ontological superiority of God over the Devil, but rather as a consequence of the self-divisive properties inherent in the nature of Evil and of Ahriman, its divine embodiment and source. To this optimistic prospect Zoroastrian teaching added the assurance that, though men would pay for their sins in the afterlife, each, as a creature of Ohrmazd, would eventually be redeemed.

Some will say that the Zoroastrian religion suffered in its long term fate for what may appear to be its over-confident identification of the interests of God and king. It survives, but as a shadow of its former glory, as the faith of perhaps ten thousand souls in Islamic Iran and among the Parsees of India, descendents of folk who fled persecution in their homeland from the 8th Century onwards. Zoroastrianism shows little of the capacity for autonomous spiritual development displayed by Judaism, another prophetic, revealed religion whose political protectors were defeated in the maelstrom of historical events. Judaism survived the loss of the Promised Land without succumbing to the dangers of syncretism, but Zoroastrianism was much more severely shaken by the defeat of the monarchy. Theologically and intellectually powerful, the Good Religion was somehow unfitted to become a religion of witness borne by the suffering servants of the Wise Lord.

History, and with it the history of the Zoroastrian faith, is unfinished, and no one can give a final judgement on the significance of this apparent fate. The end of things — the *eschaton* — might vindicate the truth which history seems to deny. On this there is nothing to say. We can only consider things in historical and phenomenological terms, as they are recorded and as they appear, and here the evidence suggests that the intimacy between religion and kingship in Zoroastrianism — an intimacy which made the political power of the king not only the expression of the will of Ohrmazd but the prime arm of religion — worked against the long-term success of the religion in a world where the temporal powers that be will not be for evermore.

The association of the religion of Zoroaster with the Persian monarchy specifically was not original. The Persians who established their hegemony over Western Asia under Cyrus the Great were one among several Iranian peoples — a sub-branch of the Indo-European or Aryan people who emerged from the Central Asian steppes to establish themselves in Northern India, Asia Minor and Europe, as well as in present-day Iran and Afghanistan. The Persians themselves were the inhabitants of Pars in the South-west of modern Iran; and their supremacy among the Iranians, and beyond, dates from the middle of the sixth century B.C., when Cyrus, having overthrown his Median overlord, Astyages, went on to conquer Asia Minor and capture Babylon.

As for Zoroaster himself, the authorities, while agreeing that he was indeed an historical figure, differ widely in ascribing dates to his life. While the late R. C. Zaehner believed that he was born about 630 B.C., Mary Boyce dates him, largely on the basis of the language of the *Gathas* — the sole part of the Zoroastrian scriptures now thought to have been composed by Zoroaster himself — some six to eight hundred years earlier.[3] The language of the *Gathas*, however ancient it may be, is more closely related to the dialects of the North-eastern Iranians than to those of the Medes and Persians who settled further to the West. In Boyce's linguistically based chronology there is therefore clearly no question of accepting the tradition, cultivated by the Magi, the Median priesthood who subsequently formed the clergy of the Zoroastrian Church, that the prophet himself was born a Mede. Zaehner, in contrast, gives more credence to the traditional account; maintaining that though Zoroaster taught among the Chorasmians, a North-eastern Iranian people, he may indeed have been a Mede exiled from his native Rhages — a town whose site is now a suburb of Teheran.

The obscurity of the historical background tells us something of the problems scholars have faced in determining the truth about the prophet and the religion he preached. The earliest Zoroastrian scriptures that survive, as opposed to Pahlavi theological works composed, even on Zaehner's dating, at least one thousand years after the prophet's death, are written in a language which is not only hard for modern scholars to understand with any great degree of certainty, but which was, in all probability, already obscure when Zoroastrianism became the preferred religion of the first, Achaemenian, Persian Empire of Cyrus and his successors.

The *Avesta*, as the scriptures are called, falls into three distinct parts; and these are far from being theologically consistent with one another. First there are the *Gathas*, odes attributed to Zoroaster himself. In the eyes of the Zoroastrian believer, these are the most sacred documents of the faith; and modern scholars agree that they must be regarded as the indispensable clue to the truth that the prophet taught. Then we have the sacrificial hymns, the *Yashts*, which are, in striking contrast to the *Gathas*, addressed to various deities apart from Ahurah Mazdah. And, finally, the *Videvdat*, "the law against the demons", a later text which, in Zaehner's judgement, "shows no spiritual life at all, only a futile legalistic dualism which, if it had ever been put into practice, would have tried the patience of even the most credulous." [4]

It is noteworthy that there is no Pahlavi translation of the *Yashts*. Their polytheism, which is close to the religious conceptions of the Indian *Rig-Veda*, was clearly and unequivocally rejected by the Zoroastrian theologians of the Second Persian Empire. Zaehner interprets the polytheistic tone of the Yashts as symptomatic of a post-*Gathic* lapse back into traditional Aryan religion that took place in the generation following the prophet's death. But, equally, the retention of a polytheistic element in the body of Zoroastrian scripture can be used to argue for Boyce's dating and placing of the prophet and religion to a time, perhaps as early as 1400 B.C., and a place, the steppes of Asia, when and where the Indian and the Iranian branches of the Aryan family had not yet gone their separate ways.

Either way, we face in the history of Zoroastrianism a situation unique in the history of religions — a faith which has endured at least two and a half thousand years; whose original deposit of revelation was not only soon overlaid with elements inimical to its fundamental message, but which was linguistically obscure to the faithful almost from the beginning.

That such a religion should have endured at all as an identifiable and self-identifying faith is in itself remarkable. But so it did, and even Zaehner, who is unimpressed with either the literary or the spiritual qualities of the late Pahlavi texts and who argues that the theologians of the Sassanid period were not philologically competent to understand the textual meaning of the *Gathas*, admits that the religious orthodoxy established under the Sassanid kings was in general conformity with the spirit of Zoroaster's original teaching.

It is true that he also seeks to show that there were differences between the two. In particular he points to what he sees as a contrast between the rigid dualism of Sassanian Zoroastrianism, which conceives Ohrmazd and Ahriman as co-eternal principles in being, and the teaching of the *Gathas*, according to which, Ahurah Mazdah, the Wise Lord, though wholly committed to the struggle of the Holy Spirit against the Spirit of Destruction, seems not to be identical with the Holy Spirit. In Zaehner's interpretation the Ahurah Mazdah of the *Gathas* is understood to be a single, primordial and, in some sense, ontologically pre-eminent God, intimately concerned with the fight of Truth against the Lie, but not himself, as it were, at first a front-line protagonist in what is essentially a battle between ontological equals.

It is because the Wise Lord of the *Gathas* is wholly good that he is, in fact and faith, at one with the Holy Spirit who is the actual protagonist in the struggle against Evil. But the Holy Spirit, through whom the battle is waged, is seen as emanating from the Wise Lord rather than being identical with him. Thus, according to this reading of the implicit theology of the *Gathas*, original Zoroastrianism, always to be the religion of free will *par excellence*, conceives even the Wise Lord, Ahurah Mazdah, as capable of choosing between Good and Evil and thus as an essentially free being. His utter goodness is itself the fruit of his own divine choice. This primordial choice determines Ahurah Mazdah's subsequent essence as all-good and thus commits him, through his emanation, the Holy Spirit, to the cosmic struggle against the Destructive Spirit, Angra Mainyu — a being who, like the Christian Lucifer, is also primordially free but has chosen to reject the regime of the creator.

In this interpretation at least, freedom is, as much or even more than goodness, an essential property of the divine as the *Gathas* reveal it. Ahurah Mazdah *chooses* to fight for the cosmic triumph of his original but self-chosen goodness; and does so by refusing to capitulate in the face of Angra Mainyu's no less free choice of evil. Ahurah Mazdah, as much as an earthly believer, chooses to defend the goodness of a creation which is his own but which, quite possibly, he might have abandoned. Again, like man, the choice he makes determines his subsequent course of action, and so the history of Being.

In later orthodoxy Ahriman is evil by nature, not by choice. Conceived as co-eternal with Ohrmazd, he is doomed to fail only because the forces of Evil are by nature confused and disordered even in their cunning. In the economy of cosmic struggle, Evil fails only because it is ultimately less efficient than Good. In contrast, the original teaching of Zoroaster, though ethically dualist in its conception of human existence in terms of choice between Good and Evil, may have been ontologically monist in conceiving Ahurah Mazdah as the one original Being and not yet the combatant god of embattled truth that he subsequently chooses to be.

The doctrine of free will remains central to later Zoroastrianism, but in the orthodoxy of the Sassanian period there is no conception that Ohrmazd himself might potentially have chosen to be other than the utterly good god that he is. It becomes the fate of man, and man alone, to choose in a cosmos primordially and ontologically riven by the conflict of equivalent and opposed divine principles.

Other differences between the teachings of the *Gathas* and later orthodoxy can be found in the doctrines of the after-life and final judgement. Here the later theologians rejected what seems to have amounted to a doctrine of eternal damnation for those who chose to serve the Lie, maintaining instead that even the worst of human sinners, as a creature of Orhmazd, would ultimately be redeemed from the consequences of his evil-doing. Even this deviation from original teaching seems mysteriously true to the spirit of Zoroaster's revelation of the goodness of God and the bounteousness of creation.

In Zaehner's words: "Holiness, for Zoroaster, also meant abundance, growth and health. The divine nature is seen as an overwhelming giving of self, as superabundant life both in the spiritual and the material realm; for Zoroastrianism is in all its phases a religion that enthusiastically and thankfully accepts and blesses all the good things of *this* world as well as those of the next: indeed, in the *Gathas*, the work of the Prophet himself, it is often exceedingly difficult to decide whether he is referring to a concrete situation here on earth or whether he is speaking of the last things." [5]

The orthodoxy of the Pahlavi texts preserves intact the goodness of Ohrmazd, even, at times, limiting his power in order to preserve him from any taint of responsibility for evil. The same doctrinal structure also enshrines the love of and gratitude for life — the "yea-saying" which is almost all the historical Zoroaster has in common with his Nietzschean homonym.

The spirit of Zoroastrian piety is well brought out in the following extracts from a catechism written after the Islamic conquest, "when the wickedness of the demons knows no limits and the Religion of Ohrmazd is much reduced and that of the unrighteous is predominant. . . . This must one know without venturing to doubt: I have come from the unseen world, nor was I always of this world. I was created and have not always been. I belong to Ohrmazd, not to Ahriman. I belong to the gods, not to the demons, to the good, not to the wicked. . . . To perform my function and to do my duty means that I should believe that Ohrmazd is, was, and evermore shall be, that his Kingdom is undying, and that he is infinite and pure; and that Ahriman is not, and is destructible. . . . My first duty on earth is to confess the Religion, to practise it, and to take part in its worship and to be steadfast in it, to keep the Faith in the Good Religion of the worshippers of Ohrmazd ever in my mind, and to distinguish profit from loss, sin from good works, goodness from evil, light from darkness, and the worship of Ohrmazd from the worship of demons. My second duty is to take a wife and to procreate earthly offspring. . . . My third is to cultivate and till the soil; my fourth is to treat all livestock justly; my fifth to spend a third of my days and nights in attending the seminary and consulting the wisdom of holy men, to spend a third of my days and nights in tilling the soil, and to spend the remaining third of my days and nights in eating, rest, and enjoyment."

The believer confesses his belief in the efficacy of good works, the essential separation of the creative and destructive principles, the resurrection and judgement of the dead, and the final banishment of Ahriman and all his works from the field of creation. He must do good not for the sake of wordly advantage but for its own sake; remembering that "the body is mortal but the soul is immortal. . . . Do not abandon the care of the soul and forget it for the body's sake. Out of respect for persons and out of forgetfulness that all the goods of the world must perish, do not lust after anything that will bring punishment on your body and retribution on your soul. Desire rather those things whose fruit is everlasting joy. Doing good is born of zeal, zeal of prayer, prayer of desire, desire of intellect, intellect of knowledge of the other world; and knowledge of the other world is a weapon that was and is and shall be. By it is He known Who creates all things anew, Who teaches all things, Who ordains all that should be done, Who wills the good of all in this world and the next." [6]

Though this text dates from at least a millennium after Zoroaster's death, and from a time of trial and persecution, it is a confession of faith utterly true to the original spirit of the prophet of Ahurah Mazdah; whose self-authenticating vision of the one Wise Lord set him apart from his contemporaries as one of the great prophetic figures in history. The essence of prophecy is not, as the modern, secular, conception of the "prophet" suggests, a predictive vision of the future events of this world, but the intimation of another; and, if the prophetic vision is to endure, the power to convey it, by word and deed, doctrine and cult, to those who come after. By this standard, as well as by its sublime harmoniousness of content, Zoroaster's revelation is among the most enduring and noblest visions of man's relationship to creator and creation that we possess.

The fact that we find such spiritual continuity is remarkable given the lack of a philologically sound interpretive tradition within the Zoroastrian community. It is more remarkable still when we consider it in relation to the history of the Iranian peoples and the obscurity surrounding the place of the religion within that history. If, with Mary Boyce, we accept the dating of the prophet to between 1400 and 1200 B.C., we must recall that we are talking of a period in the pre-history of Central Asia when the use of bronze had only just displaced the Stone Age culture of a race of semi-nomadic pastoralists. The survival of the very name of a prophet from such a time is as striking as the content of what he taught and its potential for future development into an imperial, state religion.

If, on the other hand, Zaehner's dating is accepted, we are faced, at the very start of the story, with a fact of history which is especially ironic in view of the Zoroastrian conception of the relationship between kingship and religion. For the King Vishtaspa, whom the Prophet is supposed to have converted about 588 and to whose power he looked for protection and promotion, was, in all probability, the last politically independent monarch of the Chorasmians before Cyrus incorporated them within his pan-Iranian empire. In the interpretation suggested by this chronology, the potentially deceptive promise of harmonious identity between polity and faith, which was to damage the prospects of Zoroastrian survival after the Muslim conquest of Persia, revealed its insecurity already in the sixth century B.C., when the monarchy that had been converted went down before another, as yet unconverted monarchy — one with whose fate that of the religion was to be subsequently entwined.

As Persian power extended outwards from its South-west Iranian centre, so the religion of Zoroaster penetrated westward. In the course of this process several things happened. At the level of popular religion, as described by Herodotus, the original message of the Prophet, represented by the *Gathas*, became reincorporated in a largely unreformed Iranian polytheism, whose theological expression is the *Yashts*. The clergy of the religion was now drawn from the Magi, a clan of hereditary priests of Median origin whose presence was essential at all Iranian religious ceremonies. The practices of these priests which Herodotus thought worthy of mention bear little resemblance to those enjoined upon believers by Zoroaster.

At the same time, the long-term survival and success of a recogniszably Zoroastrian religion can only be explained on the hypothesis that a significant portion of the hereditary priesthood were "converted" to the new faith — seeing in it a new revelation to be cherished rather than a variety of received and traditional Aryan polytheism. The matter is obscure, as is so much in the Zoroastrian story; and perhaps the best one can do is to be clear about where the obscurity lies. The fact is that we have no direct evidence for the existence of a purist community dedicated to keeping the legacy of the Prophet alive and uncontaminated. But if there were no such groups, how could we explain the survival of the religion in the years between the fall of the First Persian Empire in 330 B.C. and the work of King Ardashir and the priest Tansar five hundred years later?

Zoroastrianism admits to no divinely inspired prophet after the first. Also, the religious traditions which the Sassanids made their own were, on their own evidence, scattered, confused, and yet firm enough to provide the dogmatic basis for a theologically sophisticated Church. It is circumstantial evidence such as this, as well as the obviously Zoroastrian elements in the *Vis u Ramin* — a courtly romance dating from the Parthian period — that makes the existence of self-consciously "orthodox" Zoroastrians likely long before the orthodoxy was defined by the theologically inclined prelates of the Sassanian Empire.

With regard to the religion of Achaemenid kings of the First Empire matters are a bit less obscure. The inscriptions of the monarchs, from Darius I onwards, leave one in no doubt that they were worshippers of Ahurah Mazdah. Darius proclaims that he rules by the grace of the Wise Lord. He describes his enemies as followers of the Lie, and conceives his task as the promotion of the divine law of Truth, Righteousness and Right-Mindedness within the empire. These are all typical terms of the Prophet's teaching. Xerxes, son of Darius, claims to have uprooted the cult of *daevas*, gods against whom Zoroaster had preached; and Artaxerxes I introduced a calendar which bears the distinct marks of Zoroastrian teaching.

None of the surviving inscriptions of the Achaemenid kings mentions the Prophet by name; but this apparent anomaly can, I believe, be understood in terms of the relationship of Zoroaster to the traditional religion of the Iranians. Zoroaster preached in the name of Ahurah Mazdah against the worship of the *daevas*, a class of gods identical with the *devas* worshipped by the Iranians' cousins, the Aryan conquerers of India. In Zoroastrianism the *daevas* came to be regarded as demons, servants of Ahriman, father of the Lie. But in origin they may have been the class of gods especially favoured by nomadic warriors. In contrast, Ahurah Mazdah, with his injunctions to till the soil and show kindness and consideration to live-stock, was perhaps the patron adopted by tribesmen who were beginning to settle and cultivate the land.

In India, which knows of a class of gods called *asuras* distinct from the *devas*, it is the latter which become the major gods of the pantheon enshrined in the *Rig Veda*. The *asuras*, remote from the affairs of this world, are consigned to irrelevance and appear, in the warrior epic of early Hinduism, as other-worldly, almost trans-cosmic demons.

The revelation of Zoroaster led Iranian religion in precisely the opposite direction. Ahurah Mazdah is proclaimed the only creator of the cosmos, the fountain of Truth and implacable enemy of the disorder fostered by the demonic *daevas* and their followers. In sociological terms Zoroastrianism may be regarded as a religion appealing to a settled people who require the protection and assurance of a divinely ordained, lawful, political order. Whatever its origin, it enters history as a powerful religious force at a time when the Iranian peoples, having once conquered their new lands, are engaged in establishing the institutions of settled statehood. Though the Achaemenids may not have been direct disciples of the Prophet, there is, at the least, an intelligible affinity between their wish to establish universal, imperial order and the worship of Ahurah Mazdah as supreme and just god. Each represents the struggle of stable order — political or cosmic — to maintain itself against the ever-present threat of disorder. As Arnold Gehlen argued, kingship, law and religion of this type are wholly characteristic results of what he called "the agrarian revolution." That there was no equivalent development in India can be understood not only in terms of the absence of a similar prophetic figure, but also of the prolonged archaism imposed on the Indian Aryans by the desire to preserve the purity of a conquering race that remained, in contrast to Iran, an ethnic minority.

But historical and sociological factors alone cannot provide a sufficient explanation for the contrasting history of Aryan religion among the Indians and among the Persians. The figure and revelation of Zoroaster form an essential element in the story and not a mere adjunct to the process that transformed the Iranians from a group of nomadic tribes, conscious of a shared ethnic origin, into an imperial people represented by a monarch with pretensions to universal empire. At the same time, we can see in the record of this process a prime illustration of Max Scheler's point, that while spiritual movements are irreducible to the ethnic, political and economic circumstances of their origins, the success of a movement — measured by its capacity to form the ethos or spiritual substance of a people — depends upon a combination of favourable circumstances that are, in themselves, very far from being spiritual.[7]

Specifically, it seems that we can interpret the history of the Iranians and their religion in the following general terms. The revelation of Zoroaster, whose equivalents in form and content are found, if anywhere, among the Hebrew prophets and psalmists rather than among the ethnically and culturally related Indians, found worldly acceptance in a political environment increasingly subject to the effective rule of a single monarch. The single universal god, Ahurah Mazdah/Ohrmazd, proclaiming his dominion over creation and requiring the service of his creatures in the battle against demonic disorder, had a special significance for a dynasty which was seeking a spiritual principle to justify the course of imperial expansion.

I am not claiming that the Achaemenids adopted the worship of Ahurah Mazdah primarily for pragmatic, political reasons. They did not become the Mazdah worshippers they undoubtedly were because they were searching for an appropriate ideological justification for their rule; even though in the case of Darius I, whose claim to be legitimate successor to Cyrus and Cambyses was dubious, there may be an element of self-serving in his constantly reiterated claim to rule by the grace of Ahurah Mazdah. Rather, the worship of Zoroaster's god became the religion of the monarchy, if not yet of the empire, because the Great Kings and their servants could see in Zoroastrian teaching an interpretation of the cosmos and man's place within it which gave transcendent meaning to their imperial projects. Seeing themselves as bearers of universal order to a world fought over by kings, cities and tribes, each representative of and represented by a particular god, the Achaemenid kings were ripe to receive the revelation of the one Wise Lord.

The point may seem obvious; for we are used to the twin phenomena of universalizing religions that appeal to all mankind regardless of tribe or city, and of empires, of equally universal ambitions, that claim to serve a purpose transcending their immediate, pragmatic, political goals. The combination of the two was to become the historical norm in the course of what Eric Voegelin has called "the Ecumenic Age" — the period extending from the rise of the First Persian Empire to the fall of Rome. Once born, the idea of synthetic unity between universal faith and universal polity survives its effective, if never completed, embodiment in Christianized Rome. In the West it leads a shadowy afterlife in the aspirations of the Holy Roman Empire, where it is qualified rather than denied by the Christian distinction between the things of God and those of Caesar. It legitimates the pretensions and reinforces the tenacious resistance of the embattled Byzantine Emperors in Constantinople. It inspires Islam and the dream of the universal Caliphate. And, not least, it reemerges in secular form in the ideological empires of the twentieth century. An empire is no less an empire when it calls itself a "Union of Soviet Socialist Republics" and a common, legitimating faith is no less a spiritual phenomenon when its source is claimed to be the unique revelation of a "science of history".

We know the phenomenon all too well, fearing its modern embodiments even while casting our own hopes in sentimentalized visions of a universally just "democratic" world order. But time was when the idea as well as the reality of the Ecumenic Empire, conceiving and justifying its existence in terms of its service of a truth and order intended for all mankind, was new. And the Persian Empire of the Achaemenid kings was its first incarnation.

This is not, of course, to claim that it was the first empire; nor yet that its predecessors, Assyria and Babylon in particular, did not conceive their expansive ambitions in religious terms. But theirs were essentially local, ethnic and civic deities — greater in power than the gods whose peoples they delivered into the hands of the great Mesopotamian kings, but neither requiring nor even desiring anything more than formal tribute and submission from the conquered. The will of Assyria's gods, and of Babylon's Marduk, expressed itself in what Voegelin describes as "frenzied. . . outbursts of something like a pragmatic ecumenism *de facto*"; [8] but neither Semitic empire understood itself as having a mission to bring about a divinely willed, universal and just order embracing mankind.

An ecumenic empire interprets its power in terms of a form of meaning — a message for or mission to all mankind — which can, at least potentially, be embraced by conquered as well as conquerer. In fact, in the fully formed ideal of the ecumenic empire, the distinction between the original victors and vanquished is meant to disappear. The ecumenic empire discriminates in principle only between loyal and disloyal subjects of the just ruler. It was this principle that Alexander intended to establish through his much-resented efforts to break down the divisions between his Greek and his Persian subjects — an effect which was, incidentally, to be realized in part eugenically, by means of intermarriage. And later, in Rome, we find the concept and reality of a Roman citizenry whose status as "Romans" owes nothing to the ethnic or geographical origin of its members.

Earlier empires, like that of Assyria, display no such universalist features. The word of Assur is a word of force alone; and force, which ontologically belongs to and expresses itself at the physical level, rather than that of psychically and spiritually constituted meaning, is a phenomenon which, though real and thus explicable in its effects, is strictly unintelligible. The exercise of naked might by the Assyrian hosts, or the modern mugger for that matter, is experienced by the victim as a hideous intrusion in the meaningful order of life; and by the aggressor as a satisfying glorification of his possession of and, often enough, possession by a primal reality of power that neither requires nor receives verbal justification. Physical force simply *is*: to argue about what it *means* is a matter that need not concern the aggressor at all. That it sometimes does so is one of the most lasting legacies of the ecumenic age. For all the cynical brutality of its implications, the slogan "Might makes right" already represents an historically conditioned concession to the human requirement of meaning — and one that bears the marks of the legacy of the experience of the ecumenic age.

Before this the question of a meaning to conflict, transcending the balance of forces, hardly ever arises.[9] The legitimacy of the Assyrian Empire was one with the service of the god's power by the king and his armies. Assur's desires were met by the presentation of booty, slaves and sacrifices, forcefully seized from peoples whose service and worship he never sought. From the side of the potential victim, and in the light of the revelations of a God who, if not yet conceived as a universal deity, kept his distance from the pragmatic imme-diacy of Hebrew history, the prophets of Judah could impute transcendent meaning to the Assyrian destruction of the northern kingdom of Israel. Conceived as a divine chastisement visited upon the Northern tribes for their disloyalty to Yahweh, Assyrian conquest was raised by the Judaic prophets to a level of religious meaning unknown to the conquerers themselves. The Assyrians knew only that they lived and might die in a universe of hostile gods and powers. Faced with the final siege of Nineveh, they fought to the end, resisting, as they had been resisted by the Israelites and so many hapless others, with all the desperation of those who know that they can expect no mercy.[10]

When Nineveh fell no Assyrian survivor could interpret the catastrophe as anything but the shattering of the power of his gods and king alike. No Assyrian purpose survived the collapse of the empire; for there was no purpose to Assyria beyond success in arms and acquisition of power and wealth through force. With that possibility gone nothing of the substance of Assyrian nationhood survived. With some qualification the same goes for Babylon; though here the factor of sheer historical terror was mitigated by a less exclusively military conception of rulership and a distinctive cultural inheritance which made the Babylonians valued participants in a world they no longer ruled.

The Persian Empire was different from its Mesopotamian predecessors. Though the evidence is hard to evaluate, it seems that what gave it its distinction was the fact that power was conceived to be at the service of a single true god, whose will was served by the establishment of a single just order through the world. Ahurah Mazdah, by the sort of god he was, legitimized universal dominion, but only so long as dominion was itself bound to the service of his cosmic purpose, the vanquishing of demonic disorder. The Zoroastrian belief that the souls incarnate in men were created by God as warriors in a cosmic war against evil — a war waged, in part, on the field of this world — was, in itself, a powerful spur to imperial ambitions; and there is no reason to be cynical about the religious motivations of Achaemenid kings.

The Old Testament provides ample evidence that among the Hebrews at any rate Persian hegemony was seen as representing a victory for justice over naked force. And if it be objected that this was the natural and wholly selfish reaction of a people which had come close to national extinction under Assyria and Babylon, this is hardly a sufficient answer. The Persian kings are seen not merely as serving the divine purpose by punishing sinful Babylon, but as realizing certain aspects of positive justice in their rule. Additional evidence for the prominence of Zoroastrian ideas in the life of the First Persian Empire can be found in the well-known though again obscure process in which Hebrew religion made its own ideas of heaven and hell, the immortality of the soul, and the day of judgement, which are not found in the pre-exilic worship of Yahweh but which were part of Zoroastrian teaching from the beginning.

The revival of Zoroastrianism under the Sassanian Empire took place in circumstances that had changed considerably since the fall of the Achaemenid dynasty five hundred years before. It must have seemed to King Ardashir in the third century A.D., as it did to Joseph Chamberlain at the start of the twentieth, that "the day of small nations has long passed away. The day of

Empires has come." The cultural influence of Hellenism and the political example of Rome, not to mention the widespread Parthian monarchy which the Sassanids displaced, had created a new consciousness of the significance of religious, philosophical and political ideas and institutions as phenomena capable of transcending ethnic and geographical boundaries.

When Cyrus had founded his empire, the idea of synthetic unity between universal empire and universal religion had not yet fully developed. The proper form of political existence was still generally conceived in terms of ethnically compact tribes, cities and nations worshipping ethnically particular gods. Zoroaster, like the later Hebrew prophets, challenges this view of things. But the prophetic challenge is not, in itself, enough to displace the harmonious if limited vision of intrinsic co-relation between *ethnos* and *ethos*, between a people bound and bounded by kinship and an order of sacred and secular practice defining the life proper to the individual members of the race.

As the ecumenic age unfolds, the common experience that the old, compact forms of politically independent existence could no longer be effectively maintained against the ambitions of increasingly multi-ethnic empires provided a fertile ground for the spread of new prophetic religions which purported to address their message to all mankind. The clearest example of these is Manichaeism, preached by its founder as the summation of the teachings of Jesus, Zoroaster and the Buddha. The most successful of the new religions was Christianity. Without exception one important function of these religions, one that provides at least part of the reason for their success in converting people from more local cults, was that each provided a meaningful interpretation of earthly existence to people living in a world dominated by imperial powers which left no space for small, ethnically compact states, and whose authorities sought to tame, where they did not destroy, the awkward, imperially disruptive ambitions of local deities. So must Yahweh have appeared to administrators of imperial Rome.

The form taken by the Good Religion under the Sassanids was new and suited to the times, even though the content was old. The religion became a church; the beliefs a dogmatic system. The relationship between kingship and religion was formalized as part of the process of doctrinal clarification, undertaken at the behest of monarchs conscious of their Persian identity and anxious to identify the fact of imperial power with a spiritual principle universal in scope but also of undoubtedly Iranian origin. "The Creator, Ohrmazd," says the *Denkart*, "did not send down this religion to the Iranian Empire only, he sent it to the whole world and to every nation." [11] The priest Aturpat, a model of Zoroastrian orthodoxy, established a formal correspondence between the spiritual factor of religion and the material factor of kingship in the context of a theology which, in absolute opposition to all forms of world-rejecting gnosticism, and even more firmly than orthodox Christianity and Judaism, regards the material creation as intrinsically good and necessary to the ultimate victory of Ohrmazd over Ahriman.

Comparison with the Christian position on this point is particularly revealing. In *The Breaking of the Image*, David Martin discusses the essential tension present in the relationship between Christianity and the given world of society and nature. Christian signs and symbols, he argues, have never merely sacralized the world as it is: "The concept of two births, of two swords, two realms, two laws, two cities, expresses the dangerous shadow behind the established substance. Theologically it can be seen as a pervasive reserve about the 'world', and sociologically as an irreducible differentiation. Christianity creates the image of a *Doppelgänger*, a ghostly and spiritual alternative which dogs every legitimation of the principalities and the powers. Every judge, every king, every lord and every lady, is doubled by another jurisdiction as well as supported by that jurisdiction: the law of God is above the law of man. The kingdoms of this world are potentially the kingdom of Christ. There is no large concept of human authority and almost no detail of the ceremonies of legitimation which is exempt from this infiltration." [12]

Christian theory is rooted in an ambivalent rather than an ambiguous view of worldly order as both God given *and* essentially flawed by sin. This view achieves its highest articulation in St. Thomas Aquinas and, in English, in Richard Hooker's *Of the Laws of Ecclesiastical Polity*. It is beyond the powers of man to remedy this. Only an infusion of Grace can put matters to right or, at least, mitigate the effects of the separation between Creator and Creation. Grace, according to Christian doctrine, is given through the life and sacrificial death of Jesus as God incarnate; and it remains present in the world thanks to the resurrection and through the sacraments of the Church. To live as one should, within this still imperfect world, is, accordingly, to live in communion with the Church as the fount of Grace, respecting the presence of the earthly order which God has chosen to leave undisturbed, but always in the expectation of the second coming of Christ which will complete the redemption of a creation fallen from perfection through sin.

Zoroastrianism too knows that there is a gulf between the actual state of the divinely created world and the demanding standards of all-good Ohrmazd. Rejecting as the ultimate blasphemy the Gnostic and Manichaean condemnation of the material creation as the work of a lesser, demonic spirit, the Zoroastrians also refuse simply to endorse the world as it happens to be. For this is a world in which the will of Ohrmazd is continually countered by the strategies of Ahriman. But, compared with the Christian view of things — at least in its orthodox non-Pelagian form — Zoroastrian doctrine conceives of human action as an autonomously efficacious means of assuring the coming of the undisputed rule of Ohrmazd.

From this picture the notion of Grace, as the Christians conceive it, is significantly absent. No ghostly *Doppelgänger* haunted the world of the King of Kings. He knew that great things were demanded of him, and that the demonic forces of Ahriman were strong: but he knew too that, as worldly leader of God's earthly legions, guided by prudential wisdom and the teachings of the Good Religion, he had an assured place in the divine scheme of things. The Zoroastrian monarch, in contrast to his Christian counterpart, was not a temporary caretaker preserving the material fabric of a house until its owner returned, but an agent, and even an architect, doing the will of Ohrmazd in the way that Ohrmazd had himself ordained through the mouth of his prophet. In place of the Christian mystery of uncompleted redemption, we find kingship endowed with a divinely ordained role in the vanguard of the forces of Truth, battling until the end of time on the field upon which the fate of things would be decided.

In this distinction I find a key to the explanation of the fate of the Good Religion after the Muslim conquest. The reform of Iranian religion, which followed from the teachings of Zoroaster, created a religious climate in which the uncompromising monotheism of Islam was able to take root and ultimately to triumph in a way that it could not in the relatively unreformed religious environment of India. Making due allowance for political and sociological factors which differ in the two cases, it remains true that Hinduism has proved much more resistant to the assaults of an alien monotheism than Zoroastrianism: and this in spite of the fact that the Zoroastrians seem, to a Western mind at least, much better able to answer the arguments of monotheists on their own terms.

The consolidation of the Zoroastrian doctrine and church under the Sassanid kings formalized a conception of the relationship between kingship and religion which made possession of imperial power seem to be not only a test of divine favour, but an eschatological necessity. A world increasingly dominated by worshippers of a god, Allah, who in His omnipotence was source of Evil as well as Good and so, in Zoroastrian eyes, demonic, must have seemed to be slipping away from all chance of salvation. The success of Zoroastrian orthodoxy under Sassanian rule was to contribute to the undoing of the Good Religion, whose doctrines, and eschatological hopes, demanded that it be not only confessed in a church but served by the sword of the state.

Notes

1. R. C. Zaehner, *The Dawn and Twilight of Zoroastrianism*, (London: Weidenfeld and Nicolson, 1961) p.176. Hereafter Z.1.

2. Zaehner, *The Teachings of the Magi: A Compendium of Zoroastrian Beliefs*, (London, Sheldon Press, 1975) p.85. Hereafter Z.2.

3. Mary Boyce, *Textual Sources for the Study of Zoroastrianism*, (Manchester: Manchester University Press, 1984).

4. Z.1, p.171.

5. Z.1, p.45.

6. Z.2, pp.20-28.

7. Max Scheler, *Problems in a Sociology of Knowledge*, (London: Routledge and Kegan Paul, 1980).

8. Eric Voegelin, *The Ecumenic Age*, (Baton Rouge: Louisiana State University Press, 1974).

9. Whether such a question is raised by Yahweh's gift of the land of Canaan to the Hebrew tribes is a moot point and cannot be settled here. Certainly the universality of the God of later Judaism is not very apparent in the earliest expressions of Hebrew religion, which are more typical of the ethnically bound religiosity of the cults of the time.

10. David J. Levy, "Israel and Judah: Politics and Religion in the Two Hebrew Kingdoms", *Continuity*, (1986).

11. Z.1, p.299.

12. David Martin, *The Breaking of the Image: A Sociology of Christian Theory and Practice*, (Oxford: Basil Blackwell, 1980), p.161.

10

"THE RELIGION OF LIGHT"

On Mani and Manichaeism

Mani, the self-proclaimed "living Paraclete," prophet of what came to be called the religion of Light was born within the Parthian Empire at Seleucia-Ctesiphon in Babylonia on April 14 in the year A.D. 216 His father, Patek, may well have been a kinsman of the Parthian royal house and his mother, Mariam, though bearing a Jewish-Christian name, also seems to have belonged to a Parthian princely family. In the year Mani was born, King Artabanus V had been on the throne for four years. He was to be the last of the Parthian monarchs. Ten years after Mani's birth, the Parthian dynasty was overthrown by the Persian Ardashir I, founder of the second, Sassanian, Persian Empire, which was to endure from 226 until its destruction at the hands of the Muslim Arabs in 652. The period of Mani's ministry falls almost entirely within the reign of King Ardashir's successor, Shapur I, who occupied the imperial throne between 242 and 273, and who seems to have had some sympathy for the prophet's teachings. These thirty years were the years of Mani's great missionary journeys. They saw the composition of the seven books of the Manichaean canon and the founding of the Manichaean Church which was, in places, to survive the martyrdom of its founder by more than one thousand years.

On the death of Shapur I, his son Hormizd became king. He lived for scarcely a year and was succeeded by his brother Bahram I. The new king was strongly under the influence of the Zoroastrian High Priest, Karter — a determined prelate of great historical significance under whose leadership the Persian national faith became, for the first time, a persecuting religion. At the instigation of the High Priest, Mani was summoned to the royal court, where he was accused of attempting to lead the Persian people away from what had become, under the Sassanid dynasty, the established religion of the restored empire. In answer to the charge, Mani pointed to the number of times he had healed members of the king's family and household. But when he claimed that his mission was inspired by a new divine revelation, superseding that once given to Zoroaster, the king asked him, "Why was this revelation made to thee, and not to us, who are masters of the land?" Mani replied simply, "Such is the will of God." [1]

Then the king ordered the prophet to be bound with heavy shackles of a type we know also from the record of Zoroastrian Persia's Christian martyrs. Thus bound, he was taken to prison where he died after twenty-six days, on February 26, 277. Mani was sixty years old. In accordance with Persian custom, during his last days he was permitted to speak with his disciples, to whom he gave his final instructions. A Manichaean priest called Uzzai and two other disciples were present at his death, which supposedly took place at eleven o'clock in the morning, when, as the records have it, "He ascended out of his body to the dwellings of his greatness on high."

Mani's body was cut into pieces. The head was displayed at the city gate and the rest was ordered to be thrown to the dogs. However, according to Manichaean sources, the prophet's remains were gathered by the faithful, and later buried at Ctesiphon, the city of his birth. King Bahram commanded that the religion of Mani be extirpated; and thus began the first of the persecutions to which the religion of Light was to be subject throughout its history and which were, eventually, to eliminate it from the face of the earth.

Manichaeism has the dubious distinction of being the only great world religion to have been persecuted out of existence. Yet, in the 1,200 years that it endured as a distinct church, it spread to North Africa and Spain in the West and to China in the East. The two great finds of Manichaean literature that have so much increased our knowledge of the religion in this century occurred respectively in Egypt and in Chinese Turkestan. While previously our knowledge of Manichaeism depended almost entirely on the testimony of the Christians, Muslims, Zoroastrians and others who fought against its influence, we now possess significant portions of the Manichaean scriptures and a large number of psalms and hymns that bear eloquent testimony to its profound and distinctive spirituality — a spirituality that long endured the merciless persecutions of a world whose goodness Manichaean doctrine and experience alike denied.

Archaeological finds in Central Asia have also brought to light fascinating developments in an area where Manichaeism enjoyed its greatest worldly success, and where, uniquely, it was able to establish itself as the official religion of state, among the Uighur Turks. At a time, the sixth century, when the Manichaean Church was on the verge of extinction in the Christian West, it was entering a period of expansion among the peoples of the steppes that was to culminate in the conversion of the Uighur prince, Bogu Khan, in 762. This was the high point in a long-term process of missionary activity which had begun, at the latest, in the years immediately following Mani's martyrdom; when, as we know, Mar Amo, one of the prophet's closest associates and his chosen missionary to the East, was already active on the regions of Abasahr and Merv. According to a surviving fragment of the history of his mission, Mani's apostle "converted numerous kings and rulers, grandees and noblemen, queens and ladies, princes and princesses." [2] Whatever may have been the immediate effects of Mar Amo's mission, it was primarily through the medium of Sogdian merchants, an Iranian people who controlled much of the important trade between the Middle East and China, that the religion spread to the peoples of Turkestan and beyond, into China itself.

Arab sources mention the strength of Manichaeaism in the cities of Tashkent and Samarkand, where there were considerable Sogdian populations; and it was to the latter city that the seat of the Manichaean supreme pontificate was transferred from Babylon in the tenth century, following the renewal of persecution by the Abbasid Caliphs. There were colonies of Sogdian merchants in all the cities that stood along the trade route to China, and these included members of the learned "elect" of the Manichaean Church. It was following his capture of the major city of Lo-Yang that the Uighur Khan was converted by Sogdian Manichaeans. Following his own conversion, Bogu Khan instituted the religion as the state cult throughout his domains, establishing and endowing Manichaean monasteries and, in the manner of religions of state, endeavouring to root out its potential rivals. In keeping with the ascetic orientation of his new faith, his policy took a distinctly iconoclastic turn. In a royal decree, the Manichaean king declared: "All images of demons, sculptures and paintings shall be destroyed by fire; all those who venerate genii and fall down before them should. . . here the text is broken. . . and the religion of Light should be accepted." [3]

This period of Manichaean prosperity is reflected in a distinctive style of religious literature that, while never quite betraying Mani's teachings concerning the intrinsically evil character of this world, places less emphasis on the frightfulness of the human condition than do the Coptic psalms discovered in Egypt. According to H. J. Klimkeit in his study of Manichaean kingship: "The texts of Turkish Manichaeism allow us to discern an attitude to the world to be found nowhere else in the realm of Gnosticism. Being protected by a Manichaean king, the community of scribes and elect could assess the world as a place where the blessings of the gods was experienced already. Certainly ultimate salvation could only be found in the other world, but the light of that other world already shone into this world." [4]

Such periods of worldly security were rare in the history of Manichaeism, and the power of the Manichaean Uighur state was itself short-lived. In 840 it fell to Kirghiz invaders; though it seems that a smaller Manichaean kingdom was subsequently established by Uighur refugees in Kansu and the Tarim basin, in what is now Chinese Turkestan, about 850. This minor successor state survived for about four hundred years until it too was destroyed, like so many others, by the Mongol horde of Genghis Khan in the thirteenth century. Further east still, Manichaean influnce may have been responsible for the introduction of the planetary calendar into China, while two of Mani's works were incorporated into the Taoist canon. In the southern province of Fukien, in particular, where Mani was worshipped as the Buddha of Light, Manichaeism seems to have remained strong until at least the fourteenth century, but thereafter we lose sight of the religion even in its last far oriental strongholds.

Deprived of external political support and cut off from what had been its religious centre by the Mongol devastation Central Asia, the religion of Light, which had once seemed a strong and dangerous challenge to the spiritual hegemony of Chinese Buddhism, appears to have been absorbed almost without a trace in the syncretistic religious culture of China.

No one knows when the faith and church of Mani finally died out in China; but, as George Widengren remarks in what is almost an afterthought to his history of Manichaeism: "There were probably Chinese Manichees as late as modern times." [5]

In its original homeland and in the West, Manichaeism, as a distinct religion and an organized church, is long extinct. There is, though, a vast and intriguing literature devoted to possible Manichaean influences on various Muslim heresies as well as on such heretical Christian groups as the Paulicians, the Bogomols and the Albigensians. Taking their cue from the early Christian opponents of institutionalized Manichaeism as it had existed in the three centuries following Mani's death, later orthodox opponents of these sects tended to describe as "Manichaean" everything in heretical teaching that smacked of a Gnostic contempt for a world order endorsed by Western Catholicism and Eastern Orthodoxy alike. It is indeed quite possible that there was a covert, specifically Manichaean influence on some of these world-denying heresies; but interest in putative Manichaean currents in what were undoubtedly Christian heresies has sometimes distracted attention from the original phenomenon itself, and this has led to a rather loose use of terms. People sometimes use the terms "Manichaean" or "Manichee" to describe any dualist view of the world, while having little conception of Manichaeism as a religion in its own right.

The religion of Light was neither a popularized summation of pre-existing Gnostic current, nor a Christian or Zoroastrian heresy, as it has sometimes been conceived. It was a faith that aspired to be the universal church, founded upon the revelation of God to his chosen prophet Mani in Babylonia in the reign of King Ardashir I, and endowed by its founder with a powerful eschatological vision and an inclusive body of doctrine.

It is that faith and doctrine, *Manichaeism* in the strict sense of the term, that I want to examine in this essay. I undertake the task in the belief that not only is it of interest in itself but that without some knowledge of what the Manichaean Church professed, all generalizations about "Manichaean", and, perhaps more generally, Gnostic, influences in Western history, as well as loose talk about an enduring Manichaean world-view or mind-set, are necessarily premature. Since some of the most interesting work on the nature of modern, quasi-religious ideologies depends upon such references, notably the wide-ranging analyses of Eric Voegelin and Alain Besançon's brilliant study of the intellectual origins of Leninism,[6] the task in hand is intended not only as a contribution to the history of religions but also as providing a helpful side-light on some of the most pressing problems of our present political and spiritual predicament. Let us then begin by looking at the experiential sources of Mani's religion — the time and place of its founding and the revelatory events which were its specific occasion.

The Babylon of Mani's youth was a meeting place for most of the religious cross-currents of late antiquity. It was a city of individuals in search of truth and certainty in the midst of a world made uncertain by political and religious upheaval and by the perennial clash of great military powers. Within its boundaries there were Jews, Christians, Buddhists, Zoroastrians of various sects, and devotees of various mystery cults, as well as followers of many of the numerous Gnostic teachers of the time. Shortly before Mani's birth, his father, Patek, had joined a Gnostic baptizing sect —perhaps the Mandaeans but more probably the ascetic Jewish-Christian sect known as the Elkesaites.

Arab sources tell us that, while praying in "the House of Idols", Patek heard a voice calling him from the inner sanctuary. On three successive days the mysterious voice summoned him to abstain from meat, wine and women. Patek's asceticism may have influenced the attitude of the young Mani, and, together with what seems to have been a slight physical deformity in the boy, may have predisposed the future prophet to the world-rejecting faith to which his life and death bear witness.

Mani tells us that, when he was twelve, an angel appeared to him in what was to be the first of two revelations. The angel told him to forsake his father's congregation, saying: "Thou art not of its followers. The guidance of morals, the restraint of appetites, these are thy tasks. Yet because of thy youth the time is not come to stand forth openly." According to the Coptic texts, the content of the revelation was given to Mani on this first visitation; but it was not until twelve years later, in 240 or 241, that the prophet was commanded to go out and proclaim the truth to the world. This time the angel said: "Peace unto thee, Mani, from me and from the Lord who sent me to thee and who has selected thee for his apostleship. He bids thee now to call the people to the truth and to proclaim from him the good message of the truth and to dedicate thyself to this task. The time is now come for thee to stand forth openly and to preach the teaching."

In the *Kephalaia*, the "Chapters of the Teacher" found at Medinet Madi in Egypt, the first revelation is described thus: "The Living Paraclete came down to me and spoke to me. He revealed to me the hidden mystery that was hidden from the world and the generations: the mystery of the Depth and the Height. He revealed to me the mystery of the Light and the Darkness, the mystery of the conflict and the great war which the Darkness stirred up. He revealed to me how the Light overcame the Darkness by their intermingling and how (in consequence) this world was set up. . . . He enlightened me on the mystery of the forming of Adam, the first man. He instructed me on the mystery of the Tree of Knowledge, of which Adam ate, by which his eyes were made to see; the mystery of the Apostles, who were sent into this world to select the churches. . . . Thus was revealed to me by the Paraclete all that has been and that shall be, and all that the eye sees and the ear hears and the thought thinks. Through him I learned to know everything. I saw the All through him, and I became *one* body and *one* spirit." [7]

In this text Mani makes the claim that he is not merely one prophet among others but has become, in consequence of the revelatory event, somehow consubstantial with the Holy Spirit whose coming had been foretold by Jesus. Mani presents his revelation as the true Pentecost, the coming of the Holy Spirit into the world of men. But, typically, it is not only the Christian pledge that Mani claims to redeem. Christianity is only one among several sources of revelatory premonition. God had revealed his truth in part to earlier prophets, to Zoroaster and the Buddha as well as Jesus, but the religions founded by these figures had achieved only local importance. Worse than this, Mani claims, the original divinely revealed truth of their teachings had become lost or, at the least, corrupted because the prophets had not themselves committed it to writing but had entrusted the composing of the scriptures to disciples. The truth of Mani's religion was to be vouchsafed by the fact that its teachings were to be inscribed by the recipient and vehicle of revelation himself. This emphasis on the written word is characteristic of Manichaeism, which is, perhaps even more than the Koranic faith of Islam, emphatically a religion of the book. Nor is this obsession with the question of scriptural and revelatory literalism surprising when we consider the rampant sectarianism and doctrinal conflict typical of the religious traditions with which the young

Mani was familiar.

Like Muhammed after him, Mani presents himself as the last prophet of God, the successor and perfector of earlier, authentic but incomplete revelations. But, unlike the prophet of Allah, Mani did not conceive himself as emerging out of a single, historic tradition of prophecy. Rather, as Voegelin puts it, "The sequence of the messengers and their religions is not merely a succession in time but something like a confluence of independently rising waters into the one great river of truth represented by Mani." [8] Voegelin's vivid simile must of course be qualified, as his own theological observations attest, by the recognition that beneath each isolated revelatory spring lies a common divine source of the truth that is revealed. While there is no single, exclusive revelatory tradition, it is, at least according to the prophet of the religion of Light, the same God who speaks through the mouths of his various prophets. It is worth noting that, whether or not he would have included Mani among that company, this would also seem to have been Voegelin's view.

In the *Shabhuragan*, a work written in Persia by Mani for King Shaphur I, we read: "Wisdom and deeds have always from time to time been brought to mankind, by the messenger called Buddha to India, in another by Zoroaster to Persia, in another by Jesus to the West. Thereupon this revelation has come down, this prophecy in this last age, through me, Mani, messenger of the God of truth to Babylon." [9] A passage in the *Kephalaia* expands on this theme: "The writings and the wisdom and the apocalypses and the psalms of all the earlier churches have assembled with the wisdom revealed by me. As water comes to water and becomes a great water, thus have the ancient books come to my writing and become a great wisdom. The like has never been announced among the ancient generations. Never have been written nor have been revealed the books as I have written them." [10]

Living, as he thought, in the last times, when the cosmic drama of redemption was approaching its climax, Mani understood himself to be the bearer of perfect, universal truth. He conceived his church, founded as it was at the geographical meeting place of the religious cultures of East and West, to be the divinely instituted, perfected inheritor and guardian of all earlier revelations. Mani's teaching claimed to encompass all that was true in other faiths. In that sense it was perfectly attuned to the spiritual requirements of what Voegelin has called the "ecumenic age" — an age in which the military-political expansion of great imperial powers had broken down the previous order of ethnically and religiously undifferentiated, tribal or city states and incorporated their inhabitants, more or less unwillingly, in multi-ethnic and potentially universal empires. Against the background of such a world, men seem increasingly to have sought, in religious movements no less universal in intention than the contemporary empires, both a recipe for salvation that might, in principle, encompass all mankind and an explanation for the experienced disorder of the world. Manichaeism provided both in full measure, combining an ecumenic commitment to universal religious enlightenment with a characteristically Gnostic emphasis on the material world, rather than human sinfulness, as the ontological *locus* of experienced evil.

In common with earlier varieties of Gnosticism, but more ambitiously than any of them, Manichaean writings purport to convey, through the medium of a distinct myth of spiritual salvation, the inner truth of other scriptures. But, in its ecumenic ambitions, the religion of Light shows itself to be something more than simply another Gnostic sect. Mani did not, in the manner, for example, of such teachers as Valentinus, seek to tease out the esoteric meaning of pre-existing texts for the sake of the initiated few — the spiritually privileged *pneumatics* who had already found the key to salvation through coming to understand their true spiritual, immaterial and other-worldly identity. Rather, like the mainstream of Christianity, the religion was preached as a new and open message, divinely revealed to God's chosen messenger, and intended for an audience that encompassed the learned and the ignorant alike. In contrast to most other varieties of Gnosticism, Manichaeism was not intended to be a sect for the enlightened few but was to be the true religion for all.

Nor was the religion of Light a merely syncretistic phenomenon. While Mani described himself as the successor of Zoroaster, Buddha and Jesus, and while his disciples presented his truth in terms that varied depending on the religious background of the audiences they addressed, Manichaeism is emphatically not a *bricolage* of other men's beliefs and doctrines. By turns it uses the vocabulary of Zoroastrianism and Christianity, of Buddhism and of Greek philosophy, yet its core is not Zoroastrian, Christian, Buddhist or Hellenic, but is to be found in a powerful and dramatic vision of the nature and destiny of the cosmos and of the place of man within and, crucially, beyond it. This distinctive vision is unmistakably Mani's own.

Manichaeism is essentially an elaboration and explication of a central vision of struggle and redemption. Its core is expressed in what the French scholar H. C. Puech calls the "double doctrine" of the Two Principles and the Three Times.[11] The Two Principles are the radically opposed forces that make themselves known in the struggle between Light and Darkness, Good and Evil, Spirit and Matter. It is central to the Manichaean world-view that these opposed forces are seen, not as contrasting aspects of a single tensional Reality, but as manifestations of two incompatible realities. These two realities are in origin radically foreign to each other and ultimately they are to be separated once more.

The Three Times are the moments in the process in which the Two

Principles, initially isolated, come into contact with one another, intermingle in the confusion of cosmic struggle, and are finally set apart once more. Manichaeism is thus a radically dualist religion. The Two Principles have no common source and can have no common destiny — a point of great importance for the Manichaean doctrine of a purely spiritual redemption and the Manichees' consequent rejection of anything that suggested either the possibility or the desirability of the resurrection of the body. In the beginning, the First Time, the Two Principles existed, from eternity, in isolation from each other, and so they shall eternally be in the Third Time to come. It is the Second Time alone, which encompasses the whole drama of cosmic struggle and spiritual redemption, that is the major focus of Manichaean teaching.

Manichaeism is a religion concerned almost exclusively with questions of eschatology. What other religions regard as the equivalent, initial mystery of cosmic creation is, in Manichaeism, only an incident in the single drama of ultimate redemption by which Light gathers back into itself the fragments of its own substance that have become entrapped by Darkness in the course of struggle. The cosmos is not conceived as a system in equilibrium but as an unstable compound of incompatibles; and the process by which it is called into being — Mani pointedly avoids the term *creation* — is merely a relatively late moment in an eschatological process which is already under way and to whose ends it is strictly subject.

In Manichaeism the cosmos as we know it is neither, as in classical paganism, an eternal and perhaps divine reality, nor, as in Judaism and Christianity, a free manifestation of God's bounteous creativity. It is, at best, a tool or weapon of war, a necessary means to the ultimate, acosmic end of the renewal of the purity of divine Light.

It is this process that is the subject of the central Manichaean myth. Experiencing the world as the field of battle between opposite and incompatible force, the Manichaean explains the situation through a grandiose and complex mythology. We have the evidence of St. Augustine, a Manichaean for fourteen years, that this all-encompassing myth, which appears so strangely forced and artificial to the modern reader, was one of the most powerful weapons in the Manichaean missionary's armoury. To the modern consciousness, the ability of the myth to explain every mystery of existence is likely to indicate an unacceptable degree of poetic licence on the part of its Prophet-author. The story is simply too complete as well as too complex to ring true to an age which, when it admits to the reality of divine revelation at all, can hardly conceive it in terms other than stray intimations of immortality or isolated signs of God's loving care.

A myth like Mani's — especially when we know it to have been taught by one who was a sophisticated preacher and organizer, and which bears such

marks of apparently conscious craft — seems proof not of the truth but of the
falsity of the religion in which it plays so central a role. To the Neoplatonic
philosopher, Alexander of Lycopolis, it already seemed that way a generation
after Mani's death. In consequence, if we are even to begin to understand
Manichaeism as it understood itself and as it was understood by those who were
attracted to it, we have to recognize that our conceptions of what could possibly
be true are, no less than those of Mani's audience, limited ones, typical of our
own time and place; and that, as a matter of creaturely modesty, we should not
presume to prejudge *a priori* the forms that divine revelation can take.

When Mani taught that the Holy Spirit had revealed the Hidden Mysteries
to him, he was claiming the myth itself to be the very substance of the
revelation. There is, so far as we can determine, no question here of myth being
subsequent to or an elaboration upon an otherwise ineffable truth; nor, as so
often in Plato, is the myth a carefully crafted supplement to an otherwise
rationally formulated teaching. The truth of Manichaean myth is intended to
be taken literally and not metaphorically. Thus, "to reveal the hidden
mysteries" is nothing other than to identify the spiritually decisive events
recounted in the revelatory myth — events preceding the formation of the
cosmos, that could not be known apart from their revelation but which, once
revealed, explain the present state of man and the world in terms of their
necessary consequences. For such a purpose, myth may indeed be indispensable and, bearing in mind our caution regarding the unforeseeable possibilities
of divine revelation, the fact that the Manichaean myth seems unbelievable
today is not *ipso facto* proof that it is untrue.

Let us then attempt to summarize the tale in which, as men and women,
we play our allotted part. In the beginning Light and Darkness existed as
utterly separate realities. In the realm of Light all was peace and quiet, but in
the domains of Darkness there was only strife and turmoil. The disordered
motion of matter — graphically represented as a state of constant civil war
and endless battle and pursuit between dark substances that cannot even
recognize their fellowship in evil — drives the forces of Darkness to explode
beyond their original boundaries and so, eventually, to encounter the Light.
Struck by the unaccustomed beauty of what they see, the forces of Darkness
desire to conquer and possess it. The Father of Greatness, as the God of Light
is called, realizes his danger, but, by his very nature, he is unfitted and unused
to war. So he calls into being, from his own spiritual substance, a first
emanation, called the Mother of Life. She, in turn, calls into being Primal Man
who is charged to fight the forces of Darkness. Thus, proceeding herself from
pure spirit, the Mother of Life engenders an original warrior, who bears the
name of Man but is not yet the mixed compound of spirit and matter we know
today. Accompanied by his five sons — the so-called Luminous Elements of

Air, Water, Wind, Light and Fire — Primal Man battles with the Enemy but is overwhelmed. Defeated, he is captured and bound, and the five Luminous Elements are devoured by the Darkness.

However, this apparent defeat is not total; for in consuming, in the form of the Luminous Elements, what are, essentially, emanated particles of Light, Darkness has ingested elements that are opposed to its own essential nature and which will, thereafter, weaken its continuing assault upon the realm of Light. At the same time, part of the substance of the Father of Greatness has become entrapped in the Darkness, and this must be redeemed. Thus, a succession of primordial events, themselves provoked by the aggressive yet originally purposeless disorder of Darkness, events that culminate in what seems, at first sight, to be an unmitigated defeat for the forces of Light, both sets the stage for the subsequent drama of redemption and guarantees the eventual triumph of the Father of Light.

At the request of the Mother of Life, the Father then evokes another being, the Living Spirit, to rescue Primal Man from his captivity. The Living Spirit descends to the frontiers of Darkness and calls into the shadows: "Greetings O Good Man in the midst of Evil, O Creature of Light in the midst of Darkness." The call is heard and Primal Man answers: "How goes it with our Fathers, the Sons of Light in their City?"

Then the Living Spirit commands three of his sons to kill and flay the Archons, the Sons of Darkness, and to bring their bodies to the Mother of Life. Out of their skins she makes the heavens, and, casting the bodies back into the dark, she forms the Earth.

This accomplishes the rescue of Primal Man. But this first redemption of trapped elements of captured Light, in which we can recognize the common Gnostic theme of the saved saviour — the redeemer who must himself be redeemed — is incomplete. The five Luminous Elements, who are, in es-sence, not at all cosmic substances, but emanated elements of spirit ingested in Matter, remain trapped in the Darkness. At this point the macrocosm is called into being to provide what has aptly been called a machinery of salvation.

Out of the purest particles of Light the Living Spirit forms the Moon and the Sun. These are respectively to be the means of drawing light out of the darkness, and the temporary storehouse in which light can gather on its way back to its acosmic source. Mani taught that the phases of the Moon cor-respond to the rhythm of this operation. The Moon waxes as it grows full with the particles it absorbs, and wanes as these are transferred to the Sun on their way to the perfect kingdom beyond the cosmos. Thus, by a sort of cosmic water-wheel — more precisely a Light-wheel — fragments of entrapped Light, or Spirit, are lifted by the Moon to the Sun, and thence back to the pure domain of Light itself.

Even this new mechanism of redemption does not exhaust the ingenuity of the Father of Greatness in his effort to recover the still trapped particles of Light, which are, we must recall, consubstantial with him. His next move is to evoke an androgynous being of great beauty called, as the successor of Primal Man and the Living Spirit, the Third Messenger. Appearing naked to the surviving male demons as an infinitely desirable virgin, the Third Messenger causes them to ejaculate particles of Light. Falling upon the earth these particles are the seeds from which the plants of the world are generated. For this reason Manichaeism teaches that, of all the world's beings, plants contain the highest proportion of Light; and this, as we shall see, forms the justification for the strict dietary rules enjoined upon the elect of the Manichaean Church.

Appearing before the female demons, who are already pregnant, perhaps as a result of continual orgies with their male counterparts, the Third Messenger takes the form of a beautiful youth. Maddened by desire, the female demons abort, and from their offspring the animal species are said to derive. Thus, as opposed to the plants, animals are seen as purely and substantially evil in origin — creatures of pure, dark matter. Yet they too have a part to play in the redemptive scheme; for, as they consume the blossom and fruit of the plants, the beasts absorb, in turn, a certain portion of entrapped light. Thus is set the scene for the creation of man.

Here, in contrast to the formation of plants and even animals, the initiative for creation comes directly from the powers of Darkness. Fearful of losing the last of its captive Light to the ever more ingenious counter-attacks of the Father of Greatness, the Darkness, which is, we recall, identified with Matter and Evil, contrives its own final plot. Two demons, one male, the other female, are deputed to devour all the remaining fragments of Light. Having eaten most of them, the two engender between them Adam and Eve. Thus the origins of mankind are attributed to a process composed in equal parts of cannibalism and sexuality in what is, as Mircea Eliade has described, probably the most tragic and certainly the most humiliating anthropogenic myth that exists.[12]

Formed from the filth of Matter, Adam belongs to the realm of Darkness by reason of his bodily needs and carnal desires. He is created blind and deaf; unaware that there is within him anything that pertains to the realm of Spirit and Light. Yet, as the offspring of the two great Light-devouring demons, the body of Adam, the carnal form of man, has now become the prison within which the greatest proportion of the still-estranged Light particles are to be found. Thus, in Hans Jonas' words, "From now on the struggle between Light and Darkness concentrates upon man, who becomes the main prize and at the same time the main battlefield of the two contending parties. In him both sides have almost all their stakes: Light, that of its own restoration; Darkness, that of its very survival." This, Jonas claims, "is the metaphysical centre of the Manichaean religion, and it enhances the deeds and destiny of individual man to an absolute importance in the history of total existence." [13]

To redeem the Light within man, yet another new saviour is evoked. This figure, variously called the Light-Jesus or Ohrmazd, awakens Adam and tells him of his spiritual kinship and of the state of his soul's imprisonment in the world: "Then Adam examined himself and recognized who he was. And the Light-Jesus showed him the fathers in the heights and his own soul cast into the midst of all, exposed to the teeth of panthers... devoured by the devourers, consumed by the consumers, eaten by dogs, mingled with and imprisoned in everything that exists, shackled in the stench of darkness.... The Light-Jesus raised Adam up and made him eat of the Tree of Life. Then Adam glanced upward and wept, raising his voice powerfully like a lion roaring. He tore his hair, beat his breast and said: 'Woe, woe unto him, the Sculptor of my Body, woe unto him who has shackled my soul and woe to the rebellious ones who have enslaved me.'" [14]

Though the redemption of the souls of the human species is, in part, analogous to the salvation of Primal Man, there is this important distinction. While Primal Man is a spiritual being, an emanation of pure Light, who has been captured but not absorbed by matter, Adam is primordially a creature of Darkness, a being whose soul alone is worthy or capable of salvation. In Manichaeism, man as such is not truly the object of divine redemption. The offspring of Adam and Eve can never be raised to the realm of Light, for, as men and women, they do not belong there.

Indeed, even the statement that Manichaeism preaches the salvation of the soul of man may somewhat overstate the case. Some texts seem to differentiate the soul as such from the spiritual elements of which it is merely the earthly, and so irredeemable, form. Thus the Manichaean doctrine of redemption is not to be confused with the Christian doctrine of personal salvation. It is not anything distinctly pertaining to man that is to be saved from ultimate oblivion but rather a portion of God's substance lost in the world. This would seem to suggest a form of acosmic, impersonal afterlife more akin to Hindu and Buddhist conceptions than to that of Christianity. But the teachings of the religion of Light are not unequivocal on this point; and most of the surviving Coptic Psalms end with a doxology in which prayers for the souls of various Egyptian martyrs are invoked. Whether this is consistent with Mani's teaching, or whether it represents a subsequent and perhaps local concession to hopes for a personal afterlife is not altogether clear.

The ultimate redemption of entrapped Light, which is the moving force of the cosmic drama, involves a lengthy process of abstraction and refinement in which the practices of the Manichaean Church play a crucial role. Manichaeism enjoins asceticism on its followers but for reasons that are not so much ethical as eschatological. Here, as everywhere in the religion of Light, everything is subject to what we may term the eschatological imperative; and Good is simply whatever contributes to the redemption of imprisoned Light through the removal of its particles from the world. The less a man participates in the processes of the material world, the less he serves the purpose of Evil, which is to prolong the imprisonment of Light within the Darkness.

The accomplishment of the redemption of light from entrapment in the world enjoins upon the Elect of the Manichaean Church, more than a general predisposition toward asceticism, a very precise formula of living designed to ensure the maximum possible absorption and refinement of Light particles. The Manichaean Elect, the priesthood of the Church, were required to be celibate and to subsist on a diet of fruit alone; particularly on such fruits as melons and cucumbers in which, quite visibly, the particles of Light appeared to be most heavily concentrated. By living in this ascetic fashion, the Elect were not so much giving a moral example to a world held to be beyond redemption, as contributing to the ingathering of Light particles through ingestion. The digestive tract is conceived, quite literally, to be an eschatological vehicle: and the injunction to celibacy is no more than the necessary supplement to the process of light-gathering initially accomplished through eating.

Drawing on an ancient Indo-European belief according to which semen is the means by which spiritual element in man is transmitted through the generations — a widespread belief which we find, for example, in Apollo's argument for the innocence of the matricide Orestes in the final part of Aeschylus' Oresteia — the Manichaeans describe procreation as a diabolic stratagem designed by the Prince of Darkness to ensure the continued entrapment of sperm-borne Light in new material bodies. As celibates, the Manichaean Elect play no part in this process. So, in consequence of his celibacy, when one of the Manichaean priesthood died, the Light he had absorbed in life would re-enter the spiritual sphere as part of his liberated soul, even as his body went its way of stinking decay in the dank mass of matter to which it belonged. At the end of things, Mani taught, the last remaining Light within the world would be retrieved; and the Darkness, weakened by struggle, would be cast into an inescapable pit, never to emerge again.

Summarized thus, the myth is likely to strike the modern reader as a work of lurid imagination and cold artifice. As indicated earlier, the very completeness of the myth, its ability to explain everything in the most graphic terms, is, even more than its extraordinary literalism, enough to disqualify it as a serious candidate for contemporary belief. Furthermore, it is a relatively simple matter to pick apart the elements of traditional Iranian dualism from the Gnostic horror of bodily existence with which they are combined in so complex a construction. And this too, in spite of Mani's own avowal of his position as divinely appointed heir to the numerous and diverse revelations of the past, is likely to encourage scepticism with regard to the authenticity of the claim to original revelation. But there is more to the Manichaean myth than the sum of the influences —Zoroastrian, Christian and Mesopotamian —that we can detect within it. There is a unity to the whole that gives it a grandeur and pathos all its own and allows us to speak, with Eliade, of the "tragic pessimism" of the system.

The source of this unity lies not in the diversity of historical origins to which the content of the myth bears witness. Rather, the myth illuminates, in a powerful way, the experience of worldly evil and the aspiration to perfection of an imperfect form of life which is coeval with mankind. It is this, the existential rather than the historical root of the Manichaean world-view, which gives the myth its unity and even a certain outrageous plausibility.

It is easy to see why the religion of Light should have been regarded as so blasphemous by those whose religions taught them to love God by trusting in the ultimate goodness of His creation. To these, Zoroastrians and Christians alike, it must have seemed that Mani had appropriated the most precious of religious truths only to recombine them in a form in which the significance of each was reversed. In a world where faith is hard and trust so often belied, Mani's combination of explanatory myth, existential dissatisfaction and eschatological hope presented a challenge to which every established power of this world and the next was summoned to respond.

Notes

1. H. C. Puech, *Le Manicheism*, (Paris: 1949), p.51.

2. Puech, op. cit.

3. H.J. Klimkeit, "Manichaean Kingship: Gnosis at Home in the World." 29, p.20.

4. Ibid, p.30.

5. George Widengren, *Mani and Manichaeism*, (London, 1966), p.134.

6. Eric Voegelin, *Science, Politics and Gnosticism*, (Chicago, 1968). Alain Besançon, *Intellectual Foundations of Leninism*, (London, 1981).

7. Hans Jonas *The Gnostic Religion*, p.208-209.

8. Voegelin, *The Ecumeric Age*, (Baton Rouge, Louisiana University Press, 1974), p.138.

9. Ibid.

10. Ibid, p.139.

11. Puech, op. cit.
12. Mincea Eliade *A History of Religious Ideas*, (Chicago, 1982), p.393.
13. Jonas, op. cit. p.227.
14. Robert Haamdt, *Gnosis, Character and Testimony*, (Leiden, 1971).

11

PAUL RICOEUR

Christianity and the Space of Politics

Though not primarily a theorist of politics, the philosopher Paul Ricoeur has always been concerned with political questions. His involvement in politics goes well beyond the willingness, characteristic of most French intellectuals, to take a well-publicized, if not always well-considered, stance on every pressing political issue of the day. For both as a professional philosopher and as a Protestant, Christian believer, Ricoeur has been interested, throughout his long career, in reflecting seriously upon the philosophical and theological issues posed by man's political existence.

Politics obtrudes in at least three areas of Ricoeur's work. The first is in his long-lasting association with the magazine *Esprit*, a journal founded by Emmanuel Mounier in 1932 in response to the crisis of liberal democracy in Europe and intended to provide a Christian alternative to the ideological challenges of fascism and communism. *Esprit* was the main vehicle for Mounier's Christian philosophy of 'personalism' and many of Ricoeur's political essays first appeared in its pages. After Mounier's untimely death in 1950 Ricoeur published a substantial examination of his work — a study marked both by an obvious affection for the dead man and a profound sympathy with his political-philosophical outlook.[1] Second, and overlapping with the first group of writings for *Esprit*, has been a succession of lectures and articles in which Ricoeur, speaking as a Christian believer, one who attends to the kerygma, the proclamation of the gospel, has tried to clarify the significance that this gospel message has for our understanding of politics. These essentially occasional pieces combine, to a remarkable extent, a careful and devout attention to the scriptural text with repeated cautions against the perils ignoring the results of modern biblical scholarship. And third have been the points at which Ricoeur's lifelong project of developing a systematic philosophy of the will has brought him up against central questions of political philosophy.

The relationship between these three aspects of a single life's work is complex. Ricoeur's philosophy of man, centred, originally at least, upon the investigation of the enigmatic tension between human freedom and a surrounding nature, whose power also dwells forcefully within us, has been pursued along diverging paths in the various volumes of the *Philosophy of the Will*. This philosophical anthropology remains an unfinished work and certainly cannot be considered as the theoretical baseline of which the political essays are merely so many surface reflections. Nor is Ricoeur's philosophical anthropology derived in any way from a prior acceptance of Christian dogma. If he finds no ultimate incompatibility between religious faith and the secular philosophical study of man it is not because he avoids or minimizes the problems involved in their confrontation. Indeed he goes as far as he can to make it as sharp and painful as possible.

Marx, Nietzsche and Freud, the three great modern masters of suspicion, the demystifiers and would-be destroyers of the realm of the sacred, are treated in his work with the utmost sympathy and respect. The accusations they bring against religion are deadly serious and, Ricoeur repeatedly insists, all but conclusive. Ricoeur never buys the hope that rests on faith at the cost of cutting short the argument by appeal to the authoritative claims of doctrine. His faith remains a faith — a hope and trust and not a gnostic certainty. And this means that the revealed word in which Ricoeur the Christian believes cannot provide the premise from which Ricoeur the philosopher argues. Problems of philosophical anthropology can be informed by awareness of what the gospel proclaims but not resolved by appeal to its imputed status as revelation. Scriptural information is never to be misconstrued as theological instruction.

The balance struck must be a careful one for, as Ricoeur puts it: "The philosopher, even the Christian one, has a distinct task; I am not inclined to say that he brackets what he has heard and what he believes, for how could he philosophize in such a state of abstraction to what is essential? But neither am I of the opinion that he should subordinate his philosophy to theology in an ancillary relation. Between abstention and capitulation, there is the autonomous way which I have located under the heading 'the philosophical approach'. I take 'approach' in its strong sense of 'approximation'. I understand by this the incessant work of philosophical discourse to put itself into a relationship of proximity with kerygmatic and theological discourse. This work of thought is a work that begins with listening, and yet within the autonomy of responsible thought. It is an incessant reform of thinking, but within the limits of reason alone." [2]

If philosophy cannot be instructed but only informed by scripture and theology, neither can the social order be required to conform to Christian principles, at least not in the sense of those, like the French *Intégristes*, who

speak of "The Christian Social Order" as a historical configuration constituted by and requiring a distinctive cluster of institutions. "A better exegesis
and a better biblical theology," Ricoeur writes, "has almost made impossible
the search for universal principles based on scripture. Biblical criticism invites
us rather to place in their own context and to understand according to their own
intention such notions as kingdom of God, justice, law, covenant etc. It is
possible to disengage principles and eternal values, but it has become more and
more difficult — indeed impossible — to combine the kerygmatic proclamation with concepts of political and social philosophy."[3]

These remarks place Ricoeur firmly in a certain line of Christian thought.
There is a specific historical background to what he is saying — a long and
painful history of struggle between those who associate Christian social and
political teaching with support for the traditional institutions of a confessedly
Christian monarchy and those who deny that there was ever anything but an
accidental connection between the two. Some of the latter go much further and
argue that the historic alliance of throne and altar, symbolized in the
commanding image of the *Sacrum Imperium*, involved from its Constantinian
beginnings a perversion of the biblical heritage. In France the gradual
dissolution of the bond between the two has led to many bitter disputes, from
the polemics touched off by Lammenais's desertion of the legitimist cause after
the 1830 revolution through the papal condemnation of the royalist *Action
Française* movement in 1926: and while Ricoeur's own religious tradition is
Protestant, he is, as a Frenchman, especially aware of the implications of what
is sometimes pictured as the exodus of the church from the protective authority
of the confessing state — the estrangement of Christianity from Christendom.

The issues involved here are of more than local importance. They bring
into renewed focus an unsettled and unsettling problem of the relationship
between political and religious authority which lies at the heart of Western
civilization. Indeed, as my essay on politics and religion in the ancient Hebrew
kingdoms is intended to suggest,[6] the problem of the *sacrum imperium* has
roots that reach back far beyond the conversion of Constantine, to the Israelite
and Judaean monarchies and to that moment, so ambiguously recounted in the
Bible, when Samuel anointed Saul to be king over God's chosen people.

In his political essays Ricoeur's biblical references are drawn overwhelmingly from the New Testament, but the questions he considers were placed on
the Western agenda by the Hebrew prophets and scribes. They remain central
concerns of political philosophy today for they pose with dramatic clarity
fundamental problems of the range, function and legitimacy of political
projects and institutions, as well as the open question of whether there exists
beyond the space of politics a source of judgement, a scale on which every
earthly order will, like the real and metaphorical Babylon of our historical

consciousness, be weighed and found wanting.

For these reasons I will preface discussion of the politics of Ricoeur with a brief account of certain formative moments in our common history. The theme demands it. Christianity and the Christian conception of the scope and dignity of politics did not emerge in a vacuum and the texts to which Ricoeur looks for information derive from a complex and by no means unambiguous tradition. Two themes will guide me —the biblical symbol of the exodus and the Weberian concept of the disenchantment of the world. The two are more closely related than may at first appear.

At the level of pragmatic history *exodus* describes the events through which the Hebrew clans, led by the historically obscure figure of Moses, left the life of oppression they endured in Egypt to find and conquer a land promised them by their god. At this level the event is so unimportant that it has left no trace in contemporary Egyptian records. The importance of the exodus does not lie in its secular historical dimension but in the fact that out of it there emerged a new, qualitatively different conception of the relationship between man and God, world and history. A new type of man appeared on the world stage. Biologically he was the same; existentially he was different, subtly but decisively altered by his new understanding of himself amd his status in being. The event was not sudden, the results not immediate. Nor in the nature of things could the change amount to a complete transformation. The new man was not another man. His world was reconceived but there was no new creation.

For whatever reason, natural-historical or supernatural-providential, this new conception, which Eric Voegelin calls the Israelite 'leap in being',[4] was to exercise a formative, though far from exclusive influence on the future history of mankind. The emigration of an apparently insignificant population became an event of universal symbolic importance. Because a new and historically decisive conception of the human condition emerged from the exodus it came to mean more than it was at the factual level. Fact and meaning are related in ways that go beyond our knowledge and understanding. The language of revelation tells us that a mysterious God revealed himself to a hardly less mysterious man, Moses, that He commanded him to lead the children of Israel out of bondage, that He made a covenant with them and revealed His will to them through His commandments. Outside the terms of revelation we can only say that as a result of a series of events about which we have no clear evidence a specific people, an *ethnos* made perhaps newly aware of its distinct identity, began to envisage its existence in a way different from that which prevailed about it. The *ethnos* became, for itself and others, a "peculiar people" set apart by an all-encompassing ethos imposed upon it by special revelation alone. It is the long-term significance of what happened that is a matter of historical record.

Eric Voegelin's characterization of this process as the exodus of man from what he calls 'cosmological civilization' draws our attention to the heart of the matter. As Voegelin describes it in the first volume of his *Order and History*, the world of cosmological civilization, the symbolic universe of the ancient empires from which Israel defected in leaving the land of Egypt, is one in which each level of being, and of beings, gods and men, society and nature, is conceived as subject to the same all-encompassing rhythms of periodic growth, decay and renewal.

It is a world that is, in its way, as predictable and "lawful" as the conceptual universe of post-Newtonian mechanics. The priests and the astrologers, possessors of the requisite and, in principle, cumulative knowledge of 'cosmological', or in Mircea Eliade's terms, 'archaic' world order, form its pre-eminent "technological" caste. Like the possessors of modern scientific knowledge, this caste can, through knowledge of what is, in the last analysis, necessary and unalterable in the structure of the universe, guide events in an humanly favourable direction. In the ancients' interplay of human decision and cosmological necessity, as in modern science, ontological opportunism is the name of the game.

The repetitive and cyclical rhythms of the seasons and the skies provide not only a secure basis for political calculation but a universal model for the integration of life's events in a meaningful pattern. Even if it is the gods, or perhaps one great originating High-God, like the Canaanite *El*, who bear ultimate responsibility for the creation of this order, it is also true that even such divine beings are thought of as subject to the same fatal rhythms as man himself. Even though lived out on a different time scale, the nature of creator and creation are structurally identical.

In this universe, gods and men communicate within being as a matter of course, for the world order is full of signs of the divine — known conduits of theophanic power which are also, as seen from the human pole, effective channels of sacrifice and prayer. Communication takes place through participation in rites undertaken at certain fixed times of the year and in certain sacred places. Cosmological civilization expects and receives regular epiphanies. Its religions refer to the recurrent patterns of the world and not the unrepeatable encounter with the divine word.

Many of these features reappear in the religion and culture of Israel. The nomadic herdsmen conquer and settle the land. They become cultivators. They build and inhabit cities. And as they do so they are tempted by the religious and political patterns of their agricultural and urban neighbours. The tribal confederation becomes a monarchy. The worship of Yahweh is centred at the temple at Jerusalem and temple worship, with its associated burden of material tribute, becomes a requirement of the developing religion. The personality and name of *El*, the highest god in the Western Semitic pantheon, becomes identified with the originally nameless God who summoned Israel out of Egypt. In conquering Jerusalem King David lays claim to succession to Melchizadek, priest of *El 'Elyon* at Salem. In the religion of royal Judah, whose destiny is inseparable from the royal House of David, Yahweh settles in the royal temple at Jerusalem and discloses his other, speakable name as *El*, creator and sanctifier of kingship and cosmos.

But though these features are integrated with the religion of the revealed word there is no question of a wholesale return to the patterns of cosmological civilization. Sacral monarchy and priesthood in Israel, and even in Davidic Judah, exist in uneasy tension with the prophetic tradition. Aaron, the ancestor of the priestly clan, is remembered also as the builder of the Golden Calf, the properly bovine symbol of every deviation from true faith into the nature cult of the Canaanite Baals. The voice of Yahweh breaks, time and again, the holy bounds of His temple to speak, unsummoned, unwanted and, above all, untamed through the prophets. The words of the prophets, epitomized in the terrible wrath of Elijah against the prophets of Baal, keep on reminding Israel that there is no going back; that the gods of the field are, like those whose statues stand in the temple shrines, false gods betrayed for all their gilded divinity by their feet of clay.

Yahweh, unlike his erstwhile rivals whose divinity and even existence His followers are increasingly inclined to deny, does not manifest himself in the recurrent rhythms of the cosmos. He does not make Himself known only in prescribed holy places but rather at unfathomable times of His own choosing. Prophecy, in its Old Testament sense, has nothing to do with temporal calculation or prediction: and even if the eschatological and apocalyptic elements in such modern heresies as Marxism can be traced to a biblical, specifically prophetic root, the element of determinism they contain most certainly cannot. Though Yahweh is described as creator of heaven and earth He transcends them utterly. He is not so much the present powerhouse of what is, but its source, its end and its judge — the God of catastrophe as much as, or more than of order, Yahweh more than *El*. It is in relationship to this implacable, unpredictable being, a divinity conceived in essentially trans-cosmic or, as a later vocabulary would have it, transcendent terms, that the cosmos is de-sacralized.

Let us be clear about what this means. This God is trans-cosmic without being acosmic. He is neither absent from the world nor indifferent to it. Far better, perhaps, if He were. Rather He makes himself known within the world as the disturber and not the underwriter of its knowable order. The disenchant-ment of the world begins when the world is no longer reliably full of gods who are themselves reliable in their responses to sacrifice and prayer. At least initially, Yahweh can properly be identified with *El 'Elyon*, the god most high of the Canaanites, but He is, from the beginning, the destroyer of every intra-cosmic spirit or Baal.

This revelation of Yahweh, the discovery of the world-transcendent God whose revelations are tied to unique, and often humanly terrible, historical events, changes man's understanding of himself. There is a new tension in his existence rooted in the experienced break between worldly and divine order. The trappings of empire are assumed but, in contrast to the surrounding civilizations, the king can neither be a god, as in Egypt, nor, as in Mesopotamia, the privileged mediator between god and people. We are told, in words still sung in Handel's setting at every English coronation, that: "Zadok the priest and Nathan the prophet anointed Solomon king." But if Zadok is a fairly typical prelate, Nathan, in this action at least, is hardly typical of the prophets whose names have been preserved. It is not the court prophets we remember, though we know of their existence, but the voices of accusation, summons and judgement. In Hebrew civilization it is the prophet speaking the word, and not the king wielding the sceptre, who effects decisive communication between God and His people.

Before the bar of the absolute the political is relativized. Yet, in the last analysis, accusation, summons and judgement do not amount to condemnation. The tendency to condemn the secular, political order is strong but neither is nor could be dominant. So long as God is conceived as world-creator, that is, until the birth, centuries later, of a distinctively Gnostic religious consciousness, there remains a link, however hard it may be to discern, between divine will and the demands of political life. The easy analogies between god and king, powers on different but parallel cosmic levels, are put aside but in their place emerges a conception, such as we find in Ricoeur, of political order as a necessary condition of what is ultimately a God-given existence.

The biblical scholars tell us that the Old Testament shows clear signs of having been put together from conflicting traditions with different views of the worth of monarchical, that is, in the circumstances of the time, political institutions. But the ambiguities of the resulting text lose much of their potential significance, their enduring informative quality, if they are simply attributed to the interweaving of contradictory traditions in the canonical text. That is only the efficient cause of contradictions which, precisely as contradictions—textual harbingers of a lived tension that will henceforward characterize Western political consciousness — claim, in their interaction with actual historical experience, an experiential authority of their own.

The ambiguous status of political order as necessarily imperfect and perfectly necessary reflects man's discovery of his own ambiguity as a creature of dust and clay imbued with the spark of the absolute —and this discovery is mysteriously but palpably bound up with the history that is our present concern. What this means is that the political sphere is not a sacred place in human life. Politics is, nevertheless, a secular necessity of a creation granted its own life and relative autonomy by its creator. The desacralization of politics is part of the disenchantment of the previously god-filled world of cosmological civilization, and this world is disenchanted to the extent that we discover the limited autonomy and associated dissatisfactions of its given and apparently inescapable order.

It is in the light of these considerations that I understand Paul Ricoeur when he writes: "It is of decisive importance for a Christian interpretation of the State that the writers of the New Testament have bequeathed us not one but two readings of political reality: one, that of St. Paul, which offers a difficult justification, the other, that of St. John, which offers an obstinate mistrust. For the one, the State has the face of the magistrate; for the other, it is the face of the beast."[5] In the Book of Revelations the "Beast" serves as the encompassing symbol of evil, demonic power. The complementary Pauline reading is nothing like so clear-cut: "The State which carries the sword, which punishes, is 'instituted' by God and for the 'good' of its citizens. And yet that State occupies a very odd and precarious place in the economy of salvation: the apostle has just celebrated the grandeur of love—love which creates reciprocal bonds... —love which forgives and which renders good for evil. Now, the magistrate does not do that: between him and the citizens, the relation is not reciprocal; he does not forgive; he renders evil for evil. .... Through him. .. a violent pedagogy, a coercive education of men as members of historical communities that the State organizes and directs, is carried out. St. Paul does not say and perhaps does not know how that penal pedagogy is connected to the charity of Christ: he knows only that the established order. .. realizes an intention of God concerning the history of men."[6]

Yet for St. Paul as well the State is also a 'power' representing evils conquered on the Cross but not yet annihilated: "This double theological pattern," Ricoeur writes, "is full of meaning for us: we henceforth know that it is not possible to adopt for ourselves either a religiously motivated anarchism under the pretext that the State does not confess Jesus Christ, or an aopology for the State in the name of 'Be obedient to the authorities.' The State is this dual-natured reality, simultaneously instituted and fallen."[7]

The biblical theme of the dual nature of the State informs Ricoeur's treatment of what he calls the "double history of power." The benefits of institutional order and the terrible possibilities of misused power grow together: "All growth in the institution is also growth in power and in the threat of tyranny."[8] The development of the constitutional, law-governed state, beneficial in itself, can serve as an alibi for tyranny. The rationalization of administration offers the tyrant the technical means for an organized and lasting oppression. The growth of public opinion and an apparently informed discussion of politics exposes the population to ideologies extreme in their themes and rational in their outlines: "The parties become 'machines' whose organizational complexities are matched only by the spirit of abstraction that infuses its slogans, its programs, and its propaganda." [9]

The appearance of large scale planning of the economy, which Ricoeur regards as a natural extension of the same 'institutional spirit' which makes the administration of justice a state monopoly, gives the central power unprecedented means of pressure over the life of the individual. Thus Ricoeur describes the State, in a formulation that obstinately recalls the Enlightenment, but perhaps also Christian, superstition that rationality and power are, ultimately and in essence, mutually exclusive, as the unresolved 'contradiction' of rationality and power. Every growth in the one increases the other — a truth of experience that is for Ricoeur, as much as for the neo-Marxist Jürgen Habermas, also an ontological or at least sociological scandal.

Leaving this ideological element aside, it is clear that Ricoeur's treatment of the State owes as much to the analysis of social and political rationalization advanced by Max Weber as it does to the information of the Gospel, and that this double influence extends to Ricoeur's carefully modulated discussion of the specific political duty of the Christian believer. "It is not legitimate," he writes, "nor even possible to deduce a politics from a theology, for every political commitment is formed at the point of intersection of a religious or ethical conviction with information of an essentially profane character, with a situation which defines a limited field of possibilities and available means, and with a more or less hazardous choice. It is not possible to eliminate from political action the tensions which arise from the confrontation of these diverse factors. . . . Conviction, when not controlled by reflection on the possible, would tend to require the impossible to exist by requiring perfection: for if I am not perfect in everything, I am perfect in nothing. On the other hand, the logic of means, not controlled by a meditation on ends would easily lead to cynicism. Purism and cynicism are the two limits between which political action extends, navigating with its guilt calculated between the morality of all or nothing and the technique of the feasible." [10]

This, one might say, is a specifically Christian restatement of the problem of an ethics of responsibility which Weber regarded as the essential component of the authentic political vocation. Through its stress upon the inevitably situated or bounded character of moral decision, it connects as well with Ricoeur's original and broader metaphysical concern with the interplay of freedom and necessity in the structure of human existence. [11]

Political commitment, Ricoeur argues, has meaning for the individual Christian as citizen but not for the Church. There is, he says, no Christian politics as such, but there is a "style of the Christian in politics." The style is characterized by vigilance born out of the specifically Christian, perhaps more exactly Pauline, awareness of the intrinsic ambiguities of power. It "consists in finding the legitimate place of politics in life: elevated but not supreme", and "in seriousness of commitment, without the fanaticism of a faith; for the Christian knows that he is responsible for an institution which is an intention of God with regard to the history of men, but he also knows that this institution is prey to the vertigo of power, to a desire for divinization which adheres to it body and soul. Finally, this style is characterized by a vigilance which excludes sterile criticism as much as millenarian utopianism." [12]

I find in these lines a sturdy reassertion of the political realism typical of the mainstream of Christian thought down the ages. Ricoeur's remarks on politics exude the unglamorous but essential virtue of prudence, the *prudentia* on which St. Thomas Aquinas, following Aristotle, placed so much emphasis. The same strain of prudential reasoning, which is the practical issue of his appreciation of the peculiar tension involved in the biblical conception of worldly order, emerges in Ricoeur's discussion of the Marxist reduction of political to economic alienation. Today the Marxist conception of the relationship between political power and economic organization passes almost without question in wide sections of the Christian Church throughout the world in a way that would have been unthinkable little more than a generation ago. It is not, I think, unfair to suggest that the generally sloppy political and economic thinking of *marxisant* Christians reflects precisely the combination of sterile criticism with millenarian utopianism which, according to Ricoeur, the Christian's political style should exclude. Ricoeur's remarks on the Marxist conception of the relationship between politics and economics are therefore, though brief, of particular significance.

"It seems to me," he writes, "that what is most worthy of note in the Marxist critique of politics and the Hegelian State is not its explication of the State by means of the power relations among classes, which would therefore be the reduction of political evil to socio-economic evil, but rather the description of this evil as the specific evil of politics. I believe that the great error which assails the whole of Marxism-Leninism and which weighs upon the regimes engendered by Marxism is this reduction of political evil to economic evil. From this springs the illusion that a society liberated from the contradictions of bourgeois society would also be free of political aliena-tion." [13]

According to Hegel the State transcends what he calls 'civil society'. What this means, in Hegelian terms, is that the irreconcilable interests that manifest themselves in our private dealings with one another are arbitrated and rationally settled by the authority of the State. Following a line of thought that extends into the mainstream of German political and legal thought, Hegel argues that my rights and freedom achieve real existence only by virtue of State authority and, thus, I can be said to be truly free only because and insofar as I am a political animal, a citizen and subject of a sovereign state. Hegel describes the State as representative in the particular sense that, more profoundly than the wilful, self-interested individual himself, it represents, or acts in the cause of, man as a rational and free being. This exalted notion of the State provides the starting-point for Marx's critique.

In his response to Hegel, Marx points out that there is a gap between the way the State presents itself, as the impartial arbiter of interests, and the systematically unequal relationships which are sanctioned and, as it were, sanctified by the rule of law. The rationality and universality of the Hegelian State are belied by the historical contingency and particularity of the interests which are in fact dominant. However because Marx viewed the political sphere as reducible to, because derived from the economic, he attributed this contradiction between what we may term the pretence of the State and its presence — its claim to legitimacy in the light of reason and its practice in the light of experience — to specific forms of class society. "When the State is. . . conceived as the organized power of the ruling class for oppressing another, then the illusion of the State being universal conciliation is nothing but a particular instance of the vice of bourgeois societies, showing themselves unable to offset their own deficiency or to resolve their contradictions except by taking flight into the phantom of Right." [14]

Seen in this partial light, the *Rechtstaat*, the state whose commands are inscribed by established, legal right, can only seem the embodiment of universal reason to those who are, politically speaking, the Right Hegelians. To those who are not Hegelians, such as Marx's contemporaries of the German historical school, the successors of Burke's German disciples, the very requirement of universal rationality is itself thoroughly unreasonable: while to Marx's political fellows, the Left Hegelians, the State's claim to rationality is belied by the partiality of the society over which it presides.

In a famous series of early articles devoted to the legal dispute over the right to collect wood in the Rhenish forests, Marx contends that the existing law is, as a matter of fact, applied in a way biased toward the interests of property owners. But the logic of his position, the basis of his critique, is more radical than the journalistic emphasis on judgemental bias may suggest. Beneath the charge that the law is applied in a biased way, is the much more subversive contention that even the most perfectly impartial application of a law that equally defends the rights of all in a society that is itself socially and economically unequal, must favour the position of some at the expense of others. The principle of equality before the law enshrines the established inequalities of those who fall equally under the law's jurisdiction. Here, in the polemical journalism of the young Marx is the source, not only of the socialist assault on the institution of the rule of law, but of the dubious jurisprudence of what later generations have learned to call programmes of "affirmative action."

What we may think of such programmes is not in question here. What is relevant is the assumption underlying the reasoning: an assumption that Marx will only attempt to justify in his later economic and sociological writings. This is the assumption that the institution of the State and the related institution of a legal system whose sanctions are underwritten by state power — that is, as Max Weber notes, ultimately by legitimate force — are historically contingent features of human society whose existence would become unnecessary in a society characterized by social and economic equality. Or, to put it another way, that the political dimension of human existence, the sphere of the play of power and its ever-imperfect regulation by authoritative institutions, is a by-product of an economy that is not yet fully developed in either rational or even crudely productive terms. Without scarcity no conflict. Without conflict no law and no state. That is the basic formula of the anti-politics of Marx. Ricoeur stands in fundamental opposition to this seductive heresy. Both as philosopher and as believer, his position is that the political is irreducible. Political existence, and with it all the tensions and temptations of power, is constitutive of being human. If the aspiration to a fully rational power and a perfect justice is ever thwarted in the practice of politics, then this is a fact of human existence and not merely a feature of a transient form of socio-economic organization. If politics is concerned with the mediation of power relationships through institutions that must themselves ultimately rely on the potential deployment of force, it cannot be dismissed as an evil to be abolished in a coming post-political world —not, at least, so long as that world is conceived, in natural rather than supernatural terms, as an historical mutation of this one. "Politics," Ricoeur writes, "can be the seat of the greatest evil only because of its prominent place within human existence. . . . Every condemnation of politics as corrupt is itself deceitful, malevolent, and infamous, at least if it neglects to situate this description within the dimension of the political animal. The analysis of polity, as the progress of man's rationality, is not abolished but constantly presupposed by meditation on political evil. On the contrary, political evil is serious only because it is the evil of man's rationality, the specific evil of the splendor of man." [15]

Marxism denies this. It reveals its profoundly anti-political character by substituting the false problem of the withering away of the State for the traditional concerns of political philosophy with the sources and conditions of abiding order. "The theory of the withering away of the State is a logical consequence of the reduction of political alienation to economic alienation. If the State is merely an organ of repression, which springs from class antagonisms and expresses the domination of one class, then the State will disappear along with all other after-effects of the division of society into classes. But the question is whether the end of the private appropriation of the means of production can bring about the end of all alienations. Perhaps appropriation itself is but one privileged form of power of man over man; perhaps money itself is but one means of domination among others; perhaps the same spirit of domination is given expression in various forms: in economic exploitation, in bureaucratic tyranny, in intellectual dictatorship, and in clericalism." [16]

These words were first published in 1957, when, even in the wake of the suppression of the Hungarian uprising, the post-war love affair between French intellectuals of the Left — among whom Ricoeur certainly counted himself — and Marxism had hardly begun to fade. One notes in the passage the whiff of what, with caution, one may call Ricoeur's Christian Weberianism but also a pre-echo of some of the more interesting and acceptable themes that Michel Foucault was to develop a decade or so later.

It is a notable virtue of Ricoeur's examination of Marxist political theory that, unlike some other critics of the non-communist Left, he does not try to represent its actual worldly role as an accidental perversion of an essentially sound idea. His target is Marxism, not Stalinism or Leninism. He sees clearly that Marxism serves as the legitimating ideology of totalitarian regimes neither because of the evil deeds of certain pathological individuals, the thesis of Stalinist perversion, nor because the regimes have come to power in unfavourable circumstances, the thesis of Lenin's and Russia's misfortune. The flaw in the theory, from which the practical evil follows, is as essential as it is fatal. Deny, like Marx, the autonomy and permanence of the political sphere, reduce or resolve politics to the supposedly fundamental question of economic organization, and the rest will follow — the police state and the shabby fabric of lying slogans and fudged statistics.

The space of politics is an inevitable dimension of human existence. The good and evil that may be accomplished within it are permanent possibilities of life. The reduction of politics to something other than itself denies the truth that man is a political animal. Disbelieve that and, in the delusion of a fallacious anthropology, you commit yourself to a programme incapable of fulfilling its primary intention. To attempt to transcend politics is not to abolish the problem of power — still less the mystery of evil in the world — but rather to falsify its terms to an extent that makes impossible the maintenance of acceptable limits on the exercise of the force that must exist as an element of a human social order.

Ricoeur's conception of the space of politics remains true to the central insights of the biblical view of man at a time when many other Christian thinkers seem to regard its abandonment as the first word in worldly and even other-worldly wisdom. Judaism and, later, Christianity relativized the political realm by denying its claim to embody the ultimate good, but they neither questioned its present necessity nor, in any natural historical perspective, promised its abolition. To do the latter is to prepare the undoing of the good symbolized by the exodus. It is to attribute practical divinity to society by pretending to and projecting a perfection that has no place on earth except in the aspirations of our prayers.

Notes

1. Paul Ricoeur, "Emmanuel Mounier: A Personalist Philosopher" Ricoeur, *History and Truth*, Evanston, Northwestern University Press, 1965, pp. 133-165.

2. Ricoeur, "Freedom in the Light of Hope" Ricoeur, *The Conflict of Interpretations*, Evanston, Northwestern University Press, 1974, p.403.

3. Ricoeur, "The Project of a Social Ethic" Richoeur, *Political and Social Essays*, Ohio: Ohio University Press, 1974, p.162.

4. Eric Voegelin, *Israel and Revelation,* Baton Rouge and London, 1954.

5. Ricoeur, "Adventures of the State and the Task of Christians" in *Political and Social Essays*, p.201.

6. Ibid, p.202.

7. Ibid, p.203.

8. Ibid, p.207.

9. Ibid.

10. Ibid, pp. 208-9.

11. See Ricoeur, *Freedom and Nature*, Evanston, Northwestern University Press, 1966.

12. Ricoeur, "Adventures of the State", pp. 215-216.

13. Ricoeur, "The Political Paradox" in *History and Truth*, p.258.

14. Ibid, pp.259-60.

15. Ibid, pp. 260-61.

16. Ibid, p. 262.

INDEX

Aaron, 212
Absolom, 160
Absolutism of reality, 140–41, 143
Achaemenids, 182–84
Adad-Nirari, 153
Adhur-Hormizd, 172
Aeschylus, 204
Agrarian revolution, 183
Ahab, King, 153, 155, 166, 167
Ahaz, King, 154
Ahaziah, King, 167
Ahijah of Shiloh, 159
Ahriman, 172–75, 178, 182, 188–89
Ahurah Mazdah, 172, 177, 178, 180,
    182–83, 186
Albigensians, 194
Alexander of Lycopolis, 200
Alexander the Great, 170, 185
Allah, 189, 197
Alt, Albrecht, 163
Amaziah, 161
Amon, King, 162
Amos, 160–61, 165
Anahidh, 172
Anamnetic undertaking, 39–40
Anarcho-Aristotelianism, 108–9
Anaximander, 54
Animals, 129–30, 135–36, 138. *See
    also* Nature
Anthropina, 34
Anthropobiologie, 21
Anthropological constants, 128
Anthropological reflection, 14, 17
Anthropology: Aristotle's philosophical

anthropology, 42–43; Christian
anthropology, 36; Dilthey on, 13–
18; elemental anthropology, 20–28;
Gehlen on elemental anthropology, 1,
6–10, 13, 14, 17, 19–28, 72, 128,
148; Landgrebe on, 9–10; liberal
anthropology, 107; limits on elemental anthropology, 24–28; and
ontology, 74–75; Plessner on, 19–
21, 47–48; and politics, 102–4; purpose of, 74; relationship between
philosophical anthropology to hermeneutics, 5–8, 10–11, 13–16,
28–29; Ricoeur's philosophical
anthropology, 208; Scheler on, 7–9,
18–19, 44–50, 52–55, 128; scientific
anthropology, 25–26; Voegelin and
philosophical anthropology, 39–45
Apeiron, 54
Apollo, 204
Aquinas, St. Thomas, 67, 188, 216
Arche, 63, 64
Ardashir, King, 170, 171, 174, 186,
    191, 195
Arendt, Hannah, 102
Aristotle: on *anthropina,* 34;
    anthropology of, 42–43; on politics,
    102, 103, 106–11, 133–34, 216;
    practical philosophy of, 145, 146;
    Voegelin on, 42–43, 45
Aron, Raymond, 91
Artabanus V, 191
Artaxerxes I, 182
Artificial, 139

221